Witches, Druids, and Sin Eaters

Witches, Druids, and Sin Eaters

The Common Magic of the Cunning Folk of the Welsh Marches

Jon G. Hughes
with Sophie Gallagher

Destiny Books
Rochester, Vermont

Destiny Books
One Park Street
Rochester, Vermont 05767
www.DestinyBooks.com

Text stock is SFI certified

Destiny Books is a division of Inner Traditions International

Cataloging-in-Publication Data for this title is available from the Library of Congress

ISBN 978-1-64411-428-5 (print)
ISBN 978-1-64411-429-2 (ebook)

Printed and bound in the United States by Lake Book Manufacturing, Inc. The text stock is SFI certified. The Sustainable Forestry Initiative® program promotes sustainable forest management.

10 9 8 7 6 5 4 3 2 1

Text design and layout by Priscilla Harris Baker
This book was typeset in Garamond Premier Pro with Gill Sans MT Pro and Weiss Std used as display typefaces

To send correspondence to the author of this book, mail a first-class letter to the author c/o Inner Traditions • Bear & Company, One Park Street, Rochester, VT 05767, and we will forward the communication, or contact the author directly at **jongarstanhughes@gmail.com**.

Contents

Acknowledgments vii

PART I

Witchcraft and Druidic Lore of the Welsh Marches

1 A Curious Beginning 2

2 The Welsh Marches 9

3 Magic, Religion, and Ritual in the Welsh Marches 14

4 The Shropshire Amulet 23

5 Witchcraft, Christianity, and the Witch Terror 32

6 Witches of the Welsh Marches 60

7 Druids of the Welsh Marches 116

8 Other Occult Arteworkers of the Welsh Marches 132

9 Prominent Occultists of the Welsh Marches 140

10 The Legacy of the Witches and Druids of the Welsh Marches 152

PART 2

Grimoire of the Welsh Marches

Yr Llyfr Swynion Gororau Cymru

"The Book of Spells of the Welsh Borderland"

11 Finding Harmony between Two Ancient Traditions 163

12 Preparation of the Workplace and Crafting Components 170

13 Utilizing the Elements and the Will 188

14 Apotropaic Devices for Protection against Curses and Malevolent Energies 194

15 The Casting and Lifting of Spells and Curses 209

16 Elixirs of Love 252

17 Other Spells and Workings: Attachment Nosegays and Druid's Breath 273

18 Scattering the Workplace and Caching Apparatus 280

Bibliography 284

Index 285

ACKNOWLEDGMENTS

Not long after we began researching and developing the content of this book, the world was impacted by the COVID-19 pandemic, restricting movement in a way that we have never experienced before. As a result, our planned research journeys between my home in the west of Ireland and the venues and locations we had targeted in the UK were made impossible. In addition to this, all of the museums and other sites we had targeted were closed to public access, preventing us from having face-to-face meetings with the curators and managers we had been working with to that point. We are extremely grateful to those dedicated and enthusiastic curators, archivists, and local authority officers who not only provided us with unprecedented access to their collections but were kind enough to take on-site photographs especially for this publication.

Our thanks go to those individuals listed below without whose help this book would not have been created.

Sioned Williams—Principal Curator: Modern History
Museum of Wales—St Fagans Site
Sain Ffagan Amgueddfa Werin Cymru | St Fagans National Museum of History
Sain Ffagan | St Fagans
Caerdydd | Cardiff
CF5 6XB

Ben Moule—Collections Officer/Front of House
Hereford Museum
58 Friar Street
Hereford
HR4 0AS

Emma-Kate Lanyon—Curator, Shropshire Museums
Ludlow Museum
Shrewsbury Museum & Art Gallery
The Music Hall
The Square
Shrewsbury
Shropshire
SY1 1LH

Ian Andrews—*Ceidwad Arweiniol* | Lead Custodian
Llys a Chastell Tre-Twr | Tretower Court & Castle (CADW)
Tretower
Crickhowell
NP8 1RF

Alicia Jessup—Historical Interpreter
Llancaiach Fawr Manor
Cyngor Bwrdeistref Sirol Caerffili | Caerphilly County Borough Council
Trelewis
Nelson
Treharris
CF46 6ER

PART I

Witchcraft and Druidic Lore of the Welsh Marches

1
A Curious Beginning

In the depths of a very cold October in 2019, I received a call from an old friend of mine who lives near the market town of Shrewsbury, on the borders of Wales and England. He is very fortunate in having recently inherited an old farmhouse in a beautiful rural area of Shropshire and rang me because he knows well of my involvement in the Druidic community and my interest in all matters occult.

I was intrigued to hear that during the recent refurbishments at his farmhouse he had discovered a strange collection of items that had been found plastered into a void behind a mantlepiece above an old fireplace in one of the downstairs rooms of the house. The small cache contained what he called a medallion, a piece of charred paper that was completely blackened with nothing apparently written on it, and a bundle of small bent pins, tied together with thin thread.

I am sure he knew before he rang that his unexpected find would pique my interest, and he was, of course, quite right. Although none of these peculiar objects made me think of anything Druidic, hidden items like those he described certainly have a place in the broader occult practices to be found in both England and Wales in days gone by.

Understandably, in light of the age of his farmhouse, he was interested to discover if his find had any significant financial value, but as he continued to describe the items in more detail, it became obvious that the greatest value that could be attributed to his find would be in relation to its cultural significance. I suggested he show his find to members of the local archaeological societies or the regional museum, as having lived in the town of Shrewsbury for a short time, I knew that both organizations were very active and had an enthusiastic following. With an audible sigh, he told me that he had already contacted both those organizations and had been told much the same, namely that while the items were locally interesting, they had no particular financial value and therefore maybe he should hang on to them as family mementos and as interesting talking pieces for his visitors.

All the same, I asked him to send me copies of photographs of his find, as I was still very interested in seeing them for myself. He said he would do better than that and, having sent the initial pictures, he packed all the items into a padded envelope and posted them directly to me. When the package arrived a few days later, I carefully unpacked the three small boxes, each containing one of the newly discovered artifacts. It was obvious from the outset that the items had been combined to create an apotropaic device, a collection of meaningful occult items intended to protect the farmhouse and its occupants from malevolent forces and influences. These types of protective tokens were not unusual in the Welsh Marches, along the border of England and Wales, around the time that the farmhouse had been built. There were, however, two very unusual aspects to the find: the first was the intended power and potency of the combined artifacts, suggesting a dire need for powerful protection against some now-unknown threat; the second was that within the small collection of artifacts were items and images that are representative of two, normally separate, occult traditions, one being that of ancient witchcraft and the other the lore of the Druidic tradition, both combined in a way that has never been witnessed previously.

Before proceeding any further with my exploration, I decided to consult two other well-known information sources, the first an experienced and knowledgeable Witch, steeped in the tradition of the Welsh Marches, and the second the curators of the archives of the National Museum Wales, where I knew there was a rich source of relevant artifacts and contemporary texts and manuscripts. The National Museum in turn connected me to a network of regional and local museums and societies where I was later to find a wealth of exciting and eye-opening facts. Having done this and established my research resources, I invited my colleague, the aforementioned Witch researcher, to join me in my journey of exploration and become my coauthor in this eventual book. And so the stage was set and our detailed work could begin, but first an initial meeting to examine in detail the items from the find and to plan our research methodology and a timetable to proceed.

In the meantime, I returned the artifacts to their original owner, asking him to look at the walls and woodwork surrounding all the entrances to the house to see if he could find any other marks of hidden deposits that seemed out of place and to let me know immediately if he were to find any.

Around two weeks later, I received another mysterious package from Shropshire. Inside I discovered fragments of birch bark and a short length of thorn branch, two more artifacts that, found secreted behind a lintel above a doorframe, were concealed protective devices, put there with the intention of warding off Witches and their familiars.

The fragments of silver birch bark were undoubtedly the dried and shriveled parts of a silver birch bark parchment curse that had separated into thin, dried-out strips. Though there was no visible script remaining on the fragments, there were faint traces of red markings, either text or drawings long since faded. There is a well-known tradition of Witches' (and Druids') curses being written on small squares of silver birch bark, a practice that gave the silver birch tree the country name of paper birch, and the small sheets of white bark used as paper being called scholar's parchment (Welsh: *memrwn ysgolhaig*) in the Druidic tradition.

The short length of thorn branch was another common protective device hidden around the entrances of homes with the intention of warding off evil daemons and Witches. The sharp thorns from all sorts of thorny bushes and trees were thought to deter Witches, as they reputedly feared all sharp objects. On occasions, all the thorns but one were removed from a thorny twig, which then became a small pick known as a witch axe, which was used in the same way to warn away Witches and daemons. At other times, the individual thorns were removed from the branch and scattered on mantles or windowsills or even included in witch bottles with the same intention.

Fig. 1.1. The fragments of silver birch bark and thorn discovered above the entrance doorway in the Shropshire farmhouse. (See also color plate 1.)

These latest artifacts served to further intensify our curiosity, and we began to finalize our plans to visit the various sites we had identified and begin our research in earnest. Our first efforts were to decode the amulet and interpret the sigils that formed the protective power it emanated.

A FIRST MEETING: A BRIEF PREAMBLE

Living in the west of Ireland is indeed a circumstance of mixed blessings. On the one hand, we consider living in one of the most spiritual landscapes in the world a great privilege. On the other hand, living in the most westerly region of Europe, just two miles from the Atlantic Ocean—with nothing but thousands of miles of open sea between us, Newfoundland, and the Americas—does bring with it a number of disadvantages: communication and travel present frustrating though not insurmountable difficulties. Unfortunately, during the crafting of this book these normally surmountable complications were compounded by the arrival of the COVID-19 pandemic and the severe restrictions imposed in an attempt to suppress it. Fortunately, we began the initial research and our collaboration before the virus arrived, and as we were building on years of joint knowledge and experience, we were able to maintain the momentum of research and writing throughout the most difficult and restrictive period of the fight against the pandemic. But first we return to the virus-free period when we began our collaboration, a time when we were free to travel and meet people freely and without restrictions, the time when we began to define the parameters of our research and detail exactly what we were going in search of.

When we eventually met up, following a series of email exchanges, we quickly agreed that the first thing we wanted to define was the exact purpose of the book and what we were intending to achieve through the work. We knew that there was not only a treasure trove of untapped information relating to the ancient Druids and arcane witchcraft that evolved in the Welsh Marches but also a continuing, living tradition that represents a present-day manifestation of this ancient heritage. We knew immediately that we didn't want to develop yet another book on Wicca, knowing that the subject is well covered and augmented with a continuous flow of new titles, as the practice of modern Wicca continues to develop. Neither did we want to produce a theoretical history of Druidic lore and witchcraft without including a means of describing the ancient traditions in a practical, hands-on way.

We began informally exploring the differences between our two traditions, soon finding that the similarities far outnumbered the disparities and that our goal lay in developing convergence, not divergence. The history of occult practice in the Welsh Marches was one of the convergence of two arcane traditions, one emerging from ancient Druidic lore, attested to by both the physical evidence of the landscape and the unbroken line of lore and practice extending back to the origins of the land and peoples of the region, and the other evolving from the cunning women and cunning men who, living within the natural habitat of the Marches, worked with the materials and energies they found surrounding them in their immediate environment. As these two ancient traditions continued to develop, sometimes diverging and other times sharing knowledge and experience, they produced a unique brand of magicians and occult practitioners that changed and influenced the entire world of Western mysticism. Practitioners like John Dee, Thomas Vaughan, and Evan Frederick Morgan, Second Viscount of Tredegar—known as the Black Monk and called Adept of Adepts by Aleister Crowley—translated many of these practices into the burgeoning arte of Western alchemy, while others incorporated the same traditions into modern Wicca, daemonology, and other forms of natural magic.

Both traditions left a trail of evidence testifying to their work, evidence that may be seen not only in the physical landscape and the interiors of the buildings, homes, and farms of the region, but also in the continuing practices that are still maintained by both traditions in the Welsh Marches.

We decided to explore the history of the Welsh Marches and in particular the aspects of that history that contributed to the unique occult culture that defines the region. We intended to reveal the evidence hidden in the landscape and a number of museum archives that defined the progress of both traditions throughout the history of the Marches. We fully expected that many of these artifacts and texts would provide indisputable proof of the workings of Witches and Druids and their numerous contributions to the local occult culture that has changed forever the view of natural magic throughout the Western world. Part of this strange and intriguing culture was the emergence of a number of unique occult practitioners, working in a great number of ways and with a wide range of artes. Exploring the practices of the regions sin eaters, eye biters, spirit hunters, and tomb guardians was an extremely exciting prospect.

Following this, we intended to seek out contemporary interpretations of witchcraft and Druidic lore that stemmed from these ancient practices in order to examine the similarities and differences between the two traditions. Our final aim was to amalgamate the aspects of the ancient and modern traditions of witchcraft and Druidic lore within the region of the Welsh Marches and synthesize them into a working grimoire, a new practical working text that is presented in an accessible language, providing precise instruction on the use of all the methods and techniques uncovered during our intensive research.

After filling the closing hours of our first meeting with the planning of our practical methodology and the division of tasks, we returned to our respective homes filled with enthusiasm and determination, fueled by the excitement of approaching our exploration of the fascinating subject of the Witches, sin eaters, and Druids of the Welsh Marches.

2
The Welsh Marches

The Welsh Marches define the ancient borderland between Wales and England, an area that has had a profound influence on the history of the British Isles. For millennia it has marked the division between the ancient tribal principality of Celtic Wales and the Romanized lands of the Anglo-Saxons that was eventually to become known as England. Populated by a bewildering array of fortresses, castles, hillforts, and ancient fortifications, the Marches have a potent history of conflict, change, and uncertainty that has bred a unique people and culture, establishing itself as a lasting repository for ancient witchcraft, Druidic lore, and occult practice.

On the one hand, we can see the oldest and most significant locations for early witchcraft, while on the other, within a few miles, we can see the largest wooden henge in Europe that once served as the region's focal point for ancient Druidic practice. The entire area, a borderland running the entire length of the nation of Wales, is rich in occult history and mystical sites and has an uninterrupted legacy of esoteric practice. If we are to fully understand the influence that the region has had on Druidic lore and witchcraft, we should first take a brief look at the geographic location of the area and the part it has played in the history of Great Britain.

The people of Wales emerged from the amalgamation of the many individual ancient tribal societies that first populated the region following the retreat of the glaciers of the last Ice Age. It has long been the case that many, if not all, of the Welsh consider themselves, with good justification, to be a separate race to the rest of Great Britain, and like the populations of Scotland and Northern Ireland, they maintain that they have a separate heritage and culture that is still apparent up to the present day. With its own language, mythology, and belief systems, Wales has a unique history defined not only by the sea coast that delineates three-quarters of its border, but also by its only land border to the east, where it adjoins England along its entire length from Chester in the north to Newport in the south.

Originally a vague, ill-defined border, the area has been bitterly disputed by virtually every ruler of both countries until relatively recent times. It is generally accepted that the first real attempt to establish a distinct border was made by King Offa, the Anglo-Saxon king of Mercia, the English region that then bordered Wales. Around 770 CE, King Offa ordered the construction of an earthen dyke, sixty feet wide and eight feet tall, running the length of the border between the Welsh kingdom of Powys and the land of Mercia. Now commonly known as Offa's Dyke (Welsh: Clawdd Offa), it became established as the official border between the two kingdoms but never effectively eliminated the constant incursions that continued uninterrupted. It did, however, have a profound effect on the Welsh population of the region, making it fair game for any Englishman to kill any Welsh person who deliberately or accidentally strayed across the border, with no fear of prosecution or retribution. The remains of the original dyke are still visible along the old border.

In 1066, William the Conqueror successfully invaded Anglo-Saxon Britain, and he, along with his successors, spent much of the next two hundred years attempting to subdue the Welsh with very little effect, finding them a resilient and resourceful people. The efforts of the Norman invaders in the Welsh Marches reinforced the belief that it was an active frontier between the Welsh and what by then was Norman England, creating a unique society and culture that persists to the present day.

During the following two centuries, hundreds of castles, fortified houses, and other resilient fortifications were constructed by the newly

Fig. 2.1. The Welsh Marches sitting in the borderland between Wales and England.

arrived Norman lords, charged with both establishing a broad Norman culture within the region and with defending the burgeoning England of the Normans from the uncivilized and rebellious Welsh. As a result of this intensive building period, the Welsh Marches contains the largest population of motte-and-bailey castles in the British Isles. These are castles with a wooden or stone keep located on a raised area of ground called a motte with a walled courtyard or bailey.

The building of this dense concentration of fortifications and the plantation of the Norman lords who occupied them did little to unify the diverse population of the region, and the Welsh Marches (Old Welsh: Marchia Wallie) developed into a semi-independent region, the Prinicipality of Wales (Old Welsh: Pura Wallia) with its bases deep within Wales, that was governed neither by the English monarchy nor the old Welsh princes or *tywysog,* as they were known.

In an attempt to raise the Norman lords to a greater status, they were given similar rights and authority over their subjects as the Welsh princes enjoyed within Wales, though they still maintained their allegiances to their Norman king. These Marcher lords (Welsh: *barwn y Mers*), their office officially known as Lord Warden of the Marches, were appointed as noble barons directly by the king and charged with protecting the borders between England and Wales. In return for their royal support, the king granted them independent rights that were elsewhere reserved for the Crown. This meant that each lord ruled his own lands by his own law, known at the time as *sicut regale* or "just as the king does." This gave the Norman Marcher barons a unique authority, combining the privileges and power of a Norman lord with the ancient authority of the Welsh princes, which gave them the freedom to apply either English law or the much older Welsh law. Eventually, both these laws combined to become the Marches law, which was used to govern the region and settle any disputes for many years to come.

In 1284, Edward I of England conquered the principality of Wales and brought the lands previously controlled by the Welsh princes into the hands of the English Crown, at the same time creating the title of the Prince of Wales, which to this day remains the title of the oldest male heir of the English monarchy. Two centuries later, Edward IV established the Council of Wales and the Marches as the governing authority under the English Crown. Slowly, as the Marcher lords died, their lands reverted to the Crown. After the 1536 Act of Union and the introduction of the Laws in Wales Acts of 1535 and 1542, Wales was effectively adjoined to England under the legal jurisdiction of England and Wales, and the Marcher lordships were abolished and their powers returned to the Crown.

When William III (William of Orange) took the throne from James II of England (VII of Scotland) during the Glorious Revolution in 1689, the Council was finally disbanded, and both the Welsh and the English areas of the Marches were formed into the counties that we more or less see today.

The land and the people of the Welsh Marches have emerged from this turbulent history, fraught with conflict, change, and unrest, as a resilient and versatile culture with a distinct ability to adapt to changing circumstances and embrace new philosophies. Their history and worldview have included a singular acceptance of the occult and have depended upon an unwavering commitment to the pagan beliefs of the ancient Druids together with a dedication to the arcane lore of the old cunning folk, which has evolved into what we now choose to call witchcraft. The land itself holds the evidence of its ancient history and the continuous conflict that eventually bonded the inhabitants together rather than divided them. The numerous castles, manors, and fortified buildings that stand in various states of repair give evidence of the unsettled history of the region and still define the story of the changing borderland between Wales and England.

3
Magic, Religion, and Ritual in the Welsh Marches

If we are to fully understand the purpose of the protective devices, curses, and other magical workings employed in the Welsh Marches, we must briefly return to the first principles of magic as we now know them.

THE PRINCIPLES OF MAGIC

In the context of our exploration, we may consider magic to be a means of influencing the mundane world by gaining access to and the assistance of the supernatural domain. Furthermore, we can see that it is often, if not exclusively, used in circumstances where the more normal, everyday methods are inappropriate, ineffective, or both. This typically means that magic is used in unpredictable, uncertain circumstances where a high degree of risk is present and seldom in situations where the outcome may be foreseeable or within the control of the persons involved.

The relationship between magic and what may be called the scientific world, where the expectation is the known, proven, and predictable, has varied over the ages, and generally our history is one of magic receding as science and physical experimentation progressing. Even so, we can also see that where science, medicine, and physics cannot provide the solution to a specific need, the focus on magic increases and takes their place.

We need not go too far back into history to find a time when many of our everyday events were not as well understood as they may be today, and each day was filled with natural events that were neither understood nor were their outcomes predictable. The changes of the seasons, the weather, and the influence of both on crops and livestock was poorly understood, and ritual magic was used in an attempt to both predict their progress and influence their effects. At the same time, magic ritual and folk medicine were, to all intents and purposes, the same thing, with people turning to magic ritual as often as they would to the herbal folk medicine. In fact, both were usually administered by the same cunning folk and wisewomen. At times of danger and high risk, the science of the age provided neither the protection nor comfort of the magic alternatives, and most travelers, men-at-arms, and pilgrims would have taken with them as many talismans and protective amulets as they would have herbal remedies. For countryfolk and farmers, magic played an indispensable role in protecting their homes, crops, and livestock, curing diseased cattle or blighted crops, and ensuring sufficient food to sustain their families throughout the changing year.

If we then go on to consider the other side of this same coin, magic was often used as a means to curse and inflict damage upon people in a way that natural methods could not. We know that in the natural world, poison, fire, and other physical means may well have been employed to inflict hurt or damage to people and property, but magic ritual and cursing was a common, everyday method of inducing maleficent influence.

Both these positive and negative aspects of magic have their place in the history of the Welsh Marches, together with the more complex use of magical devices, charms, and amulets to protect against the most negative influences when and where they have been deployed. To fully understand how each of these aspects of magic works, we must now focus on the basic principles of magic and ritual together with its application in the ancient borderland of England and Wales.

Magic, as an arte, has been practiced since the beginning of human history, and ever since its inception we have tried in vain to understand and explain it in a way that makes sense in the mundane world. Although there are many books, ancient and relatively modern, that explore how magic may be utilized and what rituals and invocations may be used, little has been done to explain the principles underlying its process. It was not until the early twentieth century that the first definition of the tenets of magic emerged with the proposal of the laws that underpin its application.

The first and probably the most profound of these laws is the Law of Sympathy, which, as its name suggests, proposes that a magical connection between substances, objects, or people exists whether they are in close proximity or far apart. This implies that magic transcends time and space and is equally effective at any distance and at any moment in time.

This fundamental Law of Sympathy may itself be subdivided into two composite parts: the Law of Similarity (sometimes called the Law of Correspondence) and the Law of Contagion (sometimes called the Law of Contact). These are the two laws that define the practical aspects of magic and give an understanding as to exactly how it may be utilized. More simply, they propose what type of magic is most effective in each circumstance.

The Law of Similarity can be seen in almost every ancient belief system, but it is most well known for its application in magical healing and alchemy. The idea that like produces like or that a result typically resembles its cause plays a fundamental role in the Doctrine of Similarity, which is the basis of homeopathy and many other schools of herbal healing dating back to antiquity, where herbs such as wound wort were used to heal wounds because the plants themselves have holes or wounds in their leaves, or that walnuts strengthen the brain because the seeds resemble the brain itself. The extension of this form of natural magic is a form of magic that has attracted a more negative reputation.

Image magic often involves making a representational image of a thing or living person to inflict harm or even bring about the death of the person it is meant to represent. Typically, this is done by cutting the image, sticking pins in it, burning it, or mutilating it in some other fashion, with the intention of inflicting the same consequence upon the individual or item it may represent. The most well-known example of image magic is the use of a doll or poppet as a representation of a living person with the intention that when wounds are inflicted upon the poppet the victim will suffer a related pain or injury as a consequence. Other more positive examples of image magic may be readily seen with the wearing of images with the intention of attracting good fortune or protection from evil and hurt. The Christian belief that wearing a crucifix, the image of Christ being crucified on the cross, around the neck offers protection against evil, or the image of St. Christopher as a form of protection for travelers, are both examples of an adapted form of image magic, as are the many protective images in the form of medallions, amulets, and talismans that are worn by followers of most belief systems around the world. Probably the most mundane of these is the charm bracelet, which is composed of a variety of protective images drawn from ancient magic and folk culture. This form of image magic has encroached into the realm of everyday fashion and status symbol.

The Law of Similarity is also the basic principle of every alchemical working, with the fundamental tenet of alchemy: as above, then so below. It is the intention of every alchemist that through his or her work the alchemist should mirror all the aspects of heaven here on Earth below.

The second of these laws, the Law of Contagion, states that when an object or person comes into contact with another thing or person it has an influence or effect upon it and that influence is retained even when the contact no longer exists, no matter what distance or time period lies between them. It is through the use of contagious magic that we see the phenomenon of the pilgrimage where pilgrims travel huge distances through extreme conditions in the hope of simply touching a religious relic and thereby attaching to themselves some form of benefit from the contact, such as a blessing or a cure. Another product of the Law of Contagion is the use of personal possessions and bodily excreta, such as urine, blood, hair, teeth, fingernail clippings and the like, in a magic ritual as a means of affecting the original owner. Included in these items are belongings like clothing, hats, and particularly shoes, together with other personal items that may have come into close physical contact with the victim, taking on his or her shape or absorbing the victim's perspiration in the process. A more everyday example of this principle is the practice of movie-star fans collecting items of clothing or other personal possessions of their idol or of simply touching their idol in the hope of forming a personal connection or relationship. As a consequence of this belief, there are many accounts originating from the period of individuals taking great care not to discard hair trimmings, nail cuttings, clothing, shoes, and other personal belongings in case they are discovered by Witches and used to curse the individual or their home and possessions. We will see in chapters 6 and 14 how this influenced the use of witch bottles and other concealed protective devices from the early modern period (c. 1500–1800) to the present day.

Another aspect of contagious magic that is particularly germane to our investigation is what may be called transference magic. This maintains that if a person or item comes into contact with another person or item, the latter will attract or absorb any condition that the original may be suffering from and subsequently later transfer that condition to another person or item without being affected by distance or time. Alternatively, the transfer recipient may absorb the particular condition and hold on to it indefinitely unto themselves.

We shall meet all of these forms of magic again as we progress through our investigation, and we shall also discover that they are used equally by the Druids, Witches, and other workers of the occult artes we encounter in the history of the Welsh Marches.

In writing the above, we acknowledge that many readers may already be well acquainted with the principles and laws we have described, and we include them here in the pursuit of completeness and for the benefit of those new to the arte. Also, as these terms have been applied and interpreted in a number of different occult environments, it is necessary to establish a common understanding of each term in the context that we are using it here. To this end, it is also important that we establish a common understanding of a number of terms and concepts that we will encounter as we progress through the chapters that follow.

TERMINOLOGY AND INTERPRETATION

It would be impossible to explore the concept of concealed protective devices without coming across the term *apotropaic,* a word that has been used consistently throughout history to describe such devices. The word originates from the Greek *apotropaios,* which may be translated as "the turning away of evil" or "protection from evil influences or actions." Apotropaic is used to define any action or object used with the specific intention of averting or expelling malevolent intentions. The expression may also be used to define devices or activities intended to attract good fortune, health, fertility, and wealth. Popular apotropaic devices include such things as the Christian crucifix and charms depicting popular saints such as St. Christopher, St. Jude, and so on.

Another much-used term used in relation to protective devices is *superstition.* The understanding of this word will vary substantially among individuals, depending on their particular religious code and worldview. Generally, we may assume that any interaction with the supernatural that does not fall within the rituals and beliefs of the mainstream religious institutions may be defined as superstitious. Superstition comes from the Latin word *superstitio,* originally meaning "to stand over" in the context of standing over something and staring in wonder or disbelief. Later, in medieval Christian Britain, it became a description for worshipping God (the Christian God) in an inappropriate or profane way. As a result of this usage it gained a negative connotation, associated with evil, fear, and, of course, the devil.

A term that has become firmly established in our everyday language is *luck.* It first came into common usage in the English language during the 1400s CE, at the height of the witchcrafting period, originating from the German word *lucke,* which may be translated as "good fortune" and was used as an everyday salutation that we still see in our culture with expressions such as farewell and goodbye. Typically, it has a mundane usage in that it is not associated with witchcraft and magic but is more readily understood as an outcome that occurs by random chance rather than by one's own actions, whereas originally it was seen as an active force that operated beyond the individual's influence for good or bad and that had its source in the supernatural.

The word *magic* may be used in a number of different (though related) contexts. As a form of visual trickery or illusion, it is most commonly seen in what may be called stage magic. It is broadly accepted that this type of magic is purely a form of entertainment and has no direct relationship with the supernatural, though this may often be implied in order to suggest that some form of inexplicable, supernatural force is used to cause an outcome. When used in its occult sense, it has been modified into a number of different spellings such as magik, majik, and magick to differentiate it from its more mundane stage use. Some of these adapted spellings have been promoted to establish a particular association with a specific form of belief, ritual, or practice, such as Wicca, Wica, and New Age paganism. In the context of our exploration, we use the word *magic* in its definition as a belief and ritual practice used to influence and manipulate both supernatural and natural forces and beings to produce a specific outcome, with or without the direct presence of the user. Although there have been periods of history where the ideas of magic, science, and medicine have merged to a lesser or greater extent, magic in our application can be seen as being independent from science and formal mainstream Western religion.

One of the most used and well-known devices of witchcraft is the curse, and we shall see this word used over and over again in the chapters that follow. In modern uses, the word has two principal definitions. More commonly it means the use of profane, offensive, or obscene words in conversation. But this meaning is a direct result of its use in witchcraft and the word's other primary definition: the invocation of supernatural forces by a Witch or other practitioner and its projection by the invocator to his or her intended target to induce a specific result or outcome. Though that outcome may be good or bad, it was generally believed that Witches used profane language in their curses.

Curses may take many and varied forms and are not restricted by distance or time. They may or may not be closely related to the means and/or the materials used to invoke and project their influence and may be bound to a person, object, or place for an indefinite period of time, maintaining their influence throughout. In some (but not all) cases, they may be raised or removed by a countercurse, often closely related to the form of the original curse or working. They may be prevented or protection may be given to a potential recipient by the use of various protective devices, charms, amulets, talismans, and so on that counteract or inhibit the curse's effectiveness. Curses are invariably invoked as a means of producing a maleficent outcome, causing hurt or harm to an individual and his or her home and possessions. A great deal of attention and effort was expended during the period of witchcraft we are investigating in devising means and materials to either protect against curses or lift their influence by countercurses and other workings.

The final expression that we need to define is the use of the phrase *Witch's familiar*. This is most often used to describe any type of small animal that may accompany and assist the Witch in her magical workings. By essence, the familiar is typically an ordinary, unassuming animal such as a frog, toad, bird, or dog, but most often familiars are recorded as being cats. Occasionally, larger animals like a horse, donkey, pig, or cow have been known to be identified as familiars, usually because of their friendly nature and their closeness to their witch companions. Familiars can be used in a number of ways to assist the Witch in her magical endeavors, sometimes carrying spells and curses to their intended recipient, other times to venture to places where their witch companions may not go. The history of the Witch's familiar is as old as the history of the Witches themselves, and it has been suggested that the elevated cultural status of many such animals stems from their original relationship with their Witch or magician colleagues. The theory of the Witch's familiar seems to be intrinsically connected to the idea of daemonic possession, the notion of the Witch being possessed or physically and spiritually occupied by the devil as a result of a daemonic pact entered into for the mutual benefit of both parties. As part of his commitment to the pact, the devil also provided the Witch with his worldly representatives in the form of familiars to aid her in her devilish work. His familiars usually manifested themselves in familiar forms, such as cats, dogs, toads, birds, and even miniature horses and donkeys. Witches' familiars often suffered the same fate as their human companions and were typically thrown onto the fire when Witches were burned or drowned if the Witch succumbed to her dipping.

We are given to understand that a Witch's familiars were provided by the devil along with various other sprites and imps to assist the Witch in her work and accompanied her on every occasion. Records suggest that familiars were also sent on missions and tasks alone, following the instructions of either the Witch or, indeed, the devil himself. Being able to travel faster than the Witch and gain access to places and spaces that were too small and inaccessible for the Witch to enter, they were the perfect messengers for either of their masters. We shall hear more of these devoted familiars later when we examine the various protective depositions used to deter Witches and spirits from houses, farms, animals, and even common people.

4
The Shropshire Amulet

The task we had set ourselves was to interpret the meaning of the amulet and the significance of the images both cast into the original amulet and those scratched or carved onto its reverse side, and to determine just why the item was secreted within the fireplace of the farmhouse. What was the person who placed the amulet behind the mantle hoping it would achieve?

Although we had looked carefully at each of the three artifacts found at the farmhouse in our initial meeting, we needed to look much more closely at the amulet in particular to discover its source and significance and what it was intended to do.

We were able to asertain that the core of the existing farmhouse had been built in the early seventeenth century and subsequently enlarged around fifty years later. The mantle where the cache was discovered is part of the original building, and we could find nothing to challenge our belief that it was put into place when the house was first built and had remained there undisturbed for the last four hundred or so years.

We had established that the amulet itself was cast from pewter, a popular metal amalgam of the period, frequently used in the manufacture of tableware, goblets, and beakers, as well as in jewelery and decorative ornamentation. Although the surfaces of the amulet were well worn and a little distorted, remains of gold leaf were clearly visable in the recesses of the cast image, suggesting that the surface of the obverse side containing the cast image had been gilded with gold leaf either in part or as a whole.

The craftsmanship employed in creating the amulet was not inconsiderable, with both the design and execution being of a high standard. The carving of a suitable mold in which to cast the piece is a skilled craft, as is the casting of pewter itself, so it is reasonable to assume the piece was designed and cast by an artisan whitesmith, the guild name given to workers of pewter at the time. Each professional whitesmith was required by law to register his own hallmark, which identified the quality of the pewter, and also include his own identifying mark or "touch," as it was called. Though we looked closely, we could find no such mark and so remain unable to identify the maker. Our opinion is that it must have been a local craftsman with an interst in the occult who did not want to be identified or associated with the crafting of such a piece. It remains the case that making the detailed

Fig. 4.1. The front (obverse) of the amulet. (See also color plate 2.)

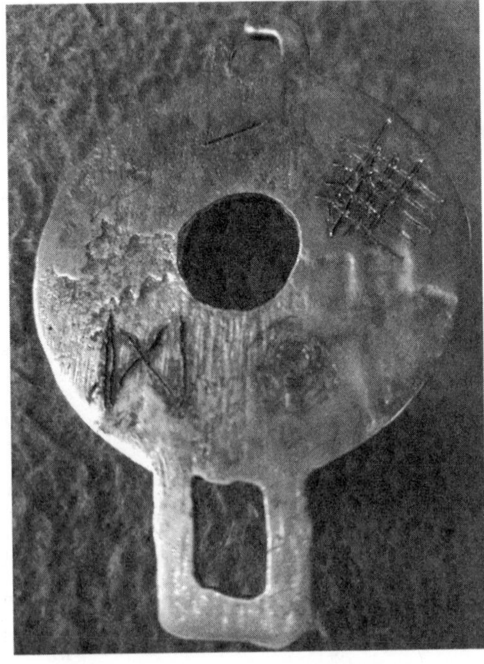

Fig. 4.2. Amulet reverse showing witch marks inscribed by the crafter. (See also color plate 3.)

mold needed to cast such a piece would only be done in anticipation of casting multiple repeat pieces, each exactly the same as the other. We can only speculate as to whether more than one piece was cast and, if so, how many more may be hidden in similar caches in other houses within the region.

DECONSTRUCTION OF THE SHADOWS OF THE SIGIL

The first step in decoding the meaning of the sigils cast into the amulet and those enscribed on the reverse as seen above is to interpret the images into schematic representations so that each individual aspect or shadow, as they are referred to in Druidic lore, may be separated from the whole and the meaning of each explained. This was a time-consuming task requiring both the coauthors' examination and interpretation. One of the surprising outcomes of this analysis was the similarity of the ancient witchcraft and Druidic traditions. To discover that the two cultures shared many of the images and understood them in the same way was a revelation, and to further establish that both cultures put them to the same use was even more remarkable. At first glance the sigils on either side of the amulet appear to be relatively simple, as can be seen from the schematic illustration in figure 4.3. But once we began our deconstruction and came to an agreement about the various interpretations of each individual shadow, we discovered that, as they were reconstructed in part and then in the whole, the meanings became more complex as each was reinforced and amplified by the other. When the whole was once again reassembled, it became apparent that the whole of the image in the obverse was an extremely powerful enabling device, and the sigils carved crudely into the reverse of the amulet at a later date are without doubt a commanding apotropaic device containing a collection of well-known protective witch marks.

In the following paragraphs we shall follow the process of deconstructing the shadows and explain the meaning of each image.

ANALYSIS OF INDIVIDUAL ELEMENTS

Here we shall examine the shadows that unite to make up and empower the final sigil and the various individual elements that blend together to create the sigil. This is the whole, and we shall return to it once we have deconstructed each of its shadows.

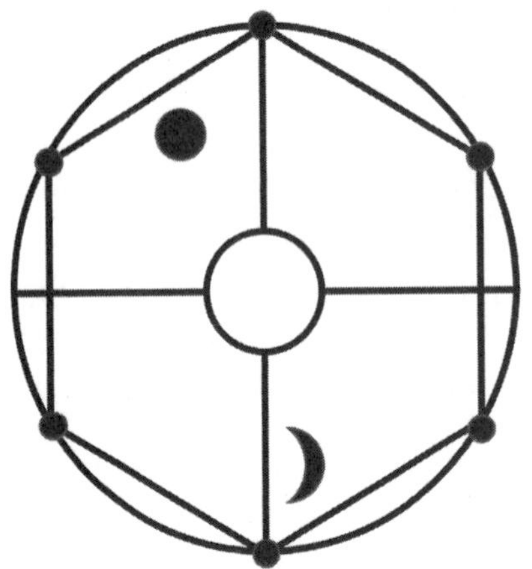

Fig. 4.3. A schematic illustration of the Shropshire amulet (obverse).

We begin at the beginning with the shadows known to ancient witchcraft and Druidic learning. First is the sigil of the Druidic sun, the male giver of life, the eternal light of knowledge and wisdom, and the symbol of the universal energy, the communal spirit, the major circle.

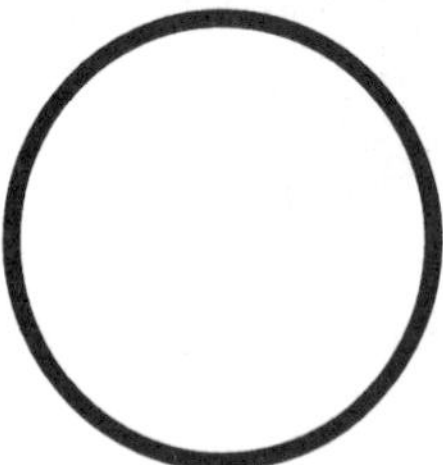

Fig. 4.4. The sigil of the Druidic sun.

Fig. 4.5. The sigil of the Druidic earth.

Next is the sigil of the Druidic earth (figure 4.5). The embodiment of long life and security, the female nature. After that is the sigil of the

Fig. 4.6. The sigil of the Druidic spirit.

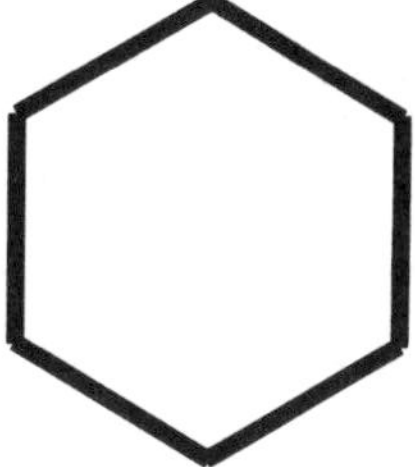

Fig. 4.7. The hexagon of the harmony of the bee.

Druidic spirit (figure 4.6), which symbolizes both male and female, and the symbol of the individual within nature and the personal spirit, the minor circle.

The sigil of the harmony of the bee is the hexagon (fig. 4.7). This is a symbol of unity, embracing the whole of the community and an image of order and dependency and represents fructivity and wholesomeness.

Next are the universal sigil of the moon, the female Mother Nature and the universe, the symbol of gestation and birth, and the giver of nourishment and nurture (fig. 4.8) and the sigil of the sun, the male provider and giver of life (fig. 4.9).

Fig. 4.8. The sigil of the moon.

Fig. 4.9. The sigil of the sun.

At each corner of the hexagon is a convergence point; these are the six points or stations (fig. 4.10 on page 28). Each represents a source of elemental energy. Each of the four major convergences embodies one of the major world essences (fig. 4.11 on page 28). The upper two, air and fire, are the male, and the lower two, water and earth, are the female.

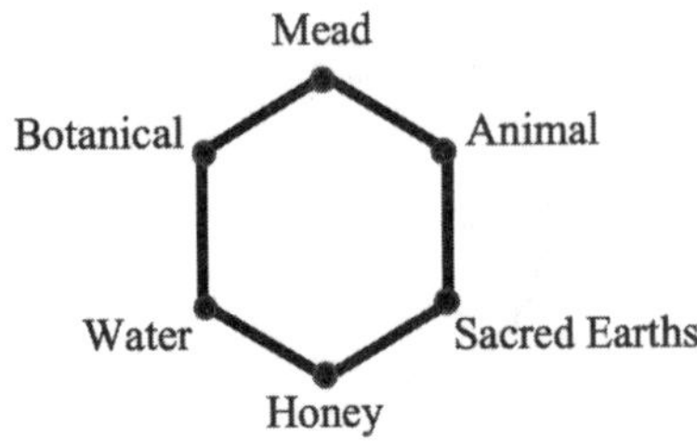

Fig. 4.10. The six convergence points or stations of the hexagon.

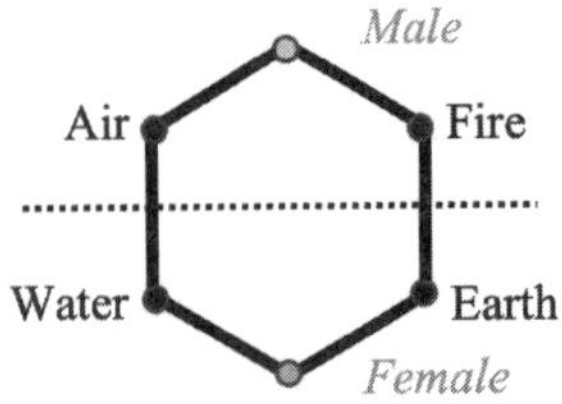

Fig. 4.11. The four major convergence points of the hexagon.

The hexagon displays the upper chevron of the male phallus, the power and force of fertilization and procreation, and the lower cup or chalice of the female vagina and the womb of creation. The two supporting pillars are knowledge and wisdom. The whole illustrates how the balance between male and female is maintained through the application of wisdom and knowledge.

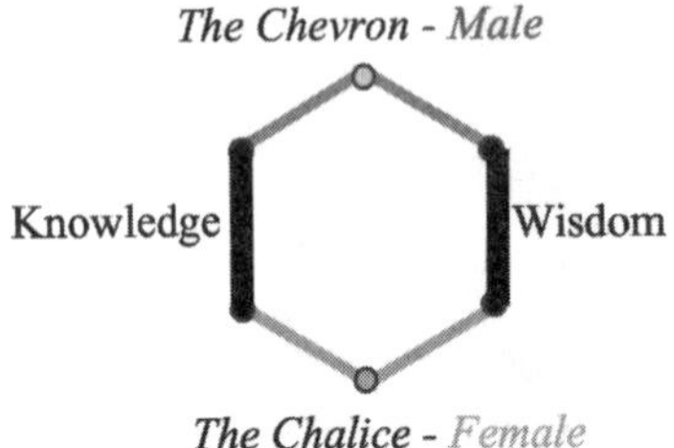

Fig. 4.12. The upper and lower sections of the hexagon and their supporting pillars.

When the sigil of Earth is combined with that of the sun, we have the sigil of eternity, the symbol of longevity, ancient wisdom, and lore and the combining of the male and female (fig. 4.13). When the sigil of the Druidic spirit is added to that of the sigil of eternity, we see the image of the individual within the whole (fig. 4.14).

The minor sigil of the individual personal energy is within the major circle of the communal energy. This represents the individual's position within eternity. The two intersecting horizons represent separation. The horizontal horizon separates the upper air and fire from

Fig. 4.13. The combination of the sigils of Earth and the sun giving the Druidic sigil of eternity.

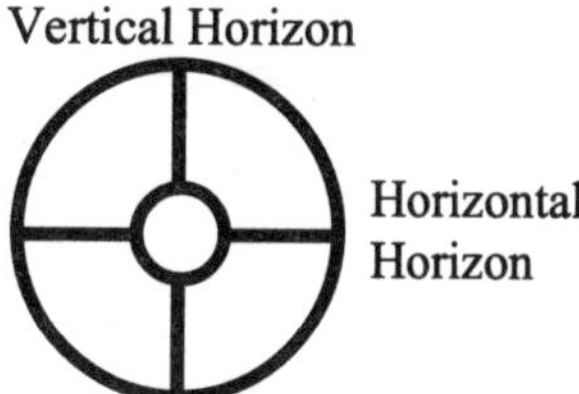

Fig. 4.14. The image of the individual within the whole.

the lower earth and water. The vertical horizon separates the day (left) from the night (right).

When the hexagon is superimposed upon the major circle (fig. 4.15), we see how all the elements of the hexagon are surrounded by the all-encompassing major circle of the communal spirit: the sun in the upper-left (day, male) above the horizon (air, fire) and the moon in the lower-right (night, female) below the horizon (earth, water).

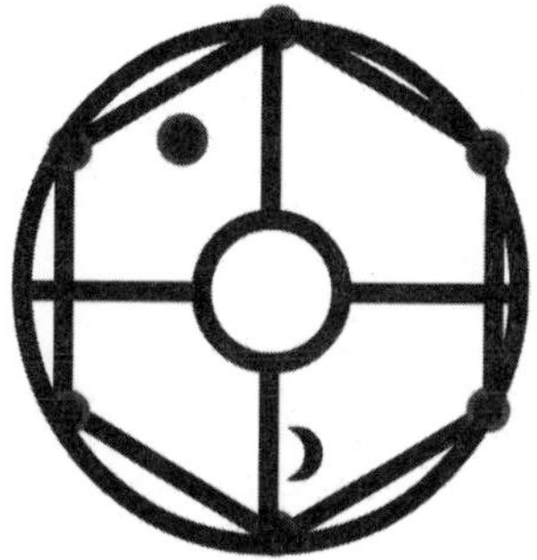

Fig. 4.15. The hexagon within the major circle.

Figure 4.16 on page 30 is the wholly restored hexagon of the beehive (*Yr Hexagon Cwch Gwenin*) with all its complexities just as it appears on the obverse face of the amulet. The synergenic composition of the shadows of the hexagon amplify the vitality of each individual sigil, as each interact with the other to form the synergy of the whole. When we look at the compound sigil as it is cast into the amulet, we see two other

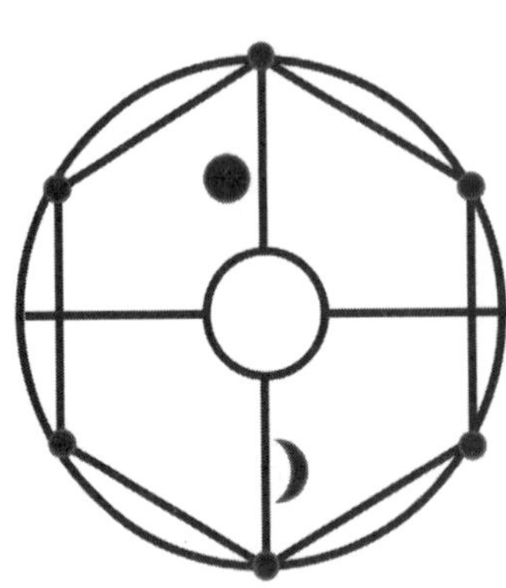

Fig. 4.16. The combined sigil as it appears on the Shropshire amulet.

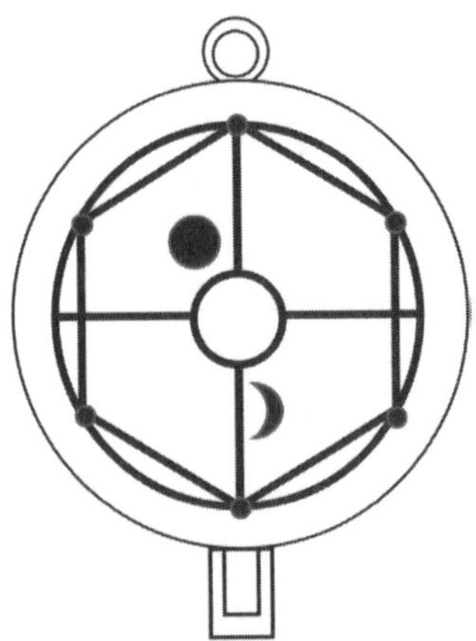

Fig. 4.17. A schematic illustration of cast Shropshire amulet.

aspects of the complete item: the first being the hanging loop at the top, assumingly included in order that the amulet may be hung around the neck and the second, a similarly cast extension at the bottom of the amulet (fig. 4.17).

At first this was confusing, as there seemed no need to have two hanging loops, one at the top and the other at the bottom. Following further research at the museum it was discovered that the bottom extension was a means of fixing the amulet to the top of a stave by means of a slot cut into the stave top to receive the extension, which is then secured by aligning the bottom loop with a similar-sized hole in the stave top and driving a wooden dowel through the hole and the amulet's loop. The result created what may be called a stave of power, an object that displayed both symbolic and practical purpose, as we shall see in later chapters.

The next step was to apply the same analytical process to the witch marks scratched onto the reverse face of the amulet (fig. 4.18). The scratched image in figure 4.19, a witch marking, is an apotropaic device designed to confuse and entrap evil spirits within the labyrinth of lines and spaces. The group of concentric circles is another witch mark (fig. 4.20), an apotropaic device designed to entrap the evil spirit within the spaces between the decreasing circles.

Fig. 4.18. A schematic illustration of the reverse of the Shropshire amulet.

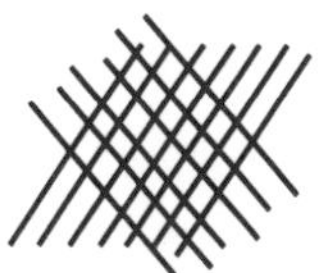

Fig. 4.19. Labyrinth witch mark.

Fig. 4.20. Concentric circles witch mark.

Fig. 4.21. The portal entry witch mark, designed to bar entry into a building.

The inscription in figure 4.21 is designed to prevent the entry of an unwanted evil spirit. The two vertical lines represent the upright portals or door jams, and the cross in between them is a very recognizable image preventing or baring entry. This is another witch mark typically seen carved into the wooden door frames or thresholds giving entry to farm buildings and homes.

Each of these witch marks is a powerful protective device in its own right and may be seen in many of the houses belonging to the same period within the Welsh Marches and beyond. To see three such witch marks used on a single amulet is a remarkable event and suggests there was a specific need for extremely powerful and robust protection, much more than either of us had previously encountered.

The amulet is a remarkable example of the syncretism of two belief systems into a new practical system, merging the tradition of beliefs from witchcraft and the Druidic traditions.

5
Witchcraft, Christianity, and the Witch Terror

When organized Christianity first established itself in Great Britain in the sixth century, it was in the form of Roman Catholicism. Every church, monastery, and Christian institution was subject to Catholic doctrine. This is important because of the Catholic Church's attitude toward Witches in particular. All across Europe and beyond, the Catholic Church showed an initial tolerance to the practice of witchcraft. It identified that many of the practices of witchcraft were common to their own rituals, and as with the earlier military conquests and land occupation by the Romans, the religious leaders were more concerned with keeping the conquered population subdued and in good order rather than needlessly imposing their politics and religion upon their new citizens in a forceful manner.

SIMILARITIES BETWEEN PRACTICES IN THE CATHOLIC CHURCH AND WITCHCRAFT

The Catholic Church appeared to have accepted witchcraft in the same way as it had other indigenous belief systems and allowed witchcraft to continue to maintain the status quo. It also appears that the familiarity of the rituals and practices of witchcraft led the early Catholic Church in Great Britain to believe they "understood" witchcraft and in doing so could absorb it into their everyday society. We must remember that at this time witchcraft was not yet seen as a fundamentally evil practice but as a relatively benign custom, engaged mainly in herbal cures, harmless fortune-telling, and other magical rituals, which the church was well aware of. Many of the customs of the wisewomen or cunning women of the time were shared by the early Catholic Church.

The wearing of talismans and charms was a well-established Catholic practice, with pilgrims wearing medals and medallions illustrating the destinations of their pilgrimage and the particular saint their journey honored in the expectation of being protected and beneficially blessed as a reward. Similarly, the veneration of relics, a well-accepted Christian preoccupation, reached its height during the same period. Every church of merit displayed a saintly relic on its altar and enjoyed a substantial income from pilgrims' donations. Many of these relics of the saints, be it a finger bone, tooth, or one of the many apparent splinters from the "true cross," were, and still are, exhibited in pride of place in rural churches and city cathedrals alike, while many are also taken on religious processions during Christian anniversaries and celebrations.

Another common feature of both practices is the importance of images and icons, be they statues, paintings, tapestries, texts, and so on. In the case of the Catholic Church, prayers are offered up to particular imagery, chosen in the hope of maximum benefit, while in witchcraft, images, texts, and artifacts (such as poppets, witch bottles, written charms, etc.) are used to cast intentions both good and evil. Libation chalices, offering plates, and sacrificial food and drink are established elements of both Christian and witchcraft rituals, and the use of ritual vessels, ritual clothing, altar trappings, and decorations would be recognizable to priest and Witch alike.

One other common aspect of both beliefs, which may seem peculiar to us today, was the use of curses as a formal means of punishment and retribution. The idea of a modern-day Christian priest or minister, no matter what their denomination, issuing blood-curdling curses from the pulpit seems very unlikely, but it was common for the priests of the time to do just that. First, we must recognize that there are a good number of curses mentioned in the Christian Bible, and within Catholic ceremonies such as excommunication (the anathema) and the ordination liturgy of nuns and bishops. In the early days of the Catholic Church in Great Britain, bishops actively encouraged their priests to both regularly reiterate the curses of the Bible and invoke their own bitter curses more attuned to their local congregation, no doubt with the idea that they would be easily recognized and feared by their followers. We shall see later a more detailed exploration of the use of curses and how the practice developed throughout the age.

All these shared ritual constituents of sympathetic magic made the witchcraft of the Welsh Marches tolerable, if not entirely acceptable, to the Christian church of the day, which itself contained more than a little hint of natural magic within its practices and rituals.

PERSECUTION OF WITCHES BY THE CATHOLIC CHURCH

The Catholic Church was, however, not entirely benign in its treatment of Witches during this period. At the beginning of the twelfth century, the church decided to take decisive action in the face of rising insurrection and what they considered to be mounting heresy against the holy Roman Church. The church, determined to stamp out all forms of heresy and opposition, instituted the Holy Inquisition, an office within the Catholic Church that was charged with rooting out and punishing heretics wherever it found them, which included Jews, Muslims, and all forms of witchcraft, sorcery, and conjuration. The Inquisition's reputation for ruthless prosecution, interrogation, and indiscriminate execution grew rapidly, and accounts of the inquisitors' fearful torture and merciless extraction of confessions struck fear into the hearts of all those who encountered them over the following centuries.

The Inquisition had its start in France and by the Late Middle Ages (1250–1500) had expanded to Spain and Portugal in response to the Protestant Reformation and Catholic Counter-Reformation. The Inquisition reached England in the mid-1500s under Mary Tudor or Mary I, daughter of Henry VII and Catherine of Aragon. Mary I, a

Catholic, briefly took power after the Protestant Reformation and was infamous for burning heretics, notably some three hundred Protestants.

It was Archbishop Thomas Arundel who passed the very first act against witchcraft in 1401 in Parliament. Called De Heretico Comburendo (Regarding the Burning of the Heretics), it was one of the most punitive regulations in England. The act formally defined witchcraft as a heretical practice and stipulated that Witches be burned so that "such punishment strike fear in the minds of others." Trials were, however, restricted to the ecclesiastical courts. Not until the witchcraft acts of the sixteenth century did witchcraft become punishable in the courts of common law.

THE PROTESTANT CHURCH AND WITCHCRAFT

This general tolerance of witchcraft by the organized church (and consequently the population as a whole) changed completely when King Henry VIII abandoned the Church of Rome so that he could divorce his wife (Catherine of Aragon) and remarry and by doing so embraced the Protestant belief system that was flooding mainland Europe, which eventually resulted in the formation of the Church of England in 1534. From this point on, Catholicism was never again the official religion of Great Britain.

The arrival of Protestant Christianity had widespread consequences for the population and landscape of the Welsh Marches and, in particular, its Witches and Druids, who, along with the Catholic priests and acolytes, were to enter a period of unparalleled persecution. With the Catholic Church outlawed, its adherents and clergy, along with its many nuns, monks, and other devotees, found shelter in the homes and manors of the old Catholic families, who sought to maintain their faith as they watched the destruction of their churches, monasteries, and abbeys. The new church's attitude to witchcraft and Witches became an important part of its efforts to distance itself from the Church of Rome and establish a new understanding of Christianity. It abandoned the pomp, flamboyant ceremony, and liturgy of the Catholic Church in favor of a simpler, less ornate form of worship and set aside the iconography and gilded artifacts, replacing them with humbler images of apocryphal stories from the Bible. It sought to teach the congregation a less formal Christianity without compromising control and authority over the population. In this new society, witchcraft and the Witch were seen in a different light. The new church's liturgy and ritual lost much of what the earlier Catholic Church had shared in common with witchcraft.

Most fundamentally, it challenged the Witch's ability to embrace nature in a way that appeared to the new church as performing magic and influencing people, things, and events in a way that, as Protestants saw it, was only possible for God. No human, no matter how powerful his or her magic may be, could shape things in a way that only God was capable of doing; therefore, they reasoned that Witches could only be frauds and charlatans, exploiting ignorant, unschooled people for their own benefit—or were they? Faced with the fact that witchcraft and the wisewoman were an established part of society and fulfilled a vital role in their community—along with the visible evidence that many of their practices, particularly those of healing and midwifery, yielded beneficial results—it was impossible for them to eliminate the rituals and practices that were both effective and widely believed, so they sought more dubious tactics.

In the absence of any meaningful understanding of how the cunning women's cures and remedies worked, they propagated the belief that only God could cure illness and it was only his will that determined whether you should live or die—a belief that is still maintained by some of the more extreme interpretations of various religions all over the world. This statement, in itself, went a long way to instilling in the church's followers a questioning or disbelief of the old ways and of the Witches who maintained them. However, there is no real evidence to suggest that prayers or appeals to the saints resulted in cures, the alleviation of pain, or the avoidance of death; neither is there anything to suggest that people changed their habits and abandoned the cures of the wisewoman. It is more likely that most people would have sought cures and remedies by combining both beliefs for their own benefit.

If, then, it was not possible for these all-too-human Witches to produce results that only God could possibly cause, how did they achieve their mysterious successes? The church saw only one way these women could achieve their supernatural outcomes: it must be the devil's work! And how did the devil achieve these works? By occupying a Witch's physical body. By possession, the devil achieved his evil intent by working through the Witch's body and spirit.

From this moment onward, the Witch was not the simple cunning woman she had previously been, she was now possessed by the devil, which explained how she could achieve results that under normal circumstances were only achievable by God. This association was the beginning of the definition of the Witch as intrinsically linked to evil and the work of the devil. As a result, Witches were to experience a long period of persecution from the church, the law, and the monarchy, a time when Witches lost their standing in their community, their freedom to practice openly, and sometimes even their lives. The Witch became a person who used magic to do evil (*maleficia*), and she became defined by her solemn pact with the devil and her obedience to his will. As the Anglican Church, the monarchy, and civil law continued to buttress one another's beliefs, it was the Witch's pact with the devil that became her greatest crime, not the activities she undertook.

With this new interpretation of witchcraft and in particular the demonological component emphasized by the church, a pan-European fear and persecution of Witches began to emerge. This witch terror or witch fear encompassed the entire population and gave rise to legislation authorizing the torture, ill treatment, and unjustified imprisonment that inflamed public opinion against Witches and encouraged so many unsubstantiated accusations and interrogations of a great number of wholly innocent women.

DEFINING WITCHES AND WITCHCRAFT IN PRINT: HISTORICAL PUBLICATIONS

Much was written about Witches and witchcraft at this time, with many of the more prominent publications having a profound influence on how Witches were perceived at all levels, from the ruling monarchy to the common folk of the Welsh Marches. A number of classic publications on witchcraft emerged during this period in which writers described what exactly constituted a witch. Their opinions proved to be hugely instrumental in formulating the opinion of the lawmakers and witchmongers as well as the general population of the Welsh Marches and beyond. These now-famous texts influenced the laws and gave detailed instructions to the witchfinders and witchmongers on how to identify, capture, interrogate, condemn, and execute those they suspected of being Witches. It is important to note here that none of these laws or instructions applied to the Druids of the era, who somehow manged to avoid the witch fears and witch hunts that condemned so many innocent women.

We investigate a few of the more famous of these publications so that we may understand just how they managed to influence so many people and how they fueled the whole nation's persecution of those women who otherwise would have been thought of as simple housewives, mothers, and ordinary citizens of England in general and of the Welsh Marches in particluar.

The Printing Revolution and the Gutenberg Bible

Ever since the invention of the printing press by German goldsmith and inventor Johannes Gutenberg (which resulted in the Printing Revolution around 1440) printed texts in the form of bound books, pamphlets, printed ballads, and broadsides became readily available to all those who were able to read. Significantly for the time, the first book to be printed and mass produced was the Christian Bible, the famous Mazarin or Gutenberg Bible, first printed in Latin in the 1450s. Gutenberg's printed Bible, even in its early Latin form, has undoubtedly influenced the Western world more than any other book, and as printing developed and subsequent translations of the Bible became available all over the world, it has established itself as the best-selling book in history, with more than 5.5 billion copies sold worldwide.

The infamous witch purge or witch terror of Western Europe and Britain began to emerge in the same decade that Gutenberg's first Bible was printed, which coincided with a growing widespread suspicion of witchcraft and the indiscriminate persecution of Witches throughout Europe.

Malleus Maleficarum

Just forty years after the Gutenberg Bible was printed, the German Catholic clergymen Heinrich Kramer (1430–1505) wrote a lesser-known work under his Latinized nom de plume, Henricus Institoris, which was to affect the history of witchcraft more than any other book. The infamous *Malleus Maleficarum,* or the Hammer of Witches, first published in the German city of Speyer in 1486, promoted the complete extermination of Witches.

The book became available all over Europe and was the guiding light for witchfinders and inquisitors throughout the Continent. Though it first experienced a mixed reception, with many Catholic theologians initially claiming that it contradicted the church's official doctrine on witchcraft and daemonology, the book soon became the main reference for all those committed to eliminating the "satanic curse" of witchcraft. It contains detailed descriptions and guidance on how to recognize Witches and the tell-tale signs that allowed readers to identify Witches, wherever they may encounter them.

> There are three sorts of witches. . . . One sort (they say) can hurt and not helpe, the second can helpe and not hurt, the third can both helpe and hurt. And among the hurtfull witches he saith there is one sort more beastlie than any kind of beasts, saving woolves: for these usually devoure and eate yong children and infants of their owne kind.

This was an opinion held by many common folk and one that formed the background for many of the witch trials that were to follow.

The book then goes on to describe the best methods of interrogation and how to formulate a conviction. Instructions on sentencing are then detailed, and the best forms of execution are recommended. One of the most distinctive elements about the text is that it elevates the crime of witchcraft and sorcery to the status of heresy, a crime

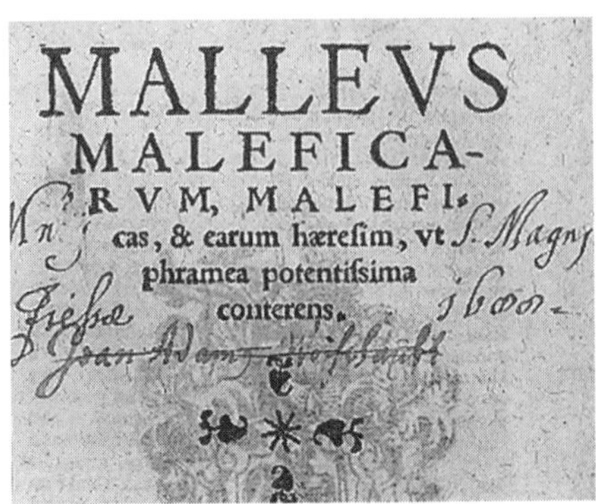
MALLEVS
MALEFICA-
RVM, MALEFI-
cas, & earum hæresim, vt
phramea potentissima
conterens.

Fig. 5.1. Original cover of the *Malleus Maleficarum.*

punishable by execution, in which case it proposes that the accused be burned alive at the stake, the most severe and feared means of execution of the time. It goes on to recommend that witchcraft trials should be conducted by civil courts and not the religious courts, where they were currently undertaken.

Malleus Maleficarum had a massive impact when it was published and went on to be the most influential authority on witchcraft for the next three centuries.

De la Démonomanie des Sorciers

For almost one hundred years, *Malleus Maleficarum* dominated the worldview on witchcraft and continued to be the seminal source for those who dedicated themselves to its eradication. It was not until 1580 that the first alternative viewpoint was published, challenging some, but not all, of the theories laid out in Kramer's major work.

When Jean Bodin (1530–1596), a French political philosopher and professor of law at the University of Toulouse, published his influential book *De la Démonomanie des Sorciers* (Of the Demon-mania of the Sorcerers) in 1580, it was the first to bring into question the propositions and instructions of Kramer's *Malleus Maleficarum.* Bodin, a lifelong Catholic, lived at a time when France was in religious turmoil, and his work staunchly maintained his religious background. Although he is best remembered for his political writings, his principal work on witchcraft and sorcery became very popular, running to ten editions during his lifetime. It may be argued that the book maintains the broadly held

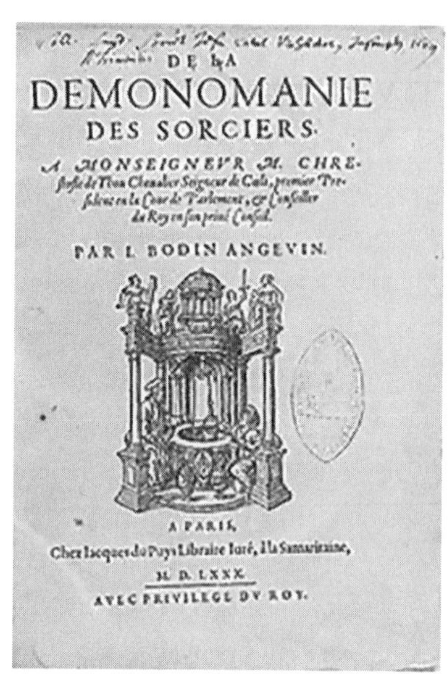

DE LA
DEMONOMANIE
DES SORCIERS.

PAR I. BODIN ANGEVIN.

A PARIS,
M. D. LXXX.
AVEC PRIVILEGE DV ROY.

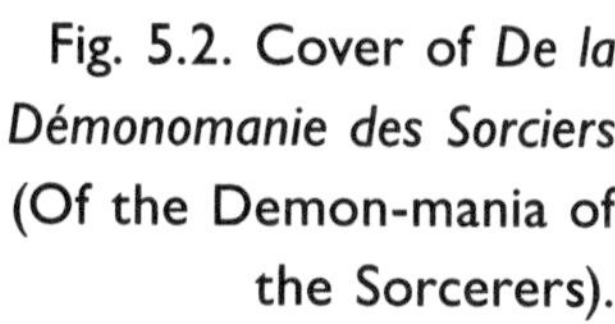

Fig. 5.2. Cover of *De la Démonomanie des Sorciers* (Of the Demon-mania of the Sorcerers).

Catholic tolerance of witchcraft while promoting the concept of the Witches' pact with the devil, extending it to suggest that the devil could influence the judges in the witchcraft trials that proliferated in Europe. Bodin suggested that accused Witches should be seen as possessed, and if they could be exorcised, they deserved compassion and forgiveness, not punishment or execution. Although Bodin's book became very popular, there is little evidence to suggest that it had any effect on the witch-hunt frenzy that preoccupied France and the whole of Europe at the time.

The Discoverie of Witchcraft

An even more critical challenge to the prevailing beliefs in witchcraft and sorcery emerged at virtually the same time but much closer to the Welsh Marches and its persecuted Witches. *The Discoverie of Witchcraft,* written by Reginald Scot (1538–1599) and published in 1584, just four years after Bodin's work, was intended to be a strong and convincing repudiation of witchcraft, sorcery, and folk magic in general, but many would argue that it ended up as the first instruction book on stage magic, illusion, and conjuring.

In his book, Scot (sometimes Scott) describes Witches and their activities, recording the common perceptions of the time.

> Those who are said to be witches are women which be commonly old, lame, bleare-eied, pale, fowle and full of wrinkles; poore, sullen, superstitious and Papist: or such as knowe no religion; in whose drousie minds the devell hath goten a fine seat: so as, what mischeefe, mischance, calamitie, or slaughter is brought to passe . . . they are leane and deformed, shewing melancholie in their faces to the horror of all that sees them.

A witch is one who can "worke miracles supernaturallie" and who "gives heed to spirits of error and doctrines of Divils which speake lies

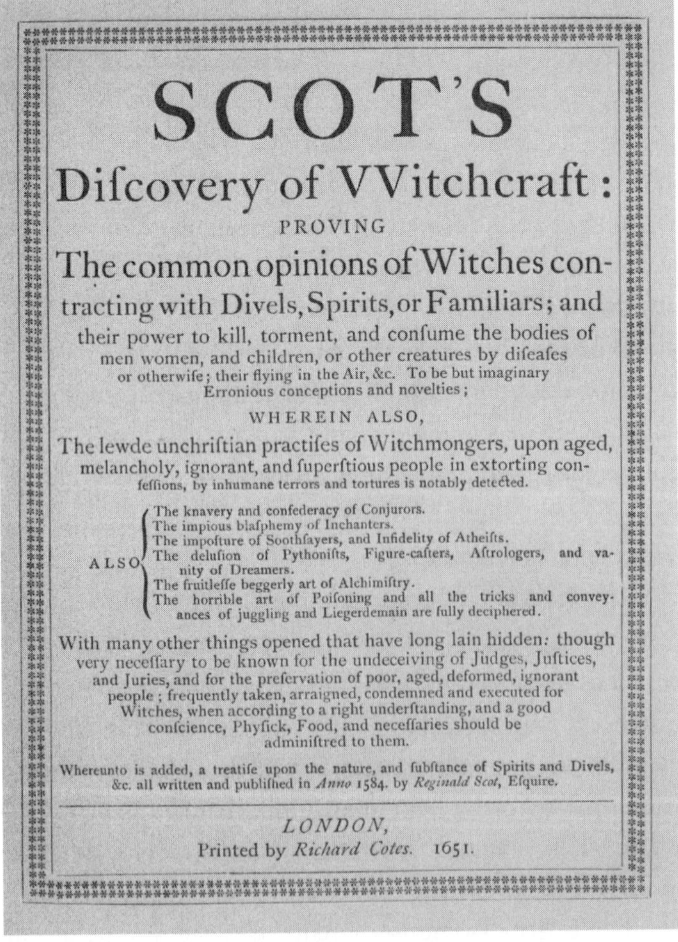

SCOT'S

Diſcovery of VVitchcraft:

PROVING

The common opinions of Witches contracting with Divels, Spirits, or Familiars; and their power to kill, torment, and conſume the bodies of men women, and children, or other creatures by diſeaſes or otherwiſe; their flying in the Air, &c. To be but imaginary Erronious conceptions and novelties;

WHEREIN ALSO,

The lewde unchriſtian practiſes of Witchmongers, upon aged, melancholy, ignorant, and ſuperſtious people in extorting confeſſions, by inhumane terrors and tortures is notably detected.

ALSO
- The knavery and confederacy of Conjurors.
- The impious blaſphemy of Inchanters.
- The impoſture of Soothſayers, and Infidelity of Atheiſts.
- The deluſion of Pythoniſts, Figure-caſters, Aſtrologers, and vanity of Dreamers.
- The fruitleſſe beggerly art of Alchimiſtry.
- The horrible art of Poiſoning and all the tricks and conveyances of juggling and Liegerdemain are fully deciphered.

With many other things opened that have long lain hidden: though very neceſſary to be known for the undeceiving of Judges, Juſtices, and Juries, and for the preſervation of poor, aged, deformed, ignorant people; frequently taken, arraigned, condemned and executed for Witches, when according to a right underſtanding, and a good conſcience, Phyſick, Food, and neceſſaries should be adminiſtred to them.

Whereunto is added, a treatiſe upon the nature, and ſubſtance of Spirits and Divels, &c. all written and publiſhed in *Anno* 1584. by *Reginald Scot*, Eſquire.

LONDON,
Printed by *Richard Cotes*. 1651.

Fig. 5.3. Cover of *The Discoverie of Witchcraft*.

as witches and conjurors do." They "can transubstantiate themselves and others, and take the forms and shapes of asses, woolves, ferrets, cowes, apes, horses, dogs, &c. Some say they can keepe divels and spirits in the likenesse of todes and cats." Furthermore:

> They can go in and out at awger holes, saile in an edde shell, a cockle or muscle shell, through and under the tempestuous sea. They can go invisible, and deprive men of their privities, and otherwise of the act and use of venerie. They can bring soules out of the graves. They can teare snakes in peeces with words, and with looks kill lambes.

Scot—the epitome of an English gentleman, a member of the British Parliament, and a confirmed Calvinist Protestant—sought to disabuse these claims and maintained that no mortal man or woman could possibly accomplish the supernatural acts that the witchfinders and courts attributed to their accused Witches, famously stating that "tis neither a witch, nor devil, but glorious God that maketh the thunder . . . God maketh the blustering tempests and whirlwinds." Unsurprisingly, he proposed that the reported daemonic acts of Witches could be easily explained either by deliberate sleight of hand on the behalf of the so-called Witch or by the deceit of Catholic clergy disguising their own acts of debauchery and sexual deviations by attributing their sins either to the actions or the influence of Witches and sorcerers. The second of these proposals he explains as being designed "specialle to excuse and mainteine the knaveries and lecheries of idle priests and bawdie monkes and cover the shame of their lovers and concubines."

To all intents and purposes Scot attempts to demonstrate that witchcraft did not exist and that the entire concept was concocted by the Church of Rome as a means of diverting attention from a corrupt and depraved priesthood. Having argued his thesis at great length, using numerous examples and anecdotal accounts, Scot then goes on the explain in infinite detail the methods and tricks that could be used to deceive the gullible onlooker and judges into believing the various apparent feats of magical witchcraft they were witnessing. The techniques he describes amount to nothing more than simple illusion and sleight of hand and in truth do nothing to explain the events and maledictions we see many of the Witches accused of as detailed in the court records of the witch trials of the same period. He seems more preoccupied in describing simple conjuring tricks like disappearing coins and producing wooden balls out of thin air. Be that as it may, Scot's book continued to be popular throughout his lifetime and beyond and played a large part in discrediting the Catholic Church's philosophy on witchcraft and its persecution of Witches.

Daemonologie

No one person has influenced the history of witchcraft in the British Isles more than the first Stuart monarch of Britain, King James VI of Scotland (1566–1625), who also became James I of England and Ireland. His seminal work, now known simply as *Daemonologie,* informed the nation's thinking on witchcraft and magic long after his burial in Westminster Abbey in 1625.

Later in this chapter, we examine the witchcraft laws that he instigated and the impact of his life and work, where we will see how his achievements and writing fit into the context of sixteenth-century Britain. Here, we will confine ourselves to *Daemonologie,* or to give it its full title: *Daemonologie, In Forme of a Dialogue, Divided into three Bookes: By the High and Mighty Prince, James &c.*

King James wrote *Daemonologie* in 1597, at the age of thirty-one, just seven years before he began work on the authorized King James Bible, completed in 1611. The work was a product of his personal involvement in the infamous North Berwick witch trials of 1590 where he presided over a number of the more notorious trials himself. Having grown up with a lifelong infatuation with black magic, necromancy, and in particular witchcraft, King James experienced a number of odd incidents in his life, which reinforced his fear and preoccupation with Witches and daemonic practice. He wrote *Daemonologie* while he was King of Scotland as a comprehensive study of witchcraft, divination, and arcane black magic, with the intention of using the Christian Bible to prove the existence of witchcraft.

The book comprises three volumes, each with a particular focus, and concludes with a summary of the North Berwick witch trials entitled *Newes from Scotland*. James's intention throughout is to present a well-informed argument based on his understanding of the history of witchcraft and his own experience of the Witches and sorcerers of the day. He uses this exposure as a justification for the witch purges and executions within his kingdom. The book is written in the form of a Socratic dialogue between two individuals, imitating the format of the classical Greek philosophers to give his argument gravitas. Though he suggests that his intention was to make the work more entertaining, most readers may not entirely agree with this assessment.

The first of the three volumes attempts to explain the various aspects of witchcraft and the practices Witches generally employ. It raises the proposal of Witches entering a contract with the devil, a belief that was to grow in the public's imagination as time progressed. Here James also outlines his overall intention to better inform an ignorant public of the practices and intention of Witches and their devilish work.

In the second book, James draws a comparison between Witches and sorcerers stemming from his belief that the former were female and the latter male. He continues to explain more of the practices of Witches, including their ability to summon the devil and transport themselves through the air. He again continues to use repeated biblical references and develops the Christian argument for the persecution of Witches.

James uses the final book to conclude and underscore his previous arguments while also including a comprehensive list of the various classifications of daemons, explaining how the devil may manifest himself in any one of four apparition forms. He then goes on to introduce a much-overlooked aspect of daemonology, the proposition that as God himself is omniscient, daemons act directly under his control and with his permission. In this way, God uses daemons as his "rod of correction" to punish the person who fails to observe his will and strays from the path of Christianity. James therefore argues that all actions of daemons are intended to further God's glory, despite the selfish daemon's attempts to disrupt God's plan and intentions. This is a convoluted argument, although James is not the first, or last, to raise this interesting philosophical thesis.

Daemonologie concludes with a final section that was originally printed as a pamphlet in England in 1591, six years before *Daemonologie*. During the period of King James, pamphlets were a common means of disseminating information to the general public and were hugely popular with everyday folk. James's *Newes from Scotland—declaring the damnable life and death of Dr, Fian, a notable sorcerer,* is a detailed account of the infamous witch trials of North Berwick, where the king himself acted as a judge for many of the individual trials, confessions, and executions that made the Scottish trials the focus of the entire country.

James himself accused almost two hundred Witches of having plotted against him and casting curses against his ships, causing them to sink in heavy storms. The most famous of these, Agnis Tompson, confessed before King James himself of sacrificing a cat familiar and casting it into the sea to raise a tempest to sink the king's fleet of ships with him on board. Only one of the ships sank during the storm, and the king's ship remained unharmed.

The Scottish doctor named in the pamphlet, one Dr. Fian, was a schoolmaster in a small Scottish village and a noted sorcerer. He was accused, along with a number of Witches who were apparently under his influence, of being the ringleader of the aforementioned ship cursing. The pamphlet gives an account of his arrest, torture, and conviction along with his accomplices, including Tompson. The doctor reportedly escaped while awaiting execution but was quickly recaptured and executed. James gives details of the doctor's torture, which included the application of the pilliwinks, a vice-like instrument with spikes on the inside of its jaws, which was clamped to a victim's feet or hands and closed slowly with a turnscrew. Similarly, iron pins (Witches and sorcerers were reputedly particularly fearful of iron) were forced under his fingernails before the nails themselves were pulled away with pliers. The pamphlet also records the use of the boot, another clamp or vice applied to the feet and tightened until the doctor's feet were entirely crushed and he could no longer walk. Quite how this fits into the story of his escape is not mentioned. Dr. Fian was eventually executed in Edinburgh, where he was drawn in a cart, garroted, revived, and then burned alive at the

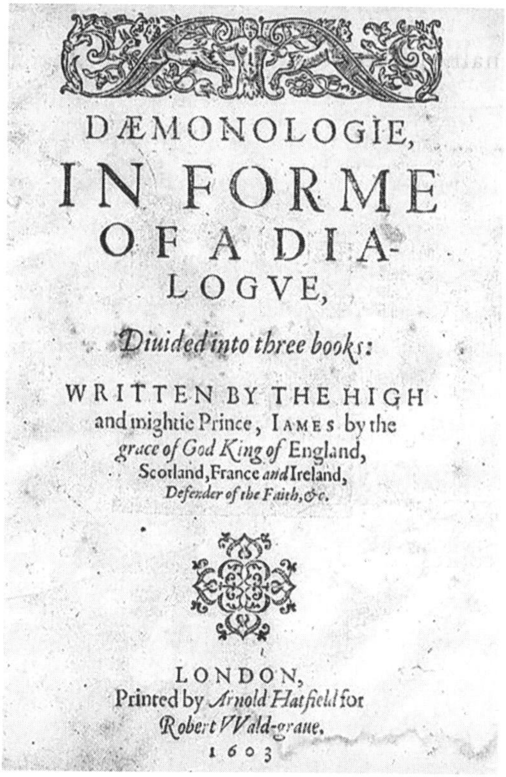

Fig. 5.4. The cover of *Daemonologie,* the full title being *Daemonologie, in Forme of a Dialogue, Divided into Three Bookes: By the High and Mighty Prince, James &c.*

DÆMONOLOGIE,
IN FORME
OF A DIA-
LOGVE,
Diuided into three books:
WRITTEN BY THE HIGH
and mightie Prince, IAMES by the
grace of God King of England,
Scotland, France *and* Ireland,
Defender of the Faith, &c.
LONDON,
Printed by *Arnold Hatfield* for
Robert VVald-graue.
1603

beginning of 1591. The pamphlet records the cost of the doctor's execution to have been five pounds, eighteen shillings, and two pence, which must have made it quite an elaborate and expensive event.

Daemonologie was one of the most read books of its age and was one of the first propaganda publications available in Great Britain. It succeeded in promoting King James's argument for the persecution and execution of Witches and sorcerers within Christian society and changing the general public's attitude to witchcraft more than any other publication of the time.

King James Bible

It is not possible to look at King James's influence on witchcraft without also taking into account his other great literary achievement. In 1603, Queen Elizabeth I of England died, and James succeeded to the throne as King James VII of Scotland and James I of England. In the same year, he began working on a new version of the Christian Bible, and it would take him more than seven years to complete the work.

James, baptized a Catholic, converted to Presbyterianism before becoming a convert to the Anglican Church. As a Protestant, James was concerned with two major aspects of the Christian Bible. The first was that there were many versions of the Bible available at the time, with differing translations and many containing different gospels and interpretation, so there was no single universally accepted version of the Bible upon which his subjects could firmly base their faith. His second concern was that, in general, the Bible was only available in its Latin form, which made it inaccessible to the great majority of the population who either participated in church ritual blindly, without any understanding of what was being said, or depended upon whatever quotation their priest or minister decided to translate.

Although literacy and reading among common folk had increased since the invention of the printing press and the distribution of popular pamphlets, ballads, and broadsheets, it was still the case that many ordinary folk were illiterate, but it was James's opinion that those who were able to read would quickly disseminate the word of the Christian Bible to those who could not, and those who, up until this point, would have only heard the word from their priest or by interpreting for themselves the allegorical paintings that decorated the walls of their simple churches would soon become aware of the message of the Christian faith.

James set about retranslating the existent biblical texts into English and selecting the text that he considered essential to what he believed to be the "true" story of Christianity. The King James Authorized Bible, as it became known, was first published in 1611 and instantly became the official Bible of the Anglican Church under the auspices of the king himself. It subsequently became the accepted version used by most churches and Christian acolytes of Western Protestantism. The King James Bible is still in widespread use and, having sold more than five billion copies worldwide, is the largest selling book in the world. It is interesting to think that the Bible most of the Christians in the world read and place at the center of their belief is the one compiled by King James and that the gospels and books that it contains are those that James selected to suit his own purposes at the beginning of the seventeenth century, having previously presided over the Great Scottish Witch Hunt of 1597—a series of witch trials that occurred from March to October 1597—and written *Daemonologie.*

Coelum Terrae: The Magician's Heavenly Chaos

One last publication worth including here was written by one of the famous Welsh occultists of the Welsh Marches, Thomas Vaughan (1621–1666). Vaughan's family owned Tretower Court, a magnificent, fortified manor at the center of the Welsh Marches. Constructed on the site of one of the Norman castles built by the Marcher lords and overlooking the single castle tower remaining from the original fortification, the manor was redeveloped by Vaughan's ancestors, who were among the most wealthy of the families of the Marches.

Known principally as a philosopher and alchemist, Vaughan was a clergyman and an outspoken Royalist, while his twin brother, Henry Vaughan, was a renowned Welsh metaphysical poet, author, and physician, known mainly for his religious poetic works. Thomas wrote his

Fig. 5.5. The cover of *Coelum Terrae: The Magician's Heavenly Chaos.*

most influential work, *Coelum Terrae: The Magician's Heavenly Chaos,* in 1650, and although it references Witches and daemonology, it is a detailed work focused on alchemy and natural magic.

I would recommend that every reader who may wish to gain an understanding of the position of Witches and witchcraft in the early modern period read as many of the books mentioned above as possible, though I will caution that they are not easy reads. They describe a ruthless history and how the view of Witches and their natural magic changed. Their perceived role changed from providers of community services on which society depended to evildoers consorting with the devil. Witchcraft became a malefaction punishable by execution, resulting in many innocent females, young and old, being burned at the stake in the name of Christian piety.

THE WITCHCRAFT ACTS, WITCH HUNTS, AND TRIALS

When Henry VIII broke away from the Roman Catholic Church to establish the Church of England in 1534, establishing Protestantism as the official religion of Britain, the roles of the inquisitors and Catholic witchfinders were eliminated and changes in the civil law became necessary. Prior to this, accusations of witchcraft and sorcery were either settled informally within the community or heard by church authorities, with punishment in both cases usually amounting to fines, confiscation of property, a period in the stocks, or a combination of any of the above.

In the midst of religious and secular pressure, King Henry finally decided that a review of the law regarding witchcraft was due and began the reform with the first of the witchcraft acts, which introduced even more punitive punishments than the Catholic Church had ever implemented. Just eight years after the establishment of the Protestant Church of England by King Henry VIII, the legislatures of England and Wales enacted the Witchcraft Act of 1542.

The act was designed to punish Witches, sorcerers, and conjurors who participated in any form of "invocations or cojuracons of Spirites, witchcrafts, enchauntements or sorceries" and was the first to define witchcraft as a crime punishable by burning at the stake, together with the forfeiture of all goods and chattels owned by the condemned. It also clearly removed the previous "benefit of clergy," which had placed all those who were accused of witchcraft under the judiciary of the church, thereby underscoring the civil courts' authority over all subsequent witchcraft trials.

Soon afterward the witchcraft trials were placed under the jurisdiction of the secular court rather than the ecclesiastical courts where they had previously been tried. As a result, from that date onward, accurate and detailed records of every matter brought before the courts were kept, immaterial of whether the case was entered for trial or dismissed as unsubstantiated.

A natural corollary of the growing concern of the public resulting from the church's propaganda against all forms of witchcraft and magic and the ever-more stringent witchcraft laws being enacted on a regular basis was the rapid increase in the number of supposed Witches who were accused of witchcraft, interrogated, tried, sentenced, and executed within all four nations of Great Britain. These trials, which were to last for a period of more than two hundred years, were provided with a continuous supply of accused Witches by witch hunters, witchmongers, and witchfinder generals who traveled the length and breadth of the British Isles in pursuit of new offenders. Many of the accused were believed to possess familiars who were the devil's minions here on Earth. These daemons took the form of animals—cats, dogs, toads, rats, birds, and even miniature horses—as well as invisible sprites, imps, and other mythical manifestations. They were nourished by the Witch, who acquired additional teats, nipples, or paps from which the daemons suckled blood. Not surprisingly, no evidence of the presence of these paps was ever submitted during any of the witchcraft trials recorded in the Welsh Marches.

Witches had now become well established as the enemies of God and the consorts of the devil. They were no longer seen as healers and helpers within their community but were now responsible for natural disasters, sickness, foul weather, and crop failures, together with any other misfortunes that befell the population. This attitude was maintained until the Church of England and the legal structure became more tolerant of Witches and abandoned the idea of daemonic possession in favor of prosecuting Witches for deceit and false claims of (or being falsely accused of) having the power of witchcraft, which by then had been declared impossible.

WITCHCRAFT LAWS AFTER HENRY VIII

When Henry VIII died in 1547, he was succeeded by Edward VI who held the throne for a brief six years before Lady Jane Grey became regent for an even briefer nine days, earning her the title of the nine-day queen. She was deposed by the infamous Mary I, known as Bloody Mary because of her ruthless executions in her attempt to reverse the Protestant Reformation and reestablish Catholicism as the official religion. Mary ruled for just five years before Queen Elizabeth I ascended to the throne in 1558 and established a more stable rule, which was to last forty-five years.

Elizabeth was a Protestant and quickly reversed Mary's attempts to restore Catholicism. She had a more tolerant attitude toward witchcraft, which resulted in a reformation of the existing witchcraft laws. In 1563, not long after taking the throne, Queen Elizabeth I, known to her subjects as Good Queen Bess or the Virgin Queen, enacted a new law: An Act Against Conjurations, Enchantments and Witchcrafts. Elizabeth's new law offered increased clemency toward those who were accused of witchcraft, stipulating that the death penalty only be applied to those cases where actual harm could be proven. If not, the accused was to receive a term in prison. It particularly specifies that "whereby any person shall happen to be killed or destroyed is guilty of a felony without benefit of clergy and is to be put to death." The act also provided for accurate records to be kept of all trials and sentences, providing the basis of much of what is known today.

During the same year, Mary Queen of Scots introduced the Scottish Witchcraft Act of 1563, which extended the existing laws by making witchcraft a separate crime with its own penalties. The act not only made witchcraft a specific crime but also made "consulting or consorting with witches" an equal offense, both being punishable by a death sentence.

When Elizabeth I died in 1603 without issue, King James VI of Scotland inherited the throne of England and, following the Union of the Crowns, was installed as King James VI of Scotland and James I of England. Within a year he decided to support the expansion of the previous Elizabethan act with the overwhelming support of the legislature of the day. James I's new act, the Witchcraft Act of 1604, known offically as An Act against Conjuration, Witchcraft and Dealing with Evil and Wicked Spirits, broadened the previous law to include those who "invoked evil spirits or communed with familiar spirits," where those found guilty of such evil would be condemned to death without the benefit of clergy. One of the main consequences of this act, along with the previous Elizabethan act, was to make witchcraft a felony, thereby making those accused of witchcraft and those who sought to use it subject to Common Law, removing them from the jurisdiction of the ecclesiastical court. The act also reduced the sentence of those found guilty from burning at the stake to that of hanging. It went on to establish a sentence for lesser witchcraft offenses, which did not result in death or destruction of property of one year imprisonment for a first offense and hanging for a subsequent conviction.

One of the most visible consequences of James I's new act was the increased profile of the witchfinder and the rise of the careers of individuals like Matthew Hopkins (1620–1647), whose brief career began in 1644 and ran until his retirement just three years later, in 1647. Self-proclaimed Witchfinder General Hopkins and his colleagues were active during the height of the witch fears in Britain and during their short period of activity are said to have been responsible for the execution of up to one hundred Witches. Taking their brief from James's law and the infamous *Malleus Maleficarum,* Hopkins and his cohorts were responsible for the apprehension, interrogation, and hanging of more Witches during the three years of their activity than in the previous one hundred years of witchcraft trials.

It is not difficult to see then that some of the men and women of a typical early modern period community may have attracted the attention of the witchfinders and clerics simply because of their trade or their everyday activities, but it was not only the witchfinders who were able to bring accusations of witchcraft or sorcery. The law allowed any citizen to bring accusations of witchcraft and daemonic works before the justices, and the court records show that by far the majority of cases were brought by fellow members of the community, neighbors, relatives, and, in many cases, individuals that had financial or other personal reasons to bring forward accusations. We can see that a good number of trials involved parties who were in dispute with those they accused, and we cannot ignore the fact that many appear to have arisen out of hatred, jealousy, or other malicious intent, resulting in many being discharged out of hand.

Following a number of years of lobbying by the Churches of Scotland, the Covenanters of Scotland, who were in dispute with James and later his son Charles I, passed the Scottish Witchcraft Act of 1649. King James had died in 1625 and had been succeeded by his son Charles I, who was executed by the Parliamentarians in 1649 at the height of the English Civil War (1642–1651) in the same year as the new law was enacted. Following his execution, his son Charles II ascended the throne until he in turn was deposed by Parliament and Britain entered a nine-year interregnum. It was during these years of turmoil that Scotland introduced its new witchcraft act, designed to impose a more sober and godly society.

The new series of acts defined new offenses, which included the worship of false gods, blasphemy, the beating or cursing of parents, and consulting with devils and familiar spirits, all punishable by execution. These additions, along with other features of the acts, reflected the growing puritanic attitudes of the legislature in Scotland, Wales, England, and Ireland. The acts of 1649 remained unchanged for more than eighty-five years of tumultuous change in the rule of the British Isles and in attitudes toward witchcraft, driven for the greater part by changes in the church's interpretation of what constituted a Witch.

WITCHCRAFT TRIALS IN WALES AND THE WELSH MARCHES

During this time, although Wales was broadly considered to be the schoolroom for magic, it was, for the most part, untroubled by the witch hunts, which scorched the rest of Britain. This was mainly due to the acceptance of Witches and witchcraft within the community and a belief in the old ways, which had prevailed in Wales for millennia, and a general belief that Witches were a benefit to their community, which depended on them in so many ways.

Nevertheless, witchcraft trials in Wales and the Welsh Marches did occur, running for a period of one hundred and fifty years, from 1550 to 1700. Although the new witchcraft acts had very specific descriptions of the offenses that came within their purview, a wide range of charges appear in the court records; these include charges of sorcery, bewitching and unlawful love, enchantment, charming, felonious witchcraft, diabolical artes, illicit acts, cozenage (deception, trickery, or fraud), and adjuration, in addition to simple witchcraft. It is difficult, if not impossible, to identify which statute each of these charges was applied to, but we can assume that all came under the auspices of the overall act as it stood.

From the evidence of the court records, it appears that throughout the period of the witch trials in the Welsh Marches there was considerable confusion created by the series of witchcraft acts that came into force, with a number of presiding magistrates putting on record their lack of understanding of how to apply the legislation, the criterion to be met to prove guilt, and the appropriate sentence that should be imposed. Having said that, the border lands of the Welsh Marches had their own system of laws, combining those of the English Star Chamber in London and the ancient Welsh Laws of Hywel Dda with the unique Welsh Law of Women, giving females specific rights within law that women outside Wales were not entitled to. These independent and unusual laws were controlled and administered by the Council of the Marches and not by the throne directly, as was the case in the rest of Britain.

It is apparent that a number of the alleged perpetrators were found guilty on the grounds of unsubstantiated accusations, sometimes borne out of spite or malice on the behalf of the accusers, combined with stereotypical expectation of age, marital status, their everyday activities, and their sincere intentions to help their neighbors by curing sickness, helping in childbirth, and curing sick livestock. There is also substantial evidence to suggest that various means of torture were used to extract confessions even though it was officially illegal and outlawed at the time. References, both recorded and allegorical, refer to pilliwinks or pilniewinks, iron caspieclaws, and witches boots—all variations of hand and foot clamps with toothed jaws that were used by interrogators—along with other "approved" methods detailed in the Hammer of Witches, the inquisitors' handbook.

The court kept meticulous records of the accused women, detailing not only their ages, marital status, and family lineage but also their occupations and often their general appearance, so we can be reasonably confident that by far the majority of accused Witches did not fit the cliché image of a Witch as an old unmarried woman as we may have become accustomed to. In the Welsh Marches, these records give us an unprecedented insight into the lives and attitudes of the people of the region and allow us to make a comparison between the trials in the Welsh Marches and those in the rest of Wales, underscoring the high level of Witches and sorcerers that were living in the Marches compared to the rest of Wales and England as a whole. With this in mind, we shall spend a little time examining some of these cases and statistics to try to gain an insight into how the courts conducted themselves, but first it is worth considering just how an ordinary farmer's wife or unassuming blacksmith could so easily be accused of witchcraft and sorcery.

If we take as an example the first forty trials recorded during this same period in this jurisdiction alone, fifteen of the accused were male and the remaining twenty-five were female, slightly more males than one may have imagined. Only ten of those accused were found guilty as charged and five of these were put to death, four women and one man. All of these were located within the Welsh Marches.

The first execution was in 1594, when the Gwen ferch Ellis, probably the most famous Witch of her day, was hanged. Gwen was born in in 1542. Her father's name was Ellis, hence Gwen ferch Ellis (in Welsh *ferch* means "daughter"); her mother's name is not recorded. By the time of her trial, Gwen had been married three times, her first two husbands having died within two years of their marriage. Gwen married her third husband when she was fifty years old, and the couple settled in the village of Betws yn Rhos in the north of the Marches. The court records tell us that Gwen earned a living by spinning and weaving but was, at the time, also considered to be a cunning woman as she would attend sick neighbors and help pregnant women giving birth as well as make cures for local cattle and pigs.

During her trial she admitted using written charms and incantations to cure her friends and neighbors and considered herself a healer. Unfortunately, one of her charms was found in the home of one Thomas Mostyn, a prominent member of the local gentry. The charm was written backward, which at the time was understood to be the method of writing curses and charms with ill intent. She was charged with "felonious witchcraft," and during her trial, a number of witnesses appeared to give evidence of other evil workings. She was found guilty and hanged in the town square at Denbigh, the local market town. As a result, Gwen entered the history books as the first woman in Wales to be tried and executed for witchcraft.

The last person to be executed for witchcraft in Wales was Margaret ferch Richard, who again lived in the north of Wales. When she was brought to trial, Margaret was a forty-four-year-old widow, typical of the expectation of a Witch at the time. She was prosecuted under King James I's new Witchcraft Act of 1694, an act that at the time was not fully understood by many local magistrates. Margaret was known to be a local "charmer," and she was found guilty of bringing about the death of a neighbor's wife by using a cursing charm, possibly because she fitted the court's stereotypical understanding of the appearance and personality of a witch. She was found guilty and hanged in the square outside the courthouse in Beaumaris.

The only man known to have been executed for sorcery in Wales was executed alongside his two sisters who were found guilty of witchcraft at the same trial in 1622 in the major north Wales fortified town of Caernarfon. Rhydderch ap Evan (Rhydderch son of Evan) and his two sisters, Loweri ferch Evan and Agnes ferch Evan, lived in Llanor, a small rural village near Caernarfon. At the time of the trial, Rhydderch was thirty years old and his trade was listed as yeoman. The trio were charged with using witchcraft and sorcery to cause the death of a local noble and to inflict harm upon his family. Found guilty, they were hanged in the shadow of Caernarfon Castle, though it appears that once again the judiciary were confused by the detail of King James I's act, and it may well have been that all three were hanged by default in the absence of an understanding of the law.

Of those individuals tried and found not guilty, twice as many were women as opposed to men, and by far the majority of the cases were dismissed as being frivolous accusations by those who had ulterior motives for wishing those accused harm.

The last witch trials in the whole of the British Isles was that of a woman named Jane Wenham, known also as the Witch of Walkerne. The trial took place in Hereford, one of the principal market towns within the Welsh Marches, and was chronicled by Sir Walter Scott, who recorded that Wenham was initially found guilty, due to her forced confession, and condemned to die, but on due consideration she was reprieved by what Scott called "a sensible judge."

THE LAW FROM KING GEORGE II TO THE PRESENT

By 1727, when King George II took the throne, the church's official attitude toward witchcraft had changed irrevocably. Church leaders now maintained that what had previously been defined as witchcraft was in fact an impossible claim. It was not possible for a human to enact supernatural events, to perform magic or summon unnatural spirits, even with the assistance of the devil or his familiars. Only God himself can do such things, and he would never allow such evil undertaking by his subjects. As a result, any person claiming to be capable of such preternatural activity and evildoing must, by simple Christian logic, be a fraudster and be punished as such. It was this revolutionary thinking that gave rise to the Witchcraft Act of 1735, which was to apply equally in Scotland and England, repealing both the 1563 Scottish act and the 1604 English act, previously discussed. The new 1735 act represented the most significant reversal of attitudes toward Witches and witchcraft in almost two hundred years, abolishing witchcraft and sorcery as capital crimes, making them minor offenses subject to fines or, in the worst cases, short-term prison sentences.

The 1735 act subdued any remaining witch frenzy and, for the majority of people, the idea of witchcraft and Witches entered the realm of fairy tales and children's ghost stories at Halloween, while witchcraft once again became a benign and beneficial practice. Surprisingly, the act of 1735 remained on the statute books of Great Britain until it was repealed by the Fraudulent Mediums Act 1951, instituted in response to an increase in fraudulent clairvoyants and mediums following the Second World War.

Finally, and in conclusion of our exploration of the changing witchcraft acts that defined a nation's attitude over a period of almost five hundred years, the act of 1951 was repealed, not by the British legislature but by a directive from the European Union while the UK was still a member. On May 26, 2008, the Consumer Protection from Unfair Trading Regulations repealed the 1951 act; this UK statutory instrument made under the European Communities Act 1972 targeted unfair marketing and sales practices. I can't help but wonder what the instigator of the first witchcraft act, Henry VIII, would have made of that.

6
Witches of the Welsh Marches

Although modern witchcraft in its various forms is considered an accepted feature of most modern communities, things were very different in the Welsh Marches of the medieval and early modern period. This was a time when the population of the Marches, along with the rest of Wales, England, Scotland, and Ireland, believed profoundly in Witches and saw very little difference between the perceived magic of witchcraft, natural medicine, and the other unexplainable events they came in contact with in their everyday lives. They understood little of the science that is now ubiquitous and accepted in our global society, and when encountering events that were beyond their ability to explain, such as failing crops, sick livestock, destructive weather events, family illness, and the like, it was common for them to turn to folk magic and witchcraft as a means of saving their livelihoods and curing illness.

Witches, and often Druids, were present in every village and town, no matter how small or remote they may have been, and when the seventeenth-century Witchcraft Acts were introduced, there was a flood of prosecutions and ill-founded accusations throughout the Welsh Marches, bearing witness not only to the number of Witches that were abroad at the time but also to just how strongly people believed in Witches' unfailing ability to influence the everyday events (for good or ill) of the community they lived in.

The power of this belief in Witches' ability to exert magical influences over people, events, and objects is one of the two fundamental elements that underscore the status of the Witch within society. An unchallenged belief in the effectiveness of Witches' abilities—the personal witnessing of their cures and remedies, together with a dependency on their ability to deal with events and circumstances that were beyond the understanding of the common villager—gave Witches a positive status within the community. This is borne out by a wealth of contemporary evidence showing that, faced with a severe illness, failing crops, or other disasters, the majority of countryfolk would consult their local Witch long before seeking assistance from the church or other local practitioners.

The other side of this positive status of Witches within their local community was, and still is, the inherent fear of Witches' ability to inflict hurt and harm whenever they may choose. This individual and communal fear of what has become known as malefice ascribes to Witches an infinite power of premeditated harm, which may be targeted at any individual, object, or activity that they may choose. This malefice may take the form of cursing a neighbor's bull, bringing ill fortune to a local farmer, or condemning a whole village to ill health and disease. These events may, of course, have occurred purely by chance, but history tells us that a Witch was rarely slow in claiming responsibility for the disaster if it suited her purpose.

The combination of these two elements—the dependence upon Witches' positive support in countering disaster and ill health (white magic) and the fear of Witches' malefice should they be offended (black magic)—resulted in both the high status they held within society and also the relentless persecution of them during the times of the witch fear, a more potent manifestation of the suspicion and mistrust that many Witches and Wiccans still experience to a lesser extent to the present day.

While much of the above applies to most Witches, no matter what their circumstance or location, there are a number of aspects of the Witches of the Welsh Marches that make them unique, both in their manner and their practices. We will see later in the chapter how these relate to their history, their association with the Druidic tradition, and the cultural background of the Welsh Marches, together with the constant political and religious conflicts that surrounded them. We will see that the sum of these influences resulted not only in the proliferation of witchcraft in the region but also in an unprecedented level of counter-witchcraft efforts and defensive practices that defined anti-witchcraft praxes for centuries to follow.

But before exploring these fascinating topics, we must first establish exactly what it means to be a Witch and, more specifically, a Witch in the Welsh Marches.

A PROFILE OF A WITCH OF THE WELSH MARCHES

We know that the spoken language of the population of the Welsh Marches was overwhelmingly Welsh (Cymraeg) and that, as well as being the language of the common folk, Welsh was also the language employed by the legal and court institutions of the day. Despite the best efforts of the Norman Marcher lords, the population of the region continued to speak Welsh in preference to English, a cultural heritage that has to some extent continued to the present day.

The use of the Welsh language at the time is significant in defining and understanding what it meant to be a Witch within the Welsh Marches. In the Welsh language of the period, a practitioner of magical artes was known either as *rheibwr* or *rheibes,* depending upon their gender. Both words are derived from the Welsh *rheibo,* which means "to conjure or beguile." At some time during the early modern period, the Welsh appropriated the word *wits* from Middle English, and we begin to see the word *witscrafft* appear in some of the Welsh manuscripts of the day, where it refers to a broad collection of practitioners of both sexes whom we may now call sorcerers, Witches, conjurors, cunning folk, and workers of charms. One of the first printed definitions of the term *wits* appeared in William Salesbury's Welsh English dictionary, published in 1547, where he defines *wits* as a *dewin wraic* (in modern Welsh: *dewin gwraig*), meaning a "woman magician." The subsequent acceptance and usage of the term *wits,* later evolving to the word *witch,* establishes that when used in the Welsh language of the period and up until the present day, the word *witch* refers specifically to a female. This early definition also has further inferences. The Old Welsh term *wraic* (Modern Welsh: *gwraig*), used in Salesbury's definition, in addition to meaning "witch or sorceress" may also mean "hag, evil crone, or ugly old woman" (unfortunately, it may also translate as "wife"). So, with this definition, the word *wits* and the later *witch* refers not only to a female magician but more pertinently to a female magician with evil and bad intention, and it is this definition that has been perpetuated from the early modern period to the present day.

In the Welsh Marches, from that time onward, the word *Witch* became permanently and inseparably associated with a female harboring the intention to inflict premeditated and intentional harm, an intention that was described as *malefice,* a term we shall see much more of as we progress through our exploration, when we will see that in the culture of the time, only women could be Witches because only women could engage in malefice.

We should also note here that male practitioners of the magical artes were commonly referred to as wizards, sorcerers, or, most often, conjurors, a word that was borrowed by the Welsh as *consuriwr.* The *consuriwrie* of the Welsh Marches were considered to be benefactors within the community who used their gifts and talents to identify thieves, recover stolen goods, and, most importantly, protect people's farms, homes, livestock, and families from the malefice of evil Witches and remove maleficent curses wherever they were thought to exist.

Having established that within the culture of the Welsh Marches a Witch by definition is female, we must now consider what other aspects of the popular culture of the time constitute a Witch and what particular characteristics were associated with a Witch of the Marches.

One may easily speculate that the general perception of a Witch of the early modern period was that of an elderly female, maybe a widow or a spinster, living in poverty on the margins of a community. In appearance, she may be a shriveled hag, dressed in tatters and preoccupied with brewing potions and ointments while chanting incomprehensible spells and curses. It was this stereotypical image that reinforced the broadly held association of the Witch with evildoing, malefice, and ill-intent, but this was not necessarily the case with the Witches of the Welsh Marches.

We are given to believe that the typical Welsh Witch did not closely fit this clichéd model but was far more likely to have been married, belonging to what we would now consider the middle class, often with a craft or trade earning her and her family a reasonable income, and to have been seen as an integral member of her community, holding considerable social standing. In appearance, the generally held idea of how a Witch of the period would have looked is not very far from the everyday dress of a typical woman living in the Welsh Marches. The traditional garb of a Welsh woman of the time would have included a long, heavy woolen skirt covered with an overskirt (Welsh: *betgwn*) and a white linen apron. A simple blouse would have been worn beneath a large woolen shawl. On her head she would have worn a white linen mobcap, topped with a tall, black felt stovepipe hat, not quite the pointed black hat of the clichéd image of the Witch but very close.

In a further comparison, the majority of these housewives would have been responsible for brewing the family's ale and mead. Some would have deliberately brewed additional ale as a means of either bartering for other household commodities or selling the excess to gain whatever income they could to help support the family. These alewives would let their community know that there was ale for sale by placing some form of signage or flagging item outside their cottages. The most popular and well remembered of these devices was a besom or broom made of twigs tied around a stick that was stuck in the edge of a thatched roof as a sign that fresh ale was available to those who were interested. These alewives had an intimate knowledge of the wild botanicals that grew in the countryside and the experience to identify the essential ingredients of the various ales and meads they concocted, often "bittered" (as hops are not indigenous to Great Britain) by the addition of psychotropic herbs growing abundantly nearby.

With this in mind, it is not difficult to see how their appearance, their intimate knowledge of nature's botanicals, and their ability to transform these ingredients into an intoxicating brew, together with their besoms and tall black hats, all combined to create an essential image of a housewife of the era. What better description of a Welsh Witch could one imagine, defined not only by what she looked like but also by what she did? As we shall see, this definition, developed from the simple, day-to-day activities of almost every housewife of the region, provided the opportunity for anyone who may have wished to accuse his or her neighbor or, for that matter, any woman of being a witch. And how do we know this was the case?

The progression of the arcane wisewoman to the Witch of the early modern period is charted in figure 6.1, where the various influences converge to arrive at the many occult practitioners of the Welsh Marches.

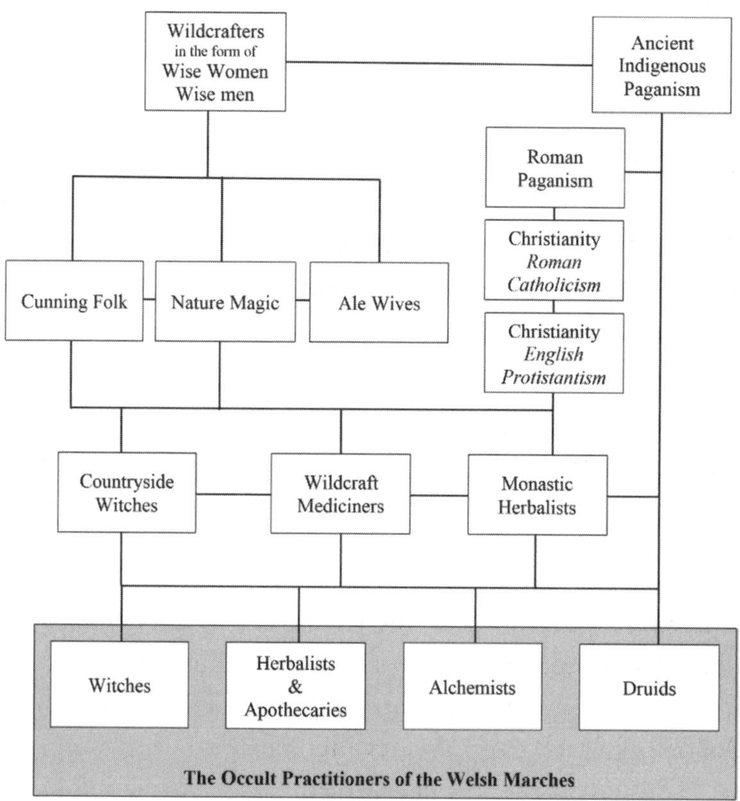

Fig. 6.1. The occult workers of the Welsh Marches and their comparative history.

The Comparative Events of the Witchcraft Terrors Period

Date	English Monarchs	Religion		Acts	Publications
1483–1485	Richard III	Catholic			1486 Malleus Maleficarum
1485–1509	Henry VII	Catholic			
1509–1547	Henry VIII	Protestant		1542	
1547–1553	Edward VI	Protestant			
1553–1553	Lady Jane Grey	Protestant	Welsh Marches Witchcraft Trials		
1553–1558	Mary I	Catholic			
1558–1603	Elizabeth I	Protestant		1563	1580 De le Demonomania
					1584 Discoverie of Witchcraft
					1597 Daemonology
1603–1625	James I/VI	Protestant		1604	
1625–1649	Charles I	Protestant			
1649–1651	Charles II	Protestant		1649	1650 Coelum Terrae
1651–1660	Commonwealth Interregna				
1660–1685	Charles II	Protestant			
1685–1688	James II/VII	Protestant			
1688–1702	William III	Protestant			
1702–1714	Anne I	Protestant			
1714–1727	George I	Protestant			
1727–1760	George II	Protestant		1735	

Fig. 6.2. The comparative events and dates of the period of the witch terror.

The comparative events of the period that significantly influenced the progression and development of witchcraft in the Welsh Marches may be seen in figure 6.2, which may help in understanding the context of the various strands and historical events of the era.

We've seen from the accounts above that the individuals who were brought before the courts in the Welsh Marches did not conform to the general profile of a typical Witch or sorcerer of the day. Many of the females were young women from reasonably affluent families, married with children and employed in what we would nowadays call a trade or profession. The males were typically middle-aged tradesmen, tenant farmers, or craftsmen from respectable households. So why were so many ordinary folk accused of witchcraft and sorcery?

For the greater part, the females involved would often have attracted suspicion because of their everyday activities. Some were, without doubt, old and unmarried, subsisting on the fringes of the community. Unquestionably, some of these "old hags" would have been considered cunning women, with a substantial knowledge of herbal lore and what we may now call natural magic, a lore they would often have learned from their mothers and grandmothers and one that was used for the benefit of their community, which normally held cunning women in great respect and depended upon their knowledge and ability as much as it did the butcher, weaver, or any other tradesperson. A number of depositions from the courts record that the majority of the people of the Welsh Marches may well have consulted their local cunning woman in times of crisis before they would have visited their physician or cleric.

It was said in the Marches that the curses to be feared the most were those cast by blacksmiths and clergymen. Practically every village had its own blacksmith, a well-established and admired trade that served to make and maintain much of the working equipment of farmers, coopers, and builders, as well as producing everyday household items such as knives, spoons, and pots. Originally, blacksmiths also smelted their own iron from locally mined ore, sometimes also casting their molten iron into useful or decorative objects. Because of their skills in extracting iron (and sometimes other metals) from what appeared to be simple stones, many civilizations considered smiths as having preternatural powers, enhanced by their ability to form useful implements from the metals they "magically" produced. Similarly, a number of cultures maintain tales of weapons, rings, and amulets with supernatural abilities, produced by master smiths using secret rituals and processes. With this in mind, it is not difficult to see how blacksmiths attracted the attention of the witchfinders or other members of their community faced with unexpected events they had no rational explanation for. The art of the blacksmith may have also played a significant role in the widely believed theory that Witches are terrified of iron, a belief that led to the use of iron nails, knives, and pins in protective devices against Witches and the making of iron amulets, charms, and talismans, which continues to the present day. Other smiths, such as silversmiths, goldsmiths, armorers, and whitesmiths (workers in pewter, as opposed to the black iron of the blacksmith), also attract special attention when it comes to supernatural influences.

WITCHES' EVIDENCE IN HOMES AND FARMS

One of the main ways we know the history of the Witches of the Welsh Marches is the evidence left by them and many ordinary people in the farms, houses, and other buildings throughout the region. There are many examples of both curse materials and protective deposits found in homes and farm buildings and even buried at farm perimeters to bring ill fortune by means of a curse or, alternatively, to protect homes and farms from either the evil intentions of Witches or to protect against any evil spirits, Witches, or sprites from entering buildings and wreaking havoc inside.

The most well known of these protective devices is the friendly horseshoe, which has permeated our popular culture and which we see hung over so many doorways all over the Western world. Popular belief would have us believe that we should hang a horseshoe over the entrance to our homes, prongs uppermost to bring good luck and prevent luck from running out. This harmless custom has existed for many generations and we can see examples in many old buildings, but if we look deeper into this ubiquitous good luck custom, we can see that its origins emerge from a pervasive fear of witchcraft, sorcery, and magic and those who were (and are) involved in effecting it. Here, it is certainly worth looking in a little more detail into the principles that underpin this common benign custom, as they also apply to a much deeper, darker history of occult practice.

In the example of the horseshoe, we can see how a practice that began as a protective device has shifted in our modern communal psyche to becoming one that attracts good luck rather than protects against a malignant force. This shift from protective magic to attractive magic may have its origins in two historical changes. The first was a movement away from witchcraft and sorcery being a fundamental element of a thriving community, as it was when many of these customs began. As a result, few of us now fear the influence of Witches and sorcerers on our everyday life and activities. But we must remember that Witches and sorceres were very much feared in the Welsh Marches and further afield during the early modern period that we are exploring, when people fervently believed in witchcraft. The second shift in popular culture is that we now predominantly choose to believe in the more benevolent form of witchcraft and magic and in general prefer the concept of bringing good luck and using lucky charms and good luck spells (like sending good luck cards, birthday cards, even Christmas cards to bring good luck at the major Christian festival) rather than dispelling bad luck. We seem to prefer reinforcing positive thoughts to protecting against evil intent. (When did you last buy a card to dispel an evil intent?) There is nothing wrong with positive thinking. In fact, I wholeheartedly encourage it in every circumstance, but in this analysis, we must consider the opposite: not positive optimism but fear; not attracting good luck but protecting against evil intent.

With this in mind, we look at the lucky horseshoe not as a means of attracting good luck but as a device that protects against malevolent evil. In doing so we begin to see the original use, not as a lucky cup form that holds our luck between its upright prongs but as a protective device with its prongs facing downward, as it was originally hung, to impale any Witches or daemons on its prongs as they attempted to pass through the doorway. This is why horseshoes are most often seen hanging over doorways or fireplaces, the two places most vulnerable to evil spirit intrusion and the two locations that need the most protection.

There are two other features of our friendly lucky horseshoe that confirm its original intention. The first is that, as we shall see in more detail later, it was often the case that people used everyday items as protective devices, adapting them for their new use. Few people could afford to buy special amulets or charms to protect their homes, so adapting everyday objects like pins, nails, shoes, and knives was common place. Hanging a horseshoe over a door has absolutely no relation to its original function; it is a cultural adaptation with no other purpose than protection against evil incursions. The second feature is that it is made of iron. Legend has it that Witches and sorcerers have a mortal fear of iron, and as a result many of the items in protective deposits are made of iron. The prevailing assumption is that many of the torture devices used to interrogate accused Witches were made of iron, as were the clamps used to secure the hands and feet of Witches when they were burned at the stake—a good enough reason to be fearful of anything made of iron. We must not forget that, as we saw earlier, blacksmiths, who worked only with iron, were also considered to have supernatural powers, and the curses of a blacksmith were, along with those of a priest, considered to be the most potent.

We can see that the intention of the iron horseshoe was to either frighten the evildoer away or to impale him or her if the evildoer tried to enter the building. We can also see why horseshoes are most often nailed (with an iron nail) over doorways and fireplaces, the most vulnerable entry points in any home.

We will see below that these principles apply not only to horseshoes but also to the vast majority of other protective deposits that appear in abundance in the homes and farms of the Welsh Marches.

The construction of the homes of the time revolved around the practice of communal living, with a large communal space where the occupants gathered around a grand fireplace that served to heat the room and as the principal cooking area where the family, along with any transient workers, extended family members, and servants assembled for meals. At the time, many families, both large and small, employed servants, often paid only with room and board, to cook, clean, and work on the farm. We can see from the remaining buildings in the Marches that the only private space an individual or married couple had was their bed chamber, with couples who had children sharing their bedrooms with up to seven or eight children of varying ages at a time. As a result, it was never a problem to identify the most vulnerable entry points in any home. By this time, despite a punitive window tax being charged for every glass window, most windows had sash fittings that allowed them to be securely locked and so were considered low risk, and we see very few protective devices deposited near or around windows. Doors were frequently very substantial, with heavy bolts and locks to secure them. However, because of the communal style of living, doors were often left unsecured or even left open to all, occupants and neighbors alike. So doorways were seen as vulnerable, and we see a history of many protective deposits and markings placed in doorjambs, over doorways, and buried beneath thresholds to prevent evil intrusions. We find protective deposits and marks not only on external doorways but also on connecting doorways within houses, particularly bedroom doors. It is not difficult to understand why people thought themselves most at risk when they were asleep, and many apparitions and visualizations happen while asleep or when going to sleep. Some marks and devices were seen as a second line of defense, and some, where there were no devices elsewhere, were seen as the only defense for those who slept within the room.

The most vulnerable place of all within the house was the chimney and fireplace—the focal point of the house where all the cooking was done and where everyone gathered to eat and rest. The chimney was never closed, as the fire was constantly lit, and the fireplace was a major portal giving access to the house. There was a constant fear that evil spirits, Witches, or sprites would enter the house via the chimney, so this became a major location for protective deposits and markings. By far, the majority of the protective devices and deposits that we shall see later were positioned over fireplaces, inside chimneys, and in nooks adjacent to chimneys or buried beneath hearthstones, often in more than one of these locations at a time. This was also the location where any conciliatory offerings were left to placate the evil spirit and distract it from its evil tasks. Food, drink, and other items were also left out near fireplaces to confuse and distract evil spirits and Witches. This is a cultural tradition that we can see all over the world. As Christianity gradually merged with pagan beliefs, maybe we could consider just how Father Christmas gains entry into our homes. Where do we hang our stockings and holly wreaths? And where do we leave his mince pie and milk along with Rudolph's carrot?

Another popular depository location was beneath floorboards, in spaces between ceilings and upper floors, or in cavities between walls, each designed to prevent spirits from traveling from room to room within the house. Many larger deposits have been found either built into stairways or hidden beneath stairs to prevent harmful spirits from using the stairway.

In addition to the items we have mentioned above such as pins, nails, knives, and so on, other items we see used as protective devices, or, as we should more formally call them, apotropaic devices, are botanical materials related directly to the lore of cunning women, healers, and Druids. Most of the ancient pagan systems held their belief in many of these herbs, barks, flowers, nuts, and fruit in common and used them in the same way, so it is not difficult to understand their application in this case.

By far, the majority of deposits are made up of or contain personal items of the occupants of the homes in which they are found. Items of clothing, decorative jewelery, and, most commonly, shoes, particularly children's shoes, are by far the most popular articles found in deposits throughout the Welsh Marches. It is believed that these personal items, particularly clothing and shoes, took on something of the spirit of the wearer, absorbing their characteristics over the time they were worn. Many are old and show signs of great wear. At the time when these deposits were hidden, shoes would have been a major investment and an item of clothing that was never shared, unlike shirts, smocks, scarves, and the like, which were often shared and worn by more than one member of the family. Shoes were worn exclusively by one person, often repeatedly repaired and adapted for all uses; however, when a child outgrew his or her shoes, they were typically handed down to the next child in line (if they had not been selected for use as a protective device, that is). All these items would have been placed in deposits to attract the evil spirit or witch who would then focus attention on the deposit and ignore the person who had donated them.

One particular custom that spans all these devices, be they pins, shoes, written charms, or household utensils, is the deliberate breaking or "killing" of the object to distinguish it from its original use and dedicate it to its new protective role. Pins, a popular protective device, are bent to prevent them for being used for their original purpose. Forks have one tine deliberately broken off. Knives have their ends bent or their cutting edge intentionally blunted or distorted so they will no longer cut. Written charms are pierced with sharp objects to kill them or burned so that the ashes may be scattered or put in witch bottles before secreting them. The old shoes are also deliberately cut apart or partly destroyed, with their uppers cut away and lacings and buckles cut off so that they can no longer be worn. This is all part of the ritual of depriving the item of its useful function and dedicating it to the sole purpose of becoming a protective device. Many smaller items are deposited in caches or assemblages to increase their potency, usually sealed in small witch bottles or pouches to keep them safe. This is discussed in greater detail in chapter 14.

Before moving on we must consider two slightly more gruesome commonly used apotropaic devices. We frequently find mummified cats deposited in familiar locations where we find other protective devices. Mostly discovered secreted between ceilings and upper flooring, mummified cats are the second-most commonly found object, second only to children's shoes. Because of this location, we can differentiate these mummified animals from what we know as foundation sacrifices that find their origin during the Roman occupation. The older tradition involved the ritual sacrifice of an animal, which was than ceremoniously buried beneath the foundations of new buildings to provide good fortune and protect the building from evil pagan gods who might otherwise destroy it. Distinguishing the protective depositions of mummified cats from these foundation ritual deposits is not difficult, as we know from many earlier examples that foundation deposits were, not surprisingly, always buried in a building's foundations, whereas mummified cats were invariably discovered between flooring spaces or hidden in wall spaces and cavities but never buried beneath the ground. We can be sure the unfortunate cats did not crawl into the spaces and, unable to escape, die of starvation because some were discovered arranged in specific poses or in spaces where they could, had they wished, have escaped without problem. Throughout history, cats have had a particular relationship with the occult in many of the world's belief systems and across many cultures. Their friendliness with their human companions, their ability to see in low light, and their increased activity at nighttime all give credence to their supernatural reputation, and, along with their association as Witches' familiars and their elevation to deity status in a number of belief structures, all compound their occult standing and reinforce their use as protective creatures when dead or alive.

The other strange animal deposits are the bleached skulls of horses, usually found buried beneath hearths and threshold slabs. Again proven not to be foundation sacrifices, as in such cases the whole animal was always used and never just the carefully cleaned and bleached skulls, these deposits have occasionally been explained as acoustic enhancement devices as they are typically discovered beneath flooring or hearth stones in public houses and inns, but such explanations have been recently discounted as they serve no real purpose and do nothing to enhance acoustics during extensive scientific testing. It is much more likely that they serve the same purpose as the mummified cat deposits, as the horse shares many of the characteristics of human familiarity, usefulness, and shared purpose as does the cat. It also has its own peculiar traits of sleeping while standing up and resting with its eyes open, which may be considered "seeing" in a different way.

Today, we find many of these old depositions kept in museum archives, but many still remain in their original locations, as do the many undiscovered deposits yet to be revealed.

Of course, some apotropaic devices cannot be removed to a museum, the most common of these being the familiar witch marks, which are either carefully inscribed into expensive pieces of furniture and panels or quickly scratched into the structure of the building. The origin of many of these witch marks varies, often dependent upon their location. As with the depositions we saw above, some of these witch marks are intended to be the means of transferring a curse, while others are designed to protect against curses. We will see how these differ when we investigate the marks and their locations in chapter 14. For now, we will focus only upon the protective witch marks. Some witch marks are made by sympathetic Witches who produced them to protect the occupiers from the evil intent of other, darker Witches. It has also been suggested that some may have been inscribed by sympathetic Druids to protect the building's occupiers, as the sigils that have been used are well known in the Druidic tradition, but we believe that the great majority are carved by the occupiers themselves or by skilled craftspeople and tradesmen commisioned by the occupant to make them at their behest, as described on the following page.

Witch marks have been found on almost every element of a building—be they stone, timber, or even iron—inscribed into the very structure of a building, on the outside surfaces and often near doorways, windows, and other entry points. They can also be found on perimeter walls enclosing courtyards, gardens, and cemeteries, in churches and monasteries, and even carved into furniture and wall paneling inside stately homes. We may also see that they are typically created in one of two ways: either skillfully carved by an artist-craftsmen into beautiful furniture, doors, and paneling, suggesting that it was a preplanned act incorporated into the building as a standard procedure at a time when such marks were a prevailing practice or even a fashionable embellishment, while others show all the signs of being hastily scratched into a convenient surface, suggesting a more urgent response to an imminent threat and a frantic need for protection against a looming danger.

Whether skillfully carved or hurriedly scratched, all the marks have a small range of sigils that are common to both styles. These sigils would have been well known to all, and their meanings and intentions have stayed with both the witchcraft and Druidic traditions right up to the present day.

The most common of these inscribed marks is the daisy wheel, also referred to as a hexafoil (fig. 6.3). We encountered the hexagon earlier when we examined the Shropshire amulet found in a cottage near Shrewsbury. The hexafoil is a similar image, but instead of being a simple

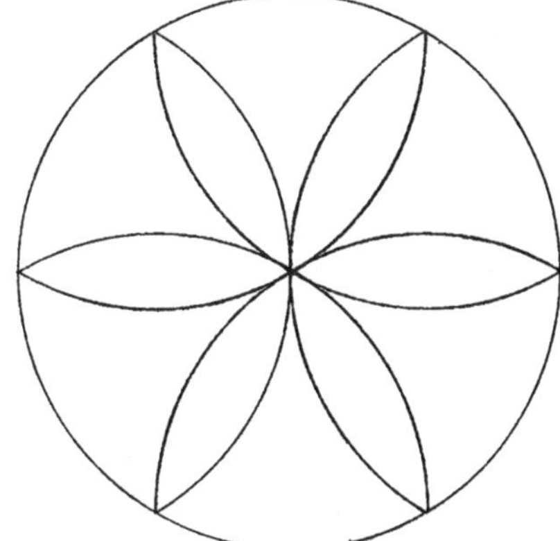

Fig. 6.3. Image of a hexafoil, commonly known as a daisy wheel.

six-sided figure it is modeled in the form of a six-petaled flower such as a daisy. Created by overlapping six circular arcs within a circle of the same diameter, the hexafoil is an ancient religious symbol relating to the six-petal lily, which in the Christian tradition symbolizes purity and has a correspondence to the Holy Trinity. In both witchcraft and Druidic traditions, the hexagon relates to a form of stability and security and also plays an important role in our relationship with the kingdom of the bee, the hexagon being the form of each individual cell within the honeycomb. In its role as a protective device, the daisy wheel is intended to scare away evil spirits because of its relationship to Christian purity, one of many protective marks having its origins in the Christian tradition.

Another common witch mark that has its origins in the Christian tradition is known as the Marian mark. Often seen as a simple M, we sometimes find it inverted to represent two overlapping V symbols, presented as a W. The two individual Vs represent the initials of the Virgin Mary, in this case presented in the Latin alias Virgo Virginum, Virgin of Virgins. Again, this witch mark is intended to scare away evil spirits with the threat of Christian retribution to those who ignore it.

An alternative means of protecting a person or building from evil intention is not to simply scare away the evil spirit but to confuse or trap it when it encounters the sigil. These types of marks are commonly known as daemon traps and may take the form of crosses, overlapping or concentric circles, meshes formed by overlapping diagonal lines, complicated mazes, coffin forms, and a simple pentagram, a form well known to Witches everywhere.

The most prolific witch mark to be found in buildings within the Welsh Marches, however, is the scorch mark or burn mark, a flame-shaped mark burned into the wooden structure of the building or sometimes into furniture and paneling. Over time, there has been speculation that these marks were the result of candle or taper burns accidentally defacing the wooden beams and doorjambs where they are found, but there is overwhelming evidence to show that these marks were deliberately made, and we can see evidence of this in the marks themselves. Many of the burn marks are seared deep into the wood, a feature that can only be obtained by repeatedly burning the wood while scratching away the burned carbon ash in between successive burnings. It appears that the burned carbon would have been removed by scratching with a fingernail, knife, or small spoon-like implement; there is no other way that such precise, contained marks can be made so deeply into the wood. If we add to this the fact that all the marks are found in places where it would be very unlikely to have appeared accidentally, such as inside the recesses of doorjambs and inside the mortice pockets of door locks, we can be confident in concluding that the burn marks were made deliberately. We also know that the people of the time lived in mortal fear of flames and fire, understandable when we consider that most houses and buildings were constructed with timber frames, often floored with straw or rushes, and, of course, there were no fire services or convenient fire extinguishers. It is no surprise that they were extremely careful around anything to do with fires and flames. It would also be inconceivable that so many accidental burn marks would appear in the most unlikely places, some houses having hundreds of burn marks scattered throughout the rooms, kitchens, and attics.

Many have wondered why people would deface their expensive property and furniture with deliberate burn marks and why such marks would prove to be a defense against witchcraft. One popular belief that has survived the test of time is that the marks, often found in corners, nooks, and crannies, were effective in deterring Witches and evil spirits because that was where any evil spirits would hide themselves. By placing these defensive marks in the dark secluded corners, the spirits would find no place to hide and thus would leave. Other theories emphasize the relationship between fire and Witches, highlighting the notion that the marks were made at a time when Witches were being tortured by fire and hot irons to extract confessions of their evildoings, for which they were subsequently burned at the stake, providing every reason for Witches to be fearful of fire, represented by the protective burn marks they encountered. One final theory we have encountered is the Christian notion of fire as a purifying force to be employed against evil, so the sight and smell of burn marks in timber would protect all innocent Christian souls.

It may never be possible for us to fully understand the reasons why people used these protective markings and deposits so often, but their ubiquitous presence throughout buildings within the Welsh Marches must surely tell us that the owners of these buildings shared a common and profound fear of being severely harmed by witchcraft. But what was it that gave rise to such widespread fear, and what physical evidence do we have to support our claims?

Being under the threat of harm or ill fortune from a curse cast or "thrown" by a Witch or sorcerer was the main reason common people resorted to the use of protective devices. Curses were seen as the foremost weapon in the armory of every Witch and, as we have already seen, every Christian priest, who in his turn was only too ready to throw curses from the pulpit whenever he thought fit. However, there is one aspect of cursing that is often overlooked.

There is ample evidence to suggest that people lived in mortal dread of being the subject of a Witch's curse and that they went to any extreme to protect themselves as best they could from what they saw as an ever-present threat. In one instance, as we shall see later, the occupant of a small attic bedroom, most likely that of a servant maid in one of the major manor houses in the Welsh Marches, had more than 130 individual protective burn marks seared deeply into the beams surrounding the entrance to her room. This starkly illustrates the individual's desperate need for personal protection, as opposed to the more general protection of the main household, and brings into focus another often overlooked aspect of cursing that goes some way toward explaining this and other examples of individual protection devices defending discreet private locations.

At the time it was generally believed within both the Christian and non-Christian sections of society that no matter how strong a curse may be, it could only attach itself and therefore be effective against a person who was guilty of the original transgression that caused the curse to be cast. If cast against an innocent person, the curse became ineffectual. No curse could harm the wholly innocent person or his or her family or possessions.

This then raises an interesting dilemma. In cases where we see these large collections of hastily created witch marks and other deposits, were they done to protect against a general fear of being randomly attacked by anonymous Witches, or, more likely, was the marker guilty of a recent trangression and so felt guilty and was concerned that a specific act of witchcraft would be aimed directly at him or her?

This potent combination of fear and guilt fed into the general zeitgeist of the witch terror and gave rise to the widespread proliferation of witch marks and protective deposits of all kinds throughout the region. One thing is very clear from the quantity and variety of protective deposits that have been discovered over the years, and that is that there was a very real and widespread fear of Witches in the region, one that appears to be greater than in any other area of Britain at the time, and this points to one undeniable conclusion: there were a great many Witches and sorcerers living in the Welsh Marches. But before we look at some of the more infamous manor houses, courts, and castles where many of these protective deposits have been discovered, we shall examine some of the specific items held in the archives of the museums of Wales and the Welsh Marches itself.

WITCH ARTIFACTS OF THE WELSH MARCHES

In researching the content of this book, we have enjoyed the cooperation of the curators and other staff members of many of the museums holding collections and individual artifacts related to our research and have been allowed unprecedented access to archived artifacts and texts not on display to the general public. We are grateful for this privilege and thank all those who have helped in our endeavors. As a result, we are able to share this unique information with our readers, and where better to begin than in the National Museum.

National Museum Wales

The National Museum Wales (Welsh: Amgueddfa Cymru) has a network of sites in various locations around the principality, each focusing on a specific aspect of Welsh history and culture. The museum's main complex is in the center of the Welsh capital, Cardiff. Because of the nature of our subject, we based the main focus of our research at St. Fagans National Museum of History (Welsh: Sain Ffagan Amgueddfa Werin Cymru) set in the grounds of St. Fagans Castle, an Elizabethan manor house to the northwest of the capital. The museum site, which covers over a hundred hectares, consists of more than forty reerected buildings, transferred brick by numbered brick from their original locations all over Wales and rebuilt in their original state within the grounds. In addition to these lovingly reconstructed buildings, the complex also has a central reception, exhibition, and educational building, which holds exhibitions, events, and an archive of texts and artifacts reflecting the history of every aspect of Welsh life, culture, and architecture. In June 2019, St. Fagans was named UK's Museum of the Year, a well-deserved accolade for such a forward-thinking enterprise. Our research at St. Fagans, along with the kind assistance of the collection curator, provided us with the first pieces of physical evidence for the presence of Witches and Druids in the Welsh Marches.

In the following section we list the photographs and the museum's own description of the items extracted from the archive collection at St. Fagan's. The museum descriptions are presented in *sans serif font* to distinguish them from the the authors' commentary.

This doll was crafted using twigs, wool, twine, and many other convenient materials, as was typical of this type of wax doll or poppet. Poppets are frequently dressed in clothing made from those previously worn by the intended recipient of the curse. It is also common to find

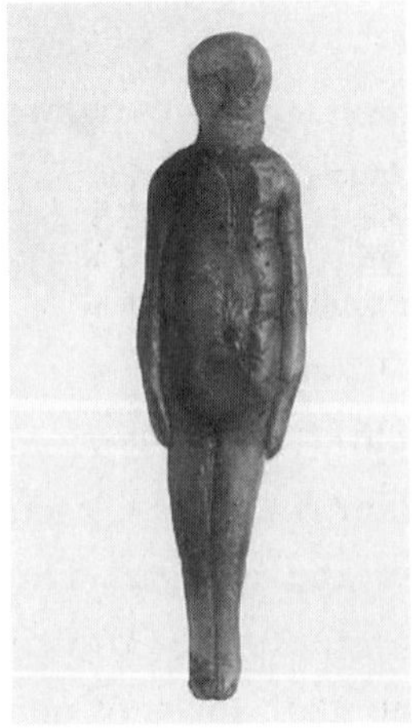

Fig. 6.4. Miniature doll in human form made entirely of wax, formerly used to work death by witchcraft. (See also color plate 4.)

poppets with nail clippings, strands of hair, and even the blood of the intended victim enclosed within the wax body, thereby making each poppet a personification of the target of the curse. Another way of potentializing the poppet is to seal a written curse or an amulet inside the body or wrap it in the doll's clothing. Poppets were also thrown in to curse wells, the intention being that the victim should drown. The crafting of miniature representations as a means of personifying the curse or spell of intention is common to both witchcraft and Druidic lore and should not be confused with the crafting of miniature representations of deities as a means of worship or as an iconic representation.

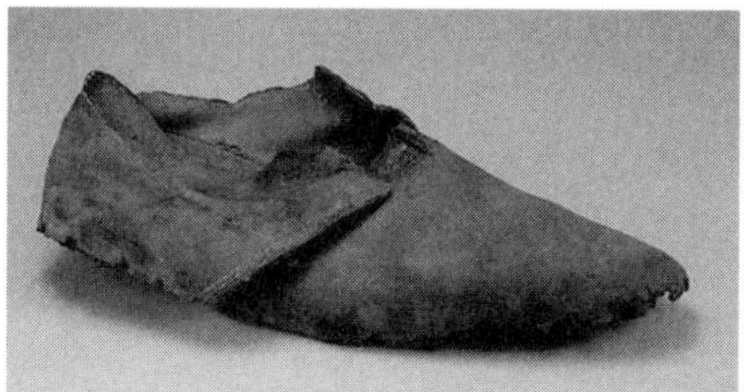

Figs. 6.5 and 6.6. Two working boots. The most frequently found hidden garments are shoes. These rusty boots were among five leather shoes discovered in 1994 behind a fireplace at a house in Llanfachreth and held in the archive collection at the National Museum Wales.

Chimneys and fireplaces were probably chosen as hiding places because they served as the main focal point in most homes—a source of heat and comfort. Shoes were also hidden under floorboards, around doorways and below staircases. Some considered these places to be the weakest part of a building, where evil spirits and witches would enter.

Many believed that hiding a child's shoe in a chimney breast or in the walls of a house increased a couple's chance of having children. A practise that could be linked to this tradition is the tying of old boots and shoes to the back of a bride and groom's wedding car.

We will encounter many more shoe deposits as we progress through the finds and collections within the buildings of the Welsh Marches.

Fig. 6.7. A small fabric bag containing the left and right feet of a mole.

Mole's feet carried in silken bag as a cure for cramps. Left and right front feet of mole (bones and nails, with skin and tissue attached) and draw-string bag made from blue silk with dots and stripes of pink silk.

Bag made from single piece of fabric, folded in half and stitched together with handstitched running stitches using black thread. The bottom of the bag is stitched in a curve.

Animal feet have long been a component of witchcraft and are said to bring good fortune and protect against evil. Most people are aware of the lucky rabbit's foot charm, which has had a place in popular culture for hundreds of years.

Fig. 6.8. Animal bone teething ring.

This dual-purpose element was the teether. These sticks or rings were not only practical aids, helping the baby's teeth to come through the gums, they were also seen as examples of sympathetic magic. Traditionally made of substances which were red or white, such as coral, they symbolised blood or bone respectively. The use of animal bone or tooth was also thought to confer the strength of the animal to fight off the pain of teething.

Teething, along with many other aspects of postnatal care, was usually the job of the Witch or cunning woman, who played the role of midwife and community nurse.

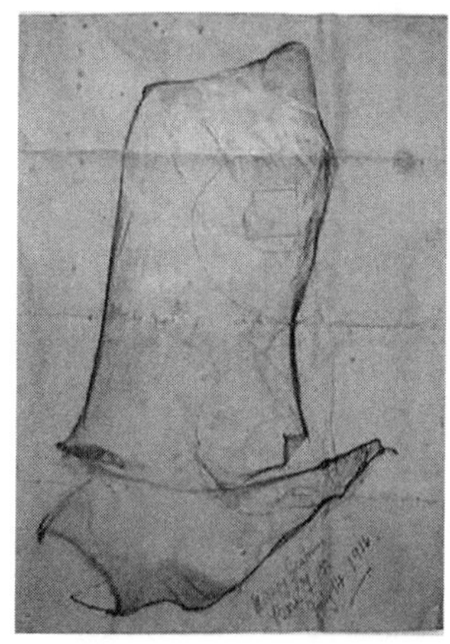

Fig. 6.9. A section of the amniotic membrane covering a baby's head (caul).

Known as a caul, this deposit is the thin, translucent tissue, which is a fragment of the amniotic membrane covering a baby's head, mounted onto a piece of paper, which is now folded. The caul was thought to have the ability to defend fertility and the harvest against the forces of evil, particularly Witches.

Possession of a baby's caul was also thought to give its bearer good luck and protect that person from death by drowning.

The use of a caul as a protective device against Witches and evil witchcraft has been recorded throughout the Welsh Marches. This tradition is shared with Druidic lore, where a caul is used as a protective device and as part of a working to increase fertility.

Fig. 6.10. An Iron Age annular blue glass bead with white wave decoration, known as an adder stone (Welsh: *glain nadredd*) and used for healing cataracts. (See also color plate 5.)

According to folklore, these "Snakestones" were thought to be dead snakes turned into stone. If found, they became prized and lucky possessions. They could be used to cure ailments such as eye infections by rubbing on the affected area.

This is another magical device that shares its origins with Druidic lore. Sometimes seen mounted on the head of Druidic staves or tied to the stave with twine, these adder stones are thought to be the shed skins of serpents that became petrified over time. This is part of the more familiar legend of the Druid's serpent egg, known to most followers of Druidic lore.

Both Witches and Druids had large collections of botanical, mineral, and animal compounds used for all sorts of cures and workings. Alabaster (fig. 6.11) was not a common mineral as it would have been imported from mainland Europe or the African continent. It became more common with the arrival of the medieval spice traders, who traded exotic materials from distant lands.

Fig. 6.11. A single piece of white alabaster from a larger collection of the same, formerly owned by Mr. William Jones, from Blaenwyre, Lledrod. Last used in the 1860s as a remedy against hydrophobia. Known in Welsh as *llaethfaern* or *carreg cynddaredd*.

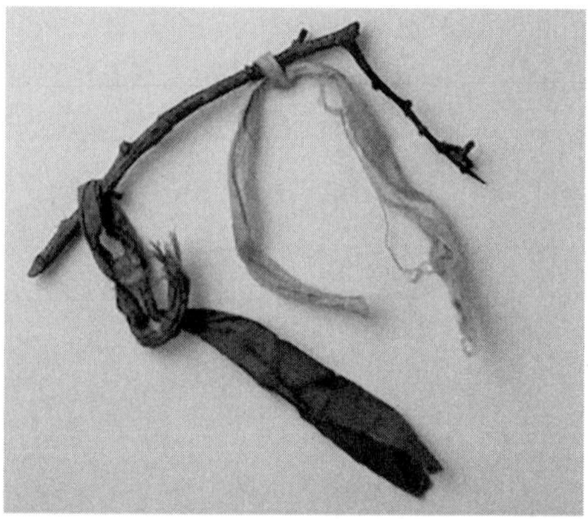

Fig. 6.12. Rag offerings like these were often tied to a hawthorn branch, and as the rag disintegrated, so the wish or spell would take effect. These are from a wishing well at Tremains near Bridgend, South Wales.

The custom of tying rags to hawthorn or blackthorn trees continues to the present day (fig. 6.12). The rag is tied to this sacred tree at the same time as the wish or intention is spoken. As the rag decays and is lost, so the wish or intention grows to fruition.

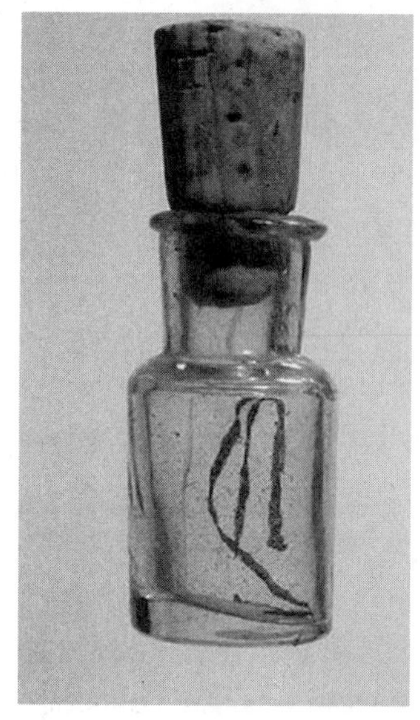

Fig. 6.13. A witch bottle.

The content of this bottle was once used to cure toothache. It was found on Barry Island, South Wales in 1895. You can still see the iron pins inside. Iron was believed to have special healing powers because it had been purified by the hot flames of the smithy. A clove oil liquid was infused with the iron pins and was rubbed on the sore area.

Figure 6.13 shows a typical witch bottle; in this case it contains a curative potion. In chapter 14 we will explore more witch bottles, which, in contrast to the ones examined here, contain a range of materials intended to either induce a curse or to be used to protect against evil intentions.

Fig. 6.14. A second witch bottle.

This plain glass bottle containing blue notepaper with undecipherable charm in brown ink. Found in Ty'n-coed, Llanymawddwy. Wales.

Similar written charms have been discovered in a variety of locations. Most contain some form of curse, either simple or more complex. Many also contain Christian references or quotations taken from the Bible, showing the extent to which both belief systems converged during the early modern period.

The collection at St. Fagans contains many more items that relate to witchcraft and Druidic lore, including texts, photographs, and physical artifacts—far too many to list here. But we can see from those detailed above that there is no doubt of the presence of Witches and Druids in all regions of the principality. Because many of the artifacts related to our research are small and considered part of the local culture of the region where they have been discovered, they rarely manage to find their way into large national collections like that of St. Fagans, but thankfully they are often held in local or regional museums, having been donated by local families, local historical societies, or archaeological groups. With this in mind, we next turned our attention to the local and regional museums within the Welsh Marches, with the intention of discovering whatever local finds they may have in their collections.

Hereford Museum

At the very heart of the Welsh Marches, we find the county town of Hereford, a town that has played a pivotal role in the history of the

Fig. 6.15. Hereford Museum. (See also color plate 6.)

region and remains a vital and vibrant market town. The museum holds an exciting collection of local folklore and cultural artifacts, and with the assistance of the museum's collections officer we were able to find a number of objects and texts that record the history of Witches and witchcraft in the region extending right up to the twentieth century.

We have listed a selection of these artifacts below, along with the comments of the museum's collections officer, Ben Moule. The descriptions in *sans serif text* are taken directly from the museum's records. We begin with a curse doll (poppet) along with the written curse found within the folds of her dress.

Fig. 6.16. Curse doll discovered in Hereford. (See also color plate 7.)

People have secretly hidden objects in their houses for centuries (things like bottles, shoes and the bodies of cats) to protect themselves and their families from various forms of supernatural menace (evil spirits, witches, hostile magic, malign influences), to influence events or to take revenge on people that may have wronged them.

This strange little 19th century doll was found in a crevice of the brickwork in the cellar of 21 East Street, Hereford. In a fold of her dress was a handwritten note which read: "Mary Ann Ward, I act this spell upon you from my whole heart wishing you to never rest nor eat nor sleep the rester part of your life. I hope your flesh will waste away and I hope you will never spend another penny I ought to have. Wishing this from my whole heart." *The body is made of wood, with arms and legs of red checked cotton material. Her head bears traces of paint; she has a string and silk pigtail and wears a red spotted dark blue cotton dress, in the folds of which the curse was hidden.*

There are a number of records of a Mary Ann Ward living in Hereford at the end of the 19th and the beginning of the 20th century, one of whom may have lived in Ryeland street at the turn of the century. From the wording of the curse Mary Ann Ward seems to have come into some money that the writer believed was theirs by right, possibly an inheritance or a controversial business transaction.

Fig. 6.17. Witch's coffin curse with small wooden poppet in coffin. (See also color plate 8.)

Witch's Coffin Curse—A roughly carved representation of a human effigy lying in a coffin. The body is pinned to the back of the coffin with a nail. It was found concealed in a wall at Woolhope, Herefordshire in 1987. No record of the written curse contained within the coffin was to be found.

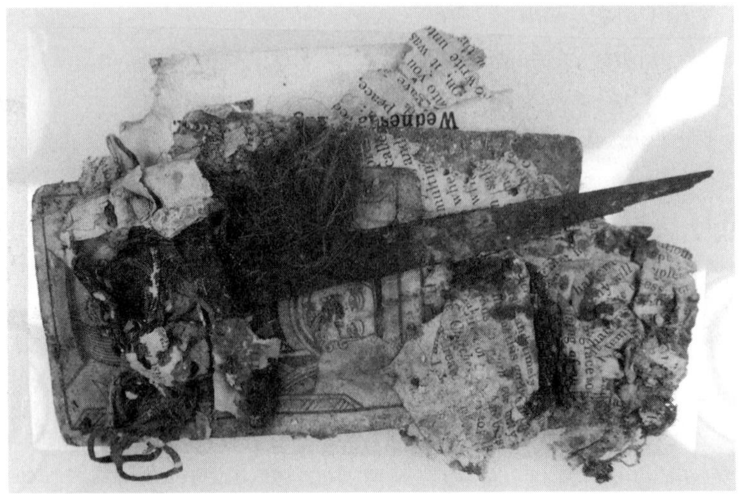

Fig. 6.18. A collection of protective devices (assemblage) deposited beneath the floorboards in a chemist shop in Hereford. (See also color plate 9.)

Possible spell/good luck charm, mid 19th Century. A splinter of wood, an iron nail, a ball of hair and a length of cord lay across a knave of Diamonds on a piece of newspaper. Beneath is a Spade playing card and a Refreshments Card with a name, message and date of 7th August 1861. Found under the floorboards of a chemists shop in St. Peters Square, Hereford.

A lady who came into the museum between 2003 and 2008 commented: "This is a good luck charm and not a spell or curse. Old Herefordians still lived much by the old ways and an Apothecary Shop/Chemist had many herbal things (i.e., natural), so a charm was made using the knave as Satan and a refreshment card/recipe tied to it as a renewal—old to new. As the old died away, new was re-born. All things bound together with a pin to prevent bad things happening via the knave and a modern piece of history, i.e., the letter or newspaper cutting. This was done to show that the church no longer ruled the Apothecary's Art, but modern grows from the old ways. If a charm was not built into a wall or floor, Herefordians would not enter the shop but go to any old lady for their herbal remedies, if she had knowledge of such."

Fig. 6.19 and Fig. 6.20. Concealed shoes.

Deliberately concealed shoes. These can often be hard to identify either within a collection or in situ as they often look like discarded objects.

Almost every museum we contacted and every manor house we investigated had either shoe deposits in their collections or accounts of shoes discovered concealed in buildings in the Marches. In Hereford, although it was difficult to confirm the purpose of these specific shoe caches, it is reasonable to conclude that they were concealed for the same purpose as the ones discovered in other locations within the Marches. Next, our investigations took us to Ludlow Museum, again at the center of the Welsh Marches.

Ludlow Museum

Ludlow (Welsh: Llwydlo) is a picturesque market town located in the county of Shropshire, just twenty-three miles north of Hereford. It is one of the major towns within Shropshire, and like Hereford, it has played an important role in the history of the Welsh Marches and the long conflict between the Marcher lords and the Welsh princes.

When we first made contact with Ludlow Museum, we were aware that it was and still is a local museum with a focus on its local culture and history, and it has every reason to be very proud of both. Ludlow is located almost halfway along the long-standing border between

England and Wales, and its castle was one of the strongest and most significant in the region. The castle's location, size, and strength were among the deciding factors when King Edward IV made it the administrative capital of the Welsh Marches and the seat of the Council of the Marches, the governing body of the Marches. In 1473 the Prince of Wales and his younger brother were imprisoned in the castle before being taken to the Tower of London, where they met their untimely death. Some years later, King Henry VII's son and heir, Arthur Tudor, Prince of Wales, and his wife, Catherine of Aragon, who was later to become the first wife of Henry VIII, took up residence in the castle, where Arthur died only six months later.

Ludlow Museum is one of more than five hundred buildings in the town that are listed as being of historical importance and is located within one of the oldest sections. Our interest in the museum stemmed from our earlier research, which suggested that they held an excellent specimen of a mummified cat (fig. 6.23), one of the infamous protective devices that we had failed to track down. The description

Fig. 6.21. Ludlow Museum at the Buttercross, Ludlow. (See also color plate 10.)

Fig. 6.22. Ludlow Castle, Ludlow. (See also color plate 11.)

that follows is taken directly from the museum records, kindly provided by Emma-Kate Lanyon, curator, Shropshire Museums.

> *Bell Lane Mummified Cat—Mummified remains of a domestic cat. Found in space of between ceiling and floor above at 1 Bell Lane, Ludlow in 1983.*
>
> *This mummified cat was found in the roof space of 1 Bell Lane, Ludlow and donated to Ludlow Museum in 1983. The house dates from the C18th but appears to have an earlier core. It is not known how or when the cat got there but it may have been put there deliberately as a good luck charm or to ward off witches.*

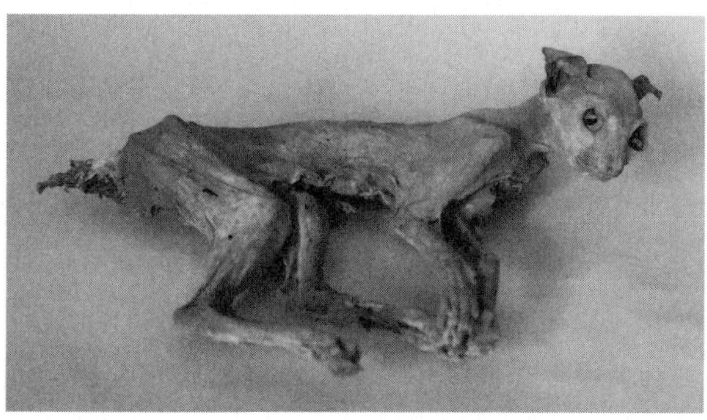

Fig. 6.23. Mummified cat found at No. 1 Bell Lane, Ludlow.

Folklore suggest that cats had a sixth sense, and in the seventeenth to nineteenth centuries, cats were often put in walls or roof spaces to ward off evil spirits and keep away anything that might threaten a house and its occupants. Although we later discovered other museum collections containing mummified cats, this one at Ludlow is by far the most impressive.

Manor Houses of the Welsh Marches

By this point we were content that we had accumulated a representative collection of artifacts that had been removed to museums from various locations within the Welsh Marches and had assembled convincing evidence of the presence of Witches and Druids in many of the towns and villages during the early modern period. Now it was time to seek out some of the evidence that could not be removed to museums because it had been permanently carved into the fabric of a building, by which we mean the witch marks, taper burns, and other protective devices within the manor houses that dominated the Welsh Marches at the time.

Although there are accounts of protective marks and deposits in virtually every manor house and noble dwelling in the region, it was impossible to investigate all the potential locations. We decided therefore to focus our attention on two of the most formidable: Tretower Court and Castle, which we have mentioned previously, and LLancaiach Fawr, a Tudor manor house near the small village of Nelson in Glamorganshire, home of Colonel Edward Prichard, a Royalist who hosted a visit by King Charles I of England in 1645. We began our exploration with the wonderful Tretower Court and Castle in the modern-day border county of Powys.

Tretower Court and Castle

Tretower Court (Welsh: Llys Tre-tŵr) is a fortified manor house in the village of Tretower, which takes its name from the original castle on the same site, located at the time in the historical county of Brecknockshire.

Following the last successful invasion of Britain by the Normans in 1066, the new king, William the Conqueror, awarded large tracts

Fig. 6.24. Tretower Court manor house.
(See also color plate 12.)

of land in the Welsh Marches to those noble families who supported his cause. One such family was the Picard family, known to the Welsh speaking community as the Pychards (a slightly corrupted contraction of the Welsh name ap-Richard, where *ap* means "son of"). Roger Picard II began building the formidable castle with its four floors and eight-foot walls and completed it around 1100, when it became one of the most substantial and impressive fortifications protecting the new Norman Marcher lords from the threat of a Welsh invasion. The Picards went on to establish themselves and their reputation within the Welsh Marches, and, through their existing wealth and generations of advantageous marriages, they soon became one of the most powerful families in the region. The family retained the castle and its extensive lands for around two hundred years; after having been in the hands of Sir William Herbert, the Earl of Pembroke, for a short time, Tretower Castle and its lands were given to Sir Roger Vaughan in 1450.

The Vaughan family soon set about building the adjoining fortified manor house known as Tretower Court, which is the focus of our investigation. The castle, court, and manor lands were to remain in the Vaughan family for successive generations, some members of which we

Fig. 6.25. Tretower Castle ruins. (See also color plate 13.)

encountered in chapter 5. Sir Roger himself became one of the most powerful men in the Marches, and his influence extended far into Wales. The family continued to improve the medieval court, filling it with fine furniture and works of art, and it soon gained a reputation as one of the most magnificent manors of its day.

Although the castle has become a ruin, with only the main tower remaining, the manor has survived its turbulent history in remarkably good condition, though at the lowest point of its decline, the splendid halls and rooms of the ground floor were used as farm buildings and even housed pigs and cattle. Fortunately, the structure of the house and court remained intact and have recently been refurbished and returned to their former glory as a historical visitor venue and educational facility.

Historical accounts tell us that the Red Book of Hergest was kept here toward the end of the Wars of the Roses when the Vaughans took over the forfeited estate and artifacts of Hopcyn ap Rhys. The Red Book is one of at least two works that are connected with the collection of legends known as the Mabinogion. Ian Andrews, the lead custodian of Tretower Court and Castle, reveals:

> *Thomas Vaughan was an elder brother of Roger Vaughan who built the Court; the Red Book apparently came to him and his part of the family, hence the "Hergest" attachment to the book title (as that's the Shropshire hamlet where Thomas lived). Thomas was executed after the Battle of Edgecote in 1469, and when his headless body was returned for burial then his spirit supposedly haunted the area for centuries. Royalists Henry Vaughan and his twin brother Thomas would have visited the Court in the 17th Century as their grandfather, uncle, and cousin were the owners; Henry returned to the area upon his release from captivity during the English Civil War, never to leave again. He was a doctor and became the vicar of Llansantffraed (5 miles from Tretower), but is now best known as "The Silurist" and one of the foremost metaphysical poets of that period; twin Thomas was an alchemist and philosopher who died in London from ingesting mercury whilst researching the means of creating gold from lead.*

We shall encounter Thomas Vaughan again in chapter 9, as one of the famous occultists of the Welsh Marches.

The court also has an infamous reputation for being haunted, most notably by the White Lady of Tretower, the ghost of Roger Vaughan's wife, Margaret Vaughan, who night after night stares out a window, waiting for her husband to return from battle, which of course he never did. The White Lady is not the only ghost who occupies the court; a young boy paces the courtroom, while yet another female apparition haunts the main bedchamber.

As one of the main centers of activity within the Welsh Marches, Tretower Court was at the peak of its power and influence during the time of the witch terror and as a result has an impressive collection of protective devices within its halls and lesser rooms.

The most common protective device we see within the court are the many witch marks that are carved or burned into the fabric of the building. These can be found not only in the kitchens of the court,

Fig. 6.26. Interior, Tretower Court manor house.

where you may expect the less sophisticated servants and estate workers to scratch protective marks on the walls to protect themselves from the Witches and sorcerers they may have gossiped about in the local village, but they can also be found in the great west range and even the great hall, which suggests that it was not only the servant and laboring classes who lived in fear of the ever-present Witches.

By far the most widespread witch marks we see are the many taper burns that cover almost every timber of the building. The taper burns at Tretower Court go a long way to dispel the theory that many of the taper burns we find in the timbers of the buildings of the period were accidental and simply burn marks resulting from the careless use of candles and tapers used at the time. This is demonstrably not the case. We can see from the closeup of the taper marks in figure 6.27 that the marks have been carefully crafted and finished in a way that suggests they have been repeatedly burned, the resulting burned ash carbon carefully scratched away, probably with a fingernail or thumbnail, and then burned and scratched over and over again until a deep, very visible burn mark is created. The burn recess has subsequently been cleaned and polished over

Fig. 6.27. Burn marks in the kitchen, Tretower Court manor house.

the centuries until we see the effect that appears today. There is practically no possibility that these are the result of accidental burning.

The taper burns we see around the kitchens are confined to the doorways, windows, and chimney opening, giving strength to the opinion that they were created to protect the building from the entry of Witches, familiars, and other evil entities who may try to enter through the most vulnerable entry points. As noted earlier, it was widely believed that because of the association of fire and flames with witch burnings and the tortures used during witch interrogation, Witches were terrified of fire and the smell of burning wood and would not cross a threshold that was protected by taper burns. Other taper marks are burned into the door and window timbers within the kitchen, sometimes in clusters rather than individually. In figure 6.29 the taper marks are clearly visible below the bolt hole, the hole in the doorjamb that receives the bolt. Again, it is difficult to imagine any reason these taper marks would be in this exact position other than as protective devices.

The manor house kitchen was an important gathering place for

Fig. 6.28 (left) and Fig. 6.29 (right).
Burn marks in the kitchen, Tretower Court manor house.

Fig. 6.30. View of the kitchen, Tretower Court manor house.

many of the servants and other staff working on the estate. It was undoubtedly a place of social interaction, gossip, and tale-telling, as well as where all the food for the entire household was prepared. It is not surprising that we see witch marks protecting the poor servant people who worked there, but it is interesting to consider that there are no records suggesting that any of the people who created the witch marks—and there are a lot of witch marks—were ever punished for making them, even though they could have been seen as damaging the owner's precious building and risking an extensive fire in a building that contained so much wood and inflammable materials. Neither do we see that any effort was made to erase the marks, which are not particularly attractive features; on the contrary, many have been repeatedly polished, varnished, and maintained along with the main timbers of the house.

As previously mentioned, taper burns and other witch marks are not confined to the servant areas of the court; they also appear in places that would be mainly the domain of the noble family. In figure 6.31 below we can see a cluster of five or more taper burns seared into the

Fig. 6.31. Burn marks in the wooden frame in the west range, Tretower Court manor house.

doorjamb in the west wing or range, again concentrated around the bolt hole, which would normally secure the door.

Other types of witch marks are more difficult to see, particularly those that have been hastily scratched into a surface rather than those carved deep into the woodwork or stone. As well as being more difficult to find, they are also notoriously difficult to photograph, as many other investigators will confirm. One such mark is a daisy wheel mark scratched into the stone of the great hall, the seat of the head of the manor (fig. 6.32). The great hall at Tretower is an impressive space that has been completely restored. The photograph in figure 6.33 shows the great hall as it is today, illustrating exactly how it would have looked when laid for a formal banquet.

There are many more examples of witch marks within Tretower Court, some already discovered and, most likely, many more to be found in the future. As the prime focus of our investigation is the presence of Witches and Druids in the Welsh Marches, accounting for the entire collection of protective marks and devices within Tretower is beyond our

Fig. 6.32. Daisy wheel mark carved into fire surround in the great hall, Tretower Court manor house.

scope. Looking at the examples shown above and in the sure knowledge that there are many more examples available, it is reasonable to assume that the residents and workers of the court had a very real fear of being affected by the evil intentions of the local Witches and sorcerers and were prepared to go to considerable efforts to protect themselves. They have left behind them very visible, permanent evidence showing just how threatened and intimidated they felt facing the ever-present terror of Witches and their daemonic crafts. The evidence shows us that this fear was not confined to the servants and underclasses but was just as valid and present to the gentry and nobility that occupied the court. There were enough Witches known to both the servant classes and the nobility to warrant such extensive protection.

Tretower Court and Castle was, however, by no means the only manor to respond so proactively to the threat of witchcraft, as we shall see when we investigate another of the manor houses of the Welsh Marches: Llancaiach Fawr, built on the border between the historic counties of Glamorganshire and Monmouthshire.

Fig. 6.33. The great hall, Tretower Court manor house.

LLancaiach Fawr

The semifortified manor house, Llancaiach Fawr, is thought to have been built around 1530 for one Dafydd ap Richard, who is recorded as being the lord of the manor in 1659, and is said to have been erected on the site of a much older medieval building. The manor is considered to be one of the most significant Tudor houses still remaining in the Marches. Now a Grade 1 listed building, it was later owned by Colonel Edward Prichard and was visited by King Charles II of England in 1645. In recent years the house has been refurbished and returned to its original splendor, showing not only the opulence that the lord of the manor enjoyed, but also the living spaces occupied by the fifteen or so live-in servants that would have been on hand to tend to the family's needs.

Our investigation into the presence of protective devices within the manor begins in the attic spaces, where the majority of the servants lived, most in the main spaces beneath the roofing timbers above the upper floor. In this main attic space, the first witch mark we find is a large Marian mark carved into a roofing timber (fig. 6.36 on page 106). Alicia Jessup, the historical interpreter at Llancaiach Fawr, told us during our tour of the manor that: "Marian marks, as we see here, are two overlapping V's, signifying Virgo Virginium or Virgin of Virgins. They are thought to be used to invoke the protection of the Virgin Mary. These marks have been found throughout the house; they were intended to stop evil entering, particularly Witches and their familiars." Alongside the Marian mark are two mesh marks, known by some as daemon traps, which could trap or confuse daemonic forces (fig. 6.37 on page 107). Both of these markings are intended to protect the servants who occupied the space, and show that they lived in fear of the evils of witchcraft that threatened them personally rather than the general occupants of the household.

Their fears, however, fall into insignificance compared to that of the occupant of the next space we investigated. In a small attic space above the entry porch, we find a small living space known as the steward's attic. Again, Jessup was able to tell us more: "The steward would have been the most important of the servants and would have

Fig. 6.34. Llancaiach Fawr Manor, near Caerphilly, Wales. (See also color plate 14.)

Fig. 6.35. Main attic space, Llancaiach Fawr Manor.

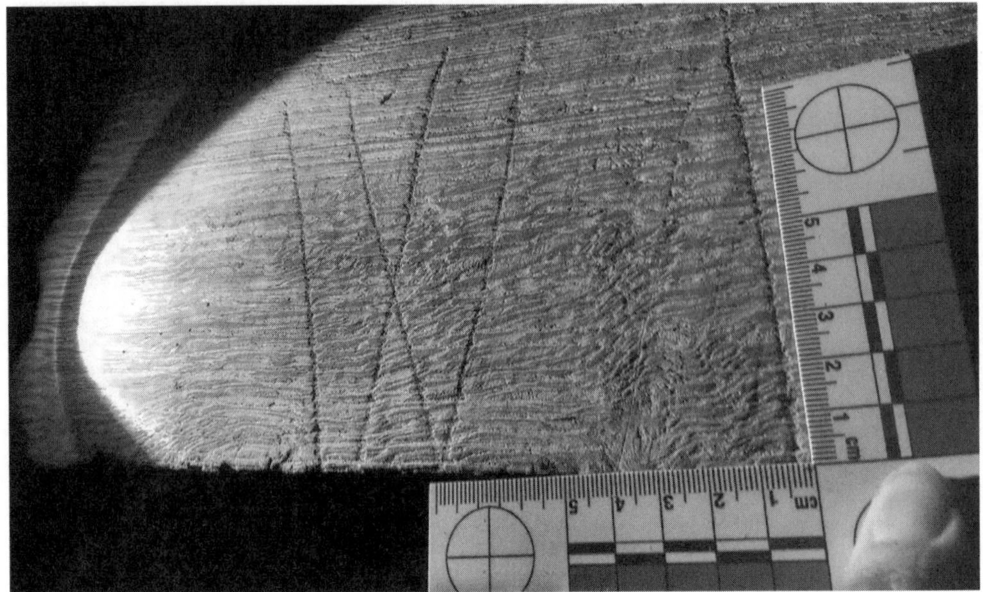

Fig. 6.36. Marian mark in the main attic space, Llancaiach Fawr Manor.

been educated and fluent in Welsh and English. He would have had an intimate knowledge of the law and a thorough insight into the comings and goings of the local tenants." Amazingly, this small attic space has the largest assemblage of witch marks in the entire manor, with more than 130 separate taper marks in the attic space alone. "Burn marks or taper marks," Jessup told us, "are found throughout the house; nearly every original door frame has one of these marks, but there is debate as to the exact purpose of these marks—they may have been used to protect against evil spirits or perhaps against fire or lightning. Whoever was sleeping there was terrified of something."

As we can see, the protection marks begin in the usual fashion, around the doorjambs and door frames. The entry to the steward's attic is covered in multiple taper marks (fig. 6.37). Even more impressive is the assemblage of taper burns in the roofing timbers above the steward's bed (fig. 6.39). As Jessup commented: "Whoever was sleeping there was terrified of something"—or maybe, as we discussed earlier, very guilty about something they had done.

Fig. 6.37. Mesh marks scratched into a beam in the main attic space, Llancaiach Fawr Manor.

If we move our focus to the kitchen of the manor house, we again find a collection of protective devices, suggesting that the servant of the household felt just as vulnerable at their work as they did while they slept. As if to reinforce this idea, the first of the witch marks we find is

Fig. 6.38. The steward's bedroom doorway, Llancaiach Fawr Manor.

Fig. 6.39. Burn marks in the roof beams in the steward's bedroom, Llancaiach Fawr Manor.

a carved cross protecting the entrance to the servants' stairs, a narrow set of stone steps leading from the kitchen to the servants' quarters (fig. 6.40). We can also see a heavily taper-burned door frame leading directly into the kitchen (fig. 6.41).

To the right of the kitchen fireplace, a spiritual midden or collection of protective magical objects was concealed (fig. 6.42 on page 110). Jessup told us that it contained "a hare's foot, large amounts of human hair from at least two different people, a twist of paper that may have contained a charm, and many other items were found. They were removed from their original hiding place when the house was being renovated. Some of these objects have now been returned to their rightful place; some members of staff felt that bad luck had befallen them after handling them and thought they should be returned as a mark of respect."

But as we have seen before, protection marks are not confined to the servants' quarters and kitchens; they are just as prolific in the quarters of the noble lord of the manor, such as the great hall, where he would have received his guests and held court. In the recess of one of the hall's windowsills we can see a small cross deeply carved into the stonework (fig. 6.44 on page 110). Again, we see the protective device carved in

Fig. 6.40. Servants' stairs in kitchen, Llancaiach Fawr Manor.

Fig. 6.41. Taper burns in the kitchen door, Llancaiach Fawr Manor.

Fig. 6.42. The main kitchen, Llancaiach Fawr Manor.

Fig. 6.43. The great hall, Llancaiach Fawr Manor.

Fig. 6.44. Cross carved into stone windowsill, Llancaiach Fawr Manor.

what one would consider a vulnerable opening, preventing incursions through the window into the hall (fig. 6.45). At one side of the hall is a small staircase that was blocked off circa 1628, when the grand staircase was installed. Below we see a large protective Marian mark, scribed into the ancient plaster; the one in figure 6.46 is the most visible, a large Marian mark.

Hidden beneath the grand staircase was an assemblage of

Fig. 6.45. Entrance to a small staircase, Llancaiach Fawr Manor.

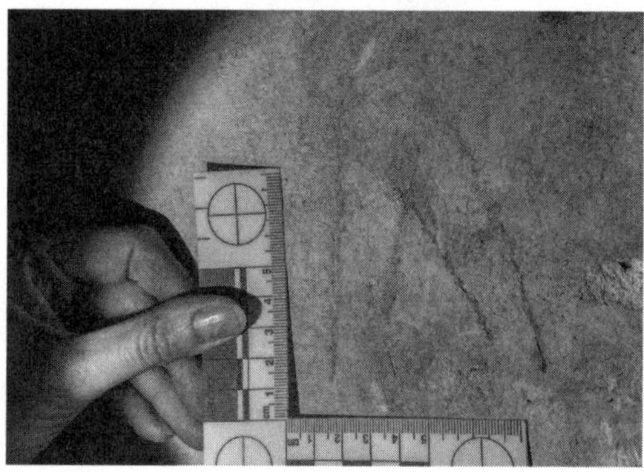

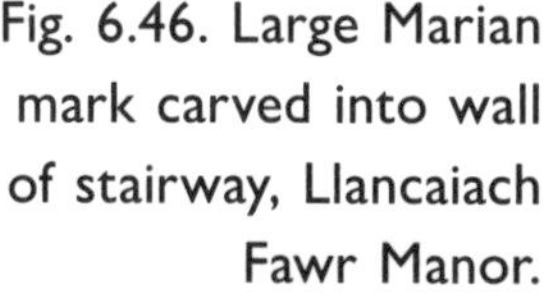

Fig. 6.46. Large Marian mark carved into wall of stairway, Llancaiach Fawr Manor.

Fig. 6.47. The grand staircase, Llancaiach Fawr Manor.

concealed items, which included parts of clothing, both high and low status, bones, wood, and the head of a crib, alongside a collection of shoes. The shoes belonged to children and had been repeatedly repaired. The earliest has been dated to circa 1600 and others have

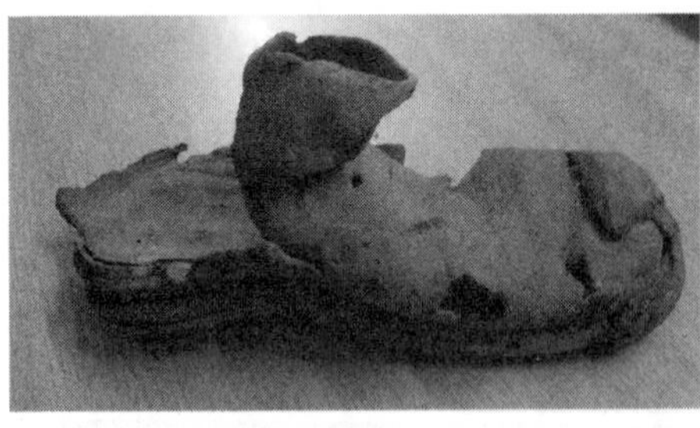

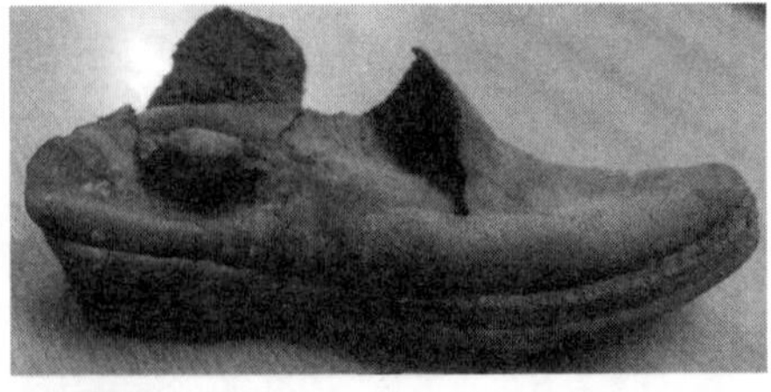

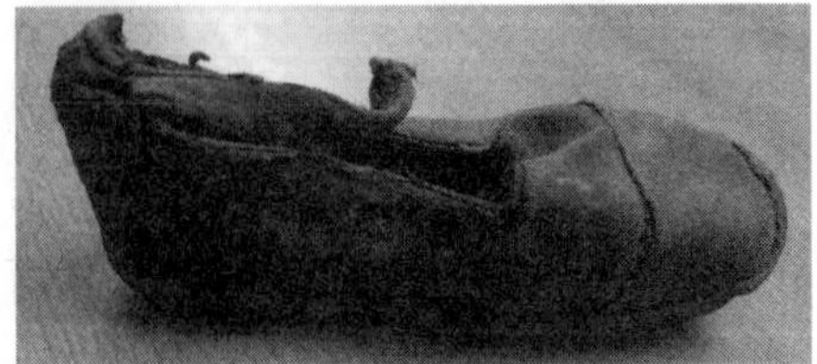

Figs. 6.48, 6.49, and 6.50. The shoes, part of an assemblage discovered beneath the grand stairway, Llancaiach Fawr Manor.

been dated to the late nineteenth century, suggesting that the assemblage had been discovered and new items added to it over a period of two to three hundred years. Again, Jessup explained the significance of the deposits: "There is a school of thought that suggests that these items could be used as decoys, as they would have taken on the essence of the wearer. The Witch's familiar or evil spirit would mistake the items for the child they wished to harm and become trapped among the confusing assemblage."

The last location we shall look at is the parlor, the highest status room in the manor and the private living space of the lord and lady. It is here that Colonel Prichard would have received King Charles I of England during his royal visit in 1645. Here we see Marian marks carved into the paneling above the splendid fireplace (fig. 6.52). The

Fig. 6.51. The parlor, Llancaiach Fawr Manor. (See also color plate 15.)

Fig. 6.52. Marian mark carved into a wooden panel in the parlor, Llancaiach Fawr Manor. (See also color plate 16.)

paneling is dated circa 1628 and the marks appear to have been carved soon after it was installed.

We can also see a St. Andrew's Cross, said to bar evil from passing through, deeply carved into the stonework of a doorjamb along with taper burns on the inner sixteenth-century door panels, again protecting those inside from any Witches, familiars, or other evil intrusions (figs. 6.53 and 6.54).

We can see from these examples from Llancaiach Fawr that the fear of Witches and witchcraft was a very real aspect of the everyday lives of both the gentry and the servant classes alike, and that people at every level of society went to great lengths to protect themselves by using every method they had at hand.

Before we leave Llancaiach Fawr, there is one more feature of the house that our host, Alicia Jessup, wanted to explain: "Llancaiach Fawr has been named in the top ten haunted locations in the UK. Our four resident ghosts are said to be Colonel Prichard, a former lord of the manor and disillusioned ally of King Charles I, who has been spotted drawing up battle plans; Mattie, a former maid who

Figs. 6.53 and 6.54. St. Andrew's cross carved into stone and taper burn marks in ancient parlor door, Llancaiach Fawr Manor. (See also color plate 17.)

burned to death in an accident; a young boy who fell to his death; and a man in black, a presumed murderer, who patrols the perimeter of the house." It appears that none of the protective deposits work against ghostly apparitions.

We began this chapter with the intention of exploring the existence of Witches in the Welsh Marches by looking for evidence of their presence in the homes and farms of the people who lived there. During our research we have seen evidence of their practices such as the curse dolls, coffin curses, written charms, and more, stored away in the archives of the National Museum Wales and the regional museums of the Marches, but even more overwhelmingly we have seen the extent to which the residents of the homes and manor houses of the region went to protect themselves from the evil intentions of the local Witches and sorcerers. Whether they resorted to hiding mummified cats under the floorboards, depositing caches of worn-out children's shoes beneath staircases, or carving magical sigils into door frames and roofing timbers, there is little doubt that the occupants of these houses and manors believed in the imminent threat of witchcraft, not in a small way, with the occasional mark or charm, but in a massive way by covering all areas of their homes with protective marks and devices of all kinds. Furthermore, we can be sure that this fear was not produced by an occasional Witch living alone in the surrounding countryside but a formidable number of Witches living in their midst—a local population of Witches and sorcerers that required a concerted effort to subdue and necessitated the application of what must have been "state of the art" methods and technology for protection.

The amount of evidence we discovered along with the extent of its distribution leaves us in no doubt of the presence of a substantial number of Witches and sorcerers in every corner of the Welsh Marches. In its day, it is likely that this concentration of Witches and sorcerers was unsurpassed anywhere in Great Britain, and we know from personal experience that this tradition remains intact through the present day, even though the number of its practitioners may be considerably reduced.

7
Druids of the Welsh Marches

How far back do the Druids go? Until recently, it has been difficult to determine when the Druids first began practicing in the British Isles because they did not keep written records. Though the Druids, along with the bards and ovates, were the learned classes of their community, they had no understanding of the concept of writing and so were required to commit all their knowledge and history to memory.

Thanks to carbondating techniques, we now know from the megalithic remains throughout Britain that communal living and a pagan belief system were established within most areas of Britain at least four thousand years before any written records began and that pagan culture has been present in the Welsh Marches for at least six thousand years. Recent carbondating techniques place the construction of some of the remaining structures at around 3800 BCE, which suggests that if these early inhabitants were constructing such sophisticated structures at that date, then they probably arrived on the British Isles many years earlier.

Later in this chapter we will examine the very visible evidence of the pagan culture that dominated the early history of the Welsh Marches, the tumultuous border region that separates England and Wales since people first began living in the area.

EARLY HISTORY OF THE DRUIDS

These early inhabitants have left evidence of their lifestyle and belief system at sites all over Britain and, significantly, scattered all about the Welsh Marches, where we find the same sorts of examples of a mature and sophisticated culture that we see in other important locations such as Avebury and Stonehenge. During this period, which runs up to the Roman conquest in 43 CE, the Druids developed a complex understanding of their relationship with nature and a variety of means that allowed them to benefit from nature's provisions. The Druids enjoyed an elevated status within the hierarchy of the tribe, often having a seat in the tribal leader's court.

At the same time, a less recognized knowledge was developing among the ordinary folk, a knowledge borne from their intimate contact with nature and the community's need for a more accessible source for healing, divination, and other forms of natural magic. These talented people became known wisewomen, cunning men, and other similar descriptive titles. For millennia the traditions of the Druid and that of these cunning folk developed in parallel, both basing their beliefs and practices upon the natural elements that surrounded them and controlled their everyday lives. These traditions evolved in unison as the practitioners of each became more knowledgeable and as each became more established within their own strata of society. Both traditions gained the respect of community members, who depended upon them to maintain their well-being and the health of their livestock and to cope with any unanticipated events that affected their lives. But everything changed forever in 43 CE when Roman soldiers landed on British soil under the command of Emperor Claudius.

THE ROMAN INVASION OF BRITAIN

The Roman Empire had invaded Britain on two previous occasions during the Gallic Wars under the command of Julius Caesar, once in 55 BCE and again in 54 BCE, when the Romans launched expeditionary forces from the European mainland. On both occasions they withdrew, but the experience opened up a range of trading opportunities and introduced Rome to the many tempting assets of the British Isles. It was almost a hundred years later that Claudius began his final invasion in 43 CE, conquering the majority of Britain and beginning an occupation that was to last for 350 years. By 50 CE, the Roman forces had begun subduing the tribes of Wales and the Marches, but it was a conflict that they never managed to complete as the fabled Welsh warriors conducted a lengthy guerrilla war, strategically retreating to the rugged Welsh hills whenever they were under threat.

The conquering Roman armies had encountered Druids early on in the Gallic Wars, when they confronted them at the head of the armies of Gaul. The Romans rapidly developed a respect for and fear of these formidable Gallic teachers and magicians. They gained a formidable reputation both for their memory skills and their dedication to learning, memorizing their whole corpus of knowledge; a task that, according to Caesar, could take twenty years or more. Most of what we now believe we know about this ancient pagan society and its Druids we have obtained from extremely meager accounts recorded by early Roman chroniclers and, of course, the living oral tradition that is maintained throughout Wales and the Welsh Marches.

As they prepared to invade Britain, one of the Romans' greatest fears was confronting the Druids of Britain and Wales, knowing that Wales was the land of origin of the Druids and, at the time, the center of Druidic training and the place where all aspiring Druids traveled to learn their art.

Persecution and Elimination

One element that is often overlooked when we consider the Roman invasion of Britain and their attitude toward the Druids is that at the time of the first invasion the Roman soldiers and their commanders were all pagans, worshipping a large pantheon of gods, so the pagan practices of the Druids were by no means totally foreign to them, and because of that, they feared them all the more. It was not until 313 CE that Emperor Constantine in the Edict of Milan accepted the Christian religion and in doing so put an end to the Roman persecution of Christians, and it was just ten years later that Christianity became the official religion of the Roman Empire.

The Roman fear of the Druids ran deep. The invading armies feared their supernatural powers along with their ability to motivate the defending tribes, while Rome's politicians feared the Druids' political prowess and their ability to influence the tribal chieftains as well as the general population. The Druids were seen as a threat to both the occupying forces and to Rome's official religion and as such they soon became one of the major focuses of the Roman forces.

Before they began their attack on Britain, the Roman armies had conquered and occupied most of northern Europe, a region predominantly belonging to the Gauls. Today, many consider the Druids to be of Celtic origin, but the Romans never used the name Celts; they knew them only as Gauls. (The word *Celt* appears in English much later and, even then, never as a name of a people but as a title for a protolanguage that developed into the languages of Wales, Ireland, and Scotland.) As the occupying Roman armies came into regular contact with the Druids in Gaul, they soon began to see their influence and the threat they posed to the security of Rome's newly acquired lands. Augustus Caesar made it illegal for Roman citizens in Gaul to be involved in Druidic practices, and soon afterward the new emperor Tiberius decreed all Druidic practices illegal, even though it was a general policy of the expanding Roman Empire to accept the regional belief systems it encountered to avoid religious and political insurrection. But when it came to the Druids, if one wished to become a Roman citizen—which the Roman Empire encouraged most of the population of their conquered lands to do—the applicant had to swear that he was not a Druid and did not participate in Druidic rites. This was the only belief system that was treated in this way, which indicates just how threatening the Romans considered the Druids to be.

Less than twenty years after the Romans subjugated the majority of the British tribes, they turned their attention to a small island just off the coast of Northern Wales known in Welsh as Ynys Mon but which the Romans knew as the island of Mona.

Gaius Suetonius Paulinus was a favored general of the emperor and became governor of Britain from 58 CE. Almost as soon as he was promoted from consul, Paulinus identified Mona as an important religious center for the Welsh pagans, the home of a large community of Druids who were living there and many more who visited to learn their arte. It was also a refuge for many of the Welsh fighters who continued to oppose the occupying Roman army. Paulinus decided to invade the small island, kill whatever rebels he could find, subjugate the remaining population, and, most significantly of all, slaughter the Druids and destroy the sacred oak groves, circles, and clearings where they practiced their rituals.

Paulinus first invaded Mona, now known as Anglesey, in 60 CE. The only written account of the invasion is recorded by the Roman historian and politician Tacitus in his history of the Roman Empire, the *Annals,* in which he tells us:

> Britain was in the hands of Suetonius Paulinus, he aspired to equal the glory of the recovery of Armenia by the subjugation of Rome's enemies. He therefore prepared to attack the island of Mona which had a powerful population and was a refuge for fugitives. He built flat-bottomed vessels to cope with the shallows, and uncertain depths of the sea. Thus the infantry crossed, while the cavalry followed by fording, or, where the water was deep, swam by the side of their horses.
>
> On the shore stood the opposing army with its dense array of armed warriors, while between the ranks dashed women, in black attire like the Furies, with hair dishevelled, waving brands. All around, the Druids, lifting up their hands to heaven, and pouring forth dreadful imprecations, scared our soldiers by the unfamiliar sight, so that, as if their limbs were paralysed, they stood motionless, and exposed to wounds. Then urged by their general's appeals and mutual encouragements not to quail before a troop of frenzied women, they bore the standards onwards, smote down all resistance, and wrapped the foe in the flames of his own brands. A force was next set over the conquered, and their groves, devoted to inhuman super-

> stitions, were destroyed. They deemed it indeed a duty to cover their altars with the blood of captives and to consult their deities through human entrails.

Paulinus's campaign was interrupted before he had fully achieved his aim when he and his army were recalled to subdue an uprising on the opposite side of Britain, where the Iceni tribal warrior queen Boudica (Buddug in Welsh) was leading a rebellion against the conquering Roman occupiers.

The Romans returned to Mona in 77 CE, this time under the command of General Agricola who was determined to subjugate the Ordovices, the Celtic tribe that held the lands across the north of Wales, now known as the county of Gwynedd, and the border region that would become the Welsh Marches. The Ordovices had given sanctuary to the famous Celtic warlord Caratacus, who had been declared a rebel and an enemy of Rome in the mid-50s CE. Tacitus, who happened to be Agricola's son-in-law, tells us once again that "the tribes being overwhelmed, and peace having been sued for and the island given up, Agricola became great and famous."

With the Druids slaughtered and the population of the sacred island subjugated, the people of Wales and the rest of Britain were deprived of their spiritual core. As the story of the mass slaughter of the Druids on Ynys Mon and the massacre of the brave warlords and tribesmen who defended them spread across the country, the remaining Druids that were scattered throughout Britain became fugitives and sought refuge in the desolate landscape of the rugged Welsh mountains and remote parts of Britain, while some crossed the Irish Sea to Ireland. Although the Roman legions feared what would happen if the Welsh magicians were to exact their revenge upon them, the Druids were never again to regain their status and power. The population of Britain had not only been deprived of its religious foundation but also of much of its history, folklore, and science and the learning of millennia, as the repositories of all this knowledge were the Druids. We can only imagine what ancient learning was lost forever with the massacre of the Druids on Ynys Mon.

REEMERGENCE OF THE DRUIDS AFTER THE ROMANS

The Roman occupation of Britain came to a slow and complicated end between 388 and 400 CE, when the transition from Roman Britain to post–Roman Britain took place. By this time, Christianity had become the official religion of the Roman Empire and was firmly established throughout Britain before the Romans left to defend a crumbling empire and a capital city that was being attacked by barbarian tribes. Britain was about to enter the Dark Ages, the period between the fifth and tenth centuries when science and the arts stagnated and Christian doctrine took precedence over every aspect of life. The Druids who remained in Wales slowly reemerged and took up their previous roles as advisers, magicians, and politicians. Over the following seven hundred years, before the Norman invasion, the Druids once again established themselves as a powerful force and influence within the community—so much so that they became a threat to the burgeoning Christian population.

The Christianity of the transition to post-Roman Britain was that propagated by the Western Catholic Church, its structure and doctrine governed by Rome. Realizing the influence of the Druids and the futility of attempting to eliminate them completely, the church needed a strategy for reducing their popularity and political influence. The method they adopted was to embrace the Druids, rather than oppose them, and bring them into the church's sphere with various inducements, which included the promise of their ascension to the Christian heaven and elevated status within the church, including becoming powerful Christian saints within their lifetime. In Wales, the period between 400 and 550 CE became known as the Age of the Saints, and much has been recorded about the exploits of these Celtic saints and their efforts to spread the Christian Gospel through Wales, Cornwall, and Ireland—but little is mentioned about their pagan origins and the motivation for their canonization.

Although many Druids reluctantly accepted their conversion—and some would suggest this included St. David and St. Illtud, the two leading Welsh saints, St. David being the patron saint of Wales—they appear never to have fully accepted the official Christian doctrine but worked to subtly amalgamate much of their original pagan beliefs into their own version of Christianity. It is here that we find the origins of Celtic Christianity, a version of Christianity that exists only in the Celtic regions of Wales, Cornwall, and Ireland with a doctrine that promulgates a visible pagan influence that exists right up to the present day. Whatever the case may have been, and we will never know for sure, we can say without fear of contradiction that the Welsh church became well established during the late Roman period and we can find the evidence in the history of the buildings of the period, which are still in daily use throughout Wales and the Welsh Marches, and the place names of the towns and villages of the region.

Many people living outside Wales assume that place names beginning with *llan,* and there are many, indicate a town or village that has grown up around an early church and that *llan* by extension is the Welsh word for "church," when in fact *eglwys* is the Welsh for "church" and *llan* has a much more complicated origin. As Christianity slowly spread across Wales, groups of believers gathered together in small communities for safety and to join together in worship. In time, these small Christian communities created enclosures, often walled with rough stones, to segregate themselves from their surrounding pagan nonbelievers. Members who died were buried within the enclosure to prevent the graves from being desecrated. When the community had accumulated sufficient resources to build a church, they did so within the confines of the enclosure. As the new religion became more widespread and the number of believers in the community grew, they gradually moved beyond the walls—vacating the enclosure, which contained the church and the graveyard—and settled in the town or village around it. So *llan* originally described the enclosure where the Christians settled and then became the name of the church and graveyard.

Eventually, the entire village adopted the name *llan* along with the name of the patron saint of the church, St. Illtud, and added the word *fawr,* which means "major, main, or big." Therefore the place name Llanilltud Fawr may be translated as "major village dedicated to St. Illtud" or simply "major village of St. Illtud." This lengthy and, hopefully, interesting explanation of the origin of the Welsh word *llan* is useful to us in that it demonstrates the distribution of the early Christian settlements and shows exactly how far the ancient Celtic Church had established itself. Some of these ancient settlements and their subsequent churches within the Welsh Marches show not only the religious development of the region but also the rebalancing of the political status quo in Wales and England as Britain entered the post-Roman era. Over time, Llanilltud Fawr became corrupted to the current Anglicized version: Llantwit Major, a village located on the coast of the ancient county of Glamorganshire.

Today, the village is a small seaside community best known for its beach and cliff-top walks, but its history stretches back to well before the Roman occupation. The oral tradition of Welsh history tells us that on the hills overlooking the village was a settlement that functioned as the major Druidic "university," drawing students and teachers from all across ancient Europe. This university existed before Illtud founded his monastery and college on the same site called Cor Tewdws, or Main University of Theodosius, believed to be Britain's earliest formal center of learning. Today, we believe the ruins of the original Druidic settlement and Illtud's monastery and college are buried beneath the existing parish church of St. Illtud.

St. Illtud was known in Welsh as Farchogor Illtud, or Illtud the Knight. The oral tradition of the Druids tells us that Illtud was a formidable Druid and political activist who had spent his early life opposing the occupying Roman army and the Romans' veneration of a Jewish magician who had been crucified in Jerusalem. As the Romans made plans to leave Britain, Illtud accepted the Christians' offer of adopting him into their faith and traveled to northern France to be trained in the ways of Christianity by the famous Bishop Germanus of Auxerre, later to become St. Germain, where he became an exemplary student. The earliest mention of St. Illtud is in *Vita Sancti Samsonis,* Life of St. Samson, a biography written about Samson of Dol by an unknown Briton in about 610 CE. According to the St. Samson biography, Samson was a student of Illtud, and Illtud was "the most learned of all the Britons in the knowledge of Scripture, both the Old Testament and the New Testament, and in every branch of philosophy—poetry and rhetoric, grammar, and arithmetic, and he was most sagacious and gifted with the power of foretelling future events."* The extensiveness of Illtud's knowledge and his power of foretelling the future described in the biography certainly agrees with the suggestion that Illtud had indeed originally been a Druid, as does his ability to memorize so much information, a skill, as noted earlier, that the Druids were renowned for.

Eventually, Illtud returned to Wales and Llanilltud Fawr to establish his Cor Tewdws monastery and university, fulfilling the role of abbot-teacher in his college, which housed more than one thousand pupils, many being other Druidic converts like St. David, St. Patrick, and Samson of Dol. All were born in Wales, together with the famous Welsh historian and monk Gildas the Wise, the son of a northern British chieftain king.

The story of Illtud, his conversion, and the establishment of his college at Llanilltud Fawr encapsulates the history of the relationship between the ancient Druids, the Roman occupation, the arrival of Christianity, and the eventual merging of the two traditions to form the Celtic Christianity we see in Wales today. This history is recorded in the landscape of the village, with the parish church of St. Illtud erected on the ruins of Illtud's Cor Tewdws, which in turn was established on the site of the original Druidic university. One tradition superimposed upon another.

We can see then that despite the massacre of the Druids at Ynys Mon in the north and the conversion of the Druids by the Christians with promises of an afterlife in heaven and a sainthood here on Earth, the Druid tradition survived intact. But we can also see the evidence of their earlier supremacy in other examples within the Welsh Marches, megalithic sites that display a splendor that has never been surpassed in the long history of pagan Britain and its Druids but is still present today in the landscape of the Welsh Marches.

*According to Emrys George Bowen, an internationally known Welsh geographer of Wales; see Bowen, "Illtud (c. 475–c. 525): A Celtic saint and one of the founders of monachism in Britain," 1959.

DRUIDIC PLACES: TIMBER ENCLOSURES, THE ROTHERWAS SERPENT, AND TEMPLE RUINS

The presence of an ancient pagan culture in the Welsh Marches, dating back to somewhere between 3800 and 2300 BCE, may be witnessed in a great many locations within the region. In this instance, however, we shall look in detail at just a few of these that have been the subject of recent archaeological investigation.

The first, situated in the Walton Basin in the county of Radnorshire on the Welsh side of the border, gives rise to the theory that it may have been a Neolithic tribal center used for religious gatherings and celebrations. The site is located in the Mid Wales region, approximately midway along the border between Wales and England at the very center of the Welsh Marches. The area of the site has been the subject of intermittent archaeological research for the last forty years.

During this time, the lengthy excavations have revealed the remains of what is claimed to be the largest Neolithic timber construction in the whole of Europe. Similar timber constructions have been identified as one of the first stages in the construction of more permanent stone circles, used to prove the seasonal alignments before the more substantial and time-consuming stone circles replaced them. Evidence of similar timber postholes has been excavated at Stonehenge and other henges around the British Isles.

Archaeologists initially revealed a series of seven Neolithic monuments, believed to have been used for tribal ceremonies at various auspicious times of the year. Along with these initial finds, the investigators went on to discover what has been dubbed the Neolithic Walton Palisaded Enclosure or Walton Basin, a circular enclosure with a diameter of around 100 meters (328 feet). The enclosure is defined by a relatively narrow ditch made up of approximately 1,200 timber logs, each about 13 feet high, which are embedded into the ground to form a wooden henge. A similar oval-shaped enclosure named the Hindwell

Palisaded Enclosure has an area equal to around six full-sized football stadiums.

The archaeological team has concluded that the whole Walton Basin site was the location of a national ceremonial center, where thousands of people gathered to build and use this monumental structure. The gathering of the timber logs and the construction of the enclosures would have taken many thousands of man hours over many years, which leads to the obvious conclusion that the whole site must have been an extremely important and significant religious location. The fact that numerous shards of pottery and examples of assorted flint tools, along with remains of plants, food, and animal bones, were found in large quantities around the site further reinforces the theory that large number of people gathered there for religious celebrations and possibly ritual animal sacrifice.

The archaeologists at the Welsh site have identified many similarities between the deposits found at this site and those discovered at Stonehenge, further enhancing the proposal that the wooden henge may well have been a prototype for a subsequent stone circle that was never erected. The site is located on a known route near the Radnor Forest leading from the hills and mountains of Mid Wales to the lowlands of central England and may well have been one of the principal meeting points for the many nomadic Neolithic tribes from across the whole of Wales and England who passed through the Welsh Marches on their journeys.

The Walton ring ditch is by far the largest such site in Wales, although there are a further thirteen ring ditches of over 30 meters in diameter (over 98 feet), with eleven ring ditches measuring more than 40 meters (about 131 feet). There are distinct clusters of these large monuments within the Walton Basin. Part of the site lies beneath two later Roman marching camps that further take advantage of the site's location within the borderlands of the Welsh Marches.

A second ancient site that demonstrates the presence of a pagan culture and the practices of the Druids in the Welsh Marches was discovered on the English side of the border, close to the county town of Hereford. Rotherwas is a small rural conurbation sitting within the suburbs of Hereford. During recent excavations for the construction of the new Rotherwas Access Road, an extraordinary Bronze Age site was discovered. The Rotherwas Ribbon or Serpent, also called the Dinedor Serpent, is a ceremonial processional roadway made from fire-cracked stones that runs along the base of Dinedor Hill. The snake-shaped processional roadway was constructed some four thousand years ago at the beginning of the early Bronze Age around 2000 BCE, approximately the same time as the construction of Stonehenge. To the naked eye the surface of the roadway looks like bright crystal or mosaic and has been made from stones brought from a site around half a mile away. The stones were heated by fire and dropped into cold water to split them open and expose their crystalline core. These crystal cobbles were then carefully laid to construct a roadway that is believed to have been used specifically for the enactment of ritual or ceremonial events.

The pathway is set into the side of the hill while close by a group of burned timber posts, set into the ground, have been discovered along with traces of a group of timber-framed round houses with stone hearths, suggesting that the whole area was once an established settlement long before the Romans and later the Norman invaders arrived in the area.

The serpent-shaped roadway has been deliberately constructed so that it undulates up and down along its length to add to its mystical appearance. To date, some sixty meters have been excavated, but as of yet no final destination point has been unearthed. Archaeologists working on the site point out that similar cobbled pavements are known to lead to ceremonial standing stones at sites in Pembrokeshire in the west of Wales and anticipate that future digs will uncover a similar destination for the Rotherwas Serpent.

When I visited the site of the Rotherwas Serpent, it was a frosty but bright early morning and I stood near the beginning of the processional route as a brilliant red sun illuminated the spring sky. Although none of the sacred pathway remains exposed, it was not difficult to imagine how the reflective crystal surface of the pathway would have looked to the ancient Druids as they began their ceremonial processions from the very point where I was standing. The pathway has been necessarily covered over with earth to protect it for future generations and investigating archaeologists, but it would be wonderful to somehow both protect it and make it visible, as it remains one of the most significant sites in the whole of Europe.

The third and final pagan site we shall explore here is located at Lydney Park, Gloucestershire, in the southern portion of the Welsh Marches. Two hills look down upon the Lydney Park Estate. On the crest of one hill, the ruins of a medieval castle are silhouetted against the sky; the crest of the other is strewn with the remains of a pagan temple, later appropriated by the Romans and dedicated to the god Nodens. Nodens correlates to Nudd, a Cymric, Irish, and Brythonic god more commonly known as Lludd or Lludd Llaw Ereint, or Ereint of the Many Hands, who appears as the spirit of water in many Welsh legends.

The hill with the pagan temple ruins, known locally as Dwarf's Hill, contains a labyrinth of tunnels and abandoned open-cast mining sites, called *scowles,* showing evidence that the original Iron Age mines were reworked by the Romans. These Roman iron mines were known as the Dwarf Mines, giving their name to the hill itself, and were said to be the home of the little people, dwarfs and goblins, making it a place that the local people would not visit after dark nor let their children play in, in case they were taken by the little people from below the hill. The tunnels and legends of the little people mean that Dwarf's Hill is steeped in folklore and fairy tales, as well as being an important archaeological site with its extensive pagan-Roman remains.

During the first major excavations of the Lydney site in the mid 1800s, the archaeologists discovered a lead curse tablet or *defixio* at the Roman temple ruins. Inscribed upon the tablet was a vengeful malediction:

> DEVO NODENTI SILVIANVS ANILVM PERDEDIT DEMEDIAM PARTEM DONA VIT NODENTI INTER QVIBVS NOMEN SENICIANI NOLLIS PETMITTAS SANITATEM DONEC PERFERA VSQVE TEMPLVM DENTIS

This translates as:

> *For the god Nodens. Silvianus has lost a ring and has donated one half of its worth to Nodens. Among those named Senicianus permit no good health until it is returned to the temple of Nodens.*

It would seem then that Silvianus, a Roman, had lost a ring and, suspecting Senicianus to be the thief, had cursed all of that name to poor health until the ring is returned to the temple at Lydney. Unbelievable as it may seem, around sixty years before the discovery of the tablet, a gold ring was discovered by a farmer ploughing a field in Silchester, the site of a major Roman settlement of the same period, Calleva Atrebatum. The ring, inscribed with the name Senicianus, bore the sentiment: *Seniciane vivas iin deo* (Eng.: Senicianus, may you abide in God). It seems more or less indisputable that this was the same ring lost at Lydney, never returned to the temple of Nodens.

We are told that the Roman temple and settlement fell out of the public consciousness for the entire medieval period when the site was considered to be the home of the dwarves and goblins of local tradition. In 1928, the eminent British archaeologist Sir Mortimer Wheeler was commissioned to examine the site of Nodens temple at Dwarf's Hill, the origin of both the curse tablet and the gold ring, and when it came to exploring the origins of the name of the god Nodens, he invited a then–professor of Anglo-Saxon at the University of Oxford to join him at the Lydney site.

The professor, one J. R. R. Tolkien, joined Sir Mortimer some weeks later, and over the next two years made many visits to the site, staying for long periods while exploring the temple, mines, and surrounding countryside and talking to many local residents about the folklore and the legends of the little people under Dwarf's Hill. Two years after beginning his research, Tolkien contributed to a report published by the Society of Antiquaries on the origin of the name Nodens. As well as formulating the association of the Roman god with his Welsh, English, and Irish counterparts, Tolkien also discovered that the colloquial name for the Roman god Nodens was the Lord of the Mines.

When, some years later, Tolkien published his famous books *The Hobbit* and the Lord of the Rings trilogy, it became impossible not to speculate upon the connection between his experiences at Lydney and his epic tales of Middle Earth. Did the Lord of the Mines inspire Tolkien's Lord of the Rings, and did the little people living under Dwarf's Hill become the indominable Hobbits? Could the Silchester gold ring with its esoteric inscription have given rise to the one ring and could the labyrinth of Iron Age mines have been the forerunner of the mines containing the ancient halls of the kingdom of the dwarves?

We began this chapter by saying that we would look at some of the more iconic archaeological sites within the Welsh Marches that demonstrate the presence of pagans and Druids in the region. But there are many other sites, be they less dramatic, that testify to the activities of these ancient pagan populations. In the light of this overwhelming evidence, absolutely no doubt remains that the occult history of the region extends as far back as its earliest settlers and has continued uninterrupted to the present day, when we will discover an occult presence that reflects the long and fascinating history of Paganism, Druidic culture, and witchcraft in the towns, villages, and countryside of the Welsh Marches.

8

Other Occult Arteworkers of the Welsh Marches

Witches, sorcercers, and Druids were not the only occult arteworkers in the Welsh Marches. The borderland was also home to a number of strange and unique occult practices and customs, among them sin eating, eye biting, and spirit hunting.

SIN EATERS

Sin eaters (Welsh: *bwytawr pechod*) are unique to Welsh culture and the region of the Welsh Marches. At one time a sin eater could be found in almost every small village and town. The function of the sin eater was to take upon himself the sins of a recently deceased person (sin eaters were always male) so that the deceased may be released from the world of mortals and find his or her place in the hereafter. Following the death of an individual, the deceased's family retained the services of the local sin eater, who attended a brief ceremony prior to the funeral.

On the night before the sin eater was due, a member of the family would bake a cake, known as a dead cake or in later days a funeral biscuit, according to a special recipe. The cake would be placed on the breast of the corpse at sunset, where it would remain until the following morning, absorbing the unabsolved sins of the deceased as it rested over the heart of the corpse. The next morning the family would assemble around the coffin of the deceased, awaiting the arrival of the sin eater. He would be given the dead cake from the body of the corpse along with a gossip's bowl—a wooden goblet filled with ale or mead. He would then eat the cake and drink the ale and thereby take upon himself the sins of the deceased that had been absorbed into the cake. In doing so he absolved the deceased from all of his or her sins.

Sin eating is one of a number of funerary customs that predates the arrival of Christianity but has since been subsumed by Christian culture. In fact, the entire concept of sin only arrived in Britain with the early Christian saints. To understand the original meaning of the custom, we must first examine its most long-lasting history in the region.

One of the earliest accounts we have of sin eating in the Welsh Marches was written by the diarist John Aubrey (1626–1697), who was a native of Wiltshire, an English shire that borders the Welsh Marches and is the county that contains Avebury and Stonehenge, two famous locations known to everyone interested in Druidic culture and witchcraft. In his book *The Remaines of Gentilisme and Judaisme,* written between 1687 and 1689, Aubrey recorded that "in the county of Hereford [in the Welsh Marches] was an old Custome at Funeralls, to hire poor people, who were to take upon them all the Sinnes of the party deceased."

Aubrey's account, although brief, accurately describes the custom of the sin eater, but for a more detailed rendition, we have to move forward to the nineteenth century. In 1926, Bertram S. Puckle researched and wrote a book on the origin of funerary customs. He wrote that in 1825 a Professor Evans of the Presbyterian College, Carmarthen, actually saw a sin eater, who was then living near Llanwenog, Cardiganshire.

> Abhorred by the superstitious villagers as a thing unclean, the sin-eater cut himself off from all social intercourse with his fellow creatures by reason of the life he had chosen; he lived as a rule in a remote place by himself, and those who chanced to meet him avoided him as they would a leper. This unfortunate was held to be the associate of evil spirits, and given to witchcraft, incantations and unholy practices; only when a death took place did they seek

> him out, and when his purpose was accomplished they burned the wooden bowl and platter from which he had eaten the food handed across, or placed on the corpse for his consumption.*

Puckle also quotes a William Howlett, who mentions an old custom in Hereford in the center of the Welsh Marches: "The corpse being taken out of the house, and laid on a bier, a loaf of bread was given to the sin-eater over the corpse, also a maga-bowl of maple, full of beer. These consumed, a fee of sixpence was given him for the consideration of his taking upon himself the sins of the deceased, who, thus freed, would not walk after death."

When the Scottish novelist Catherine Sinclair visited the Welsh Marches in 1838, she observed that the practice, though in decline, still survived. She noted that "a strange popish custom prevailed in Monmouthshire and other Western counties until recently. Many funerals were attended by a professed 'sin-eater,' hired to take upon him the sins of the deceased."†

The last surviving practicing sin eater in Britain, a farmer named Richard Munslow, died as recently as 1905 in the small Shropshire village of Ratlinghope, twenty-five miles south of Shrewsbury. Remarkably, Munslow's grave in the small village churchyard was refurbished in 2010, when a formal funeral and ceremonial commemoration took place, a recognition that none of his predecessors would have received in their day.

In the Christian context, it may be argued that Jesus Christ was the ultimate sin eater, giving up his earthly life to atone for the sins of mankind and absolving them for their individual transgressions. It could also be suggested that the Anglican Church may also have seen the eating of bread to absolve one from sin as a substitute for the sacrament lost when it abandoned its Catholic doctrines, but it must be said that the church has never officially sanctioned or promoted the act of sin eating, though it definitely demonstrated a good deal of tolerance, on occasions allowing the sin eater to conduct his ritual in

*Puckle, "Wakes, Mutes, Wailers, Sin-Eating, Totemism, Death-Taxes."

†Sinclair, *Hill and Valley: Or, Hours in England and Wales,* 336.

graveyards and within the sanctified grounds of Anglican churches.

When we consider the similar, but much older, tradition maintained within the Druidic oral tradition, we see a comparable ritual enacted in a much less sanitized fashion. When the Romans first observed the Druids and their rituals, their early historians recorded what they saw through the lens of an aggressive, invading force who for a number of reasons benefited from the demonization of everything Druidic. They repeatedly failed to understand the direct association the Druids had (and still have) with nature and the environment that surrounded them, and as a result they consistently misinterpreted what they observed, either deliberately or accidentally from lack of understanding. We can see this in a wide range of circumstances including a ritual that is much akin to sin eating, which we shall look at later. First, it is worth looking at another example that epitomizes how the Romans misinterpreted the Druids.

One of the few contemporary accounts we have of the Druids recorded by the early Roman historians is that of the Druids' use of what they called "their Sacred Oak Groves" to conduct their rituals. From this we can see that when the Romans first encountered the Druids and their rituals, they were totally unaware of the fundamental belief of the Druids—that they, and the rest of humanity, are an inseparable part of nature and that all their actions and rituals are designed to engage with nature from within, not as a separate external agent. As such, Druids do not worship any anthropomorphic gods or deities as they have never chosen to use any intermediaries when they connect with nature, electing instead to engage directly with nature itself. When the Roman historians saw the Druids conducting their rituals, they failed to see that they were communing directly with the forces of nature, assuming instead that they were seeking the intercession of their gods just as the Romans did themselves in the same circumstances. The Roman observers assumed, incorrectly, that instead of engaging directly with the natural force of thunder and rain, the Druids were summoning their gods of thunder and rain, just as their own priests would have done, even recording these imagined gods in their accounts by using their Roman names.

In the same way, when it came to recording the Druidic rituals involving the use of body fluids and parts, the Romans immediately related it to the animal sacrificial rites of their own pagan priests. They further reported that the Druids engaged in human sacrifice, using human organs for divination and eating the flesh of slaughtered babies; the Romans officially condemned human sacrifice but on rare occasions had performed it themselves. Druids did, and still do, use bodily fluids and internal organs in rituals, but unlike the Romans, they only harvested animals killed for human consumption, not through ritual slaughter. Indeed, some of these rituals may, in particular cases, be identified as the forerunners of sin eating.

Finally, to return to sin eating as viewed through the Christian lens, we have already drawn parallels between the Catholic Eucharist and sin eating, in as much as both are enacted to absolve sin. In the case of sin eating, it absolves the deceased, not the recipient of the offering; in the case of the Catholic Eucharist, it is part of the absolution of the recipients themselves, and we should acknowledge this distinction. But the main difference in the two rituals is that the bread consumed by the sin eater has absorbed the sins of the deceased, while the Host consumed by the Catholic acolyte, through the fundamental doctrine of transubstantiation, has been transformed into the actual flesh of their savior, again another act of intercession unfamiliar to Druidic lore. Transubstantiation in this context means that the Host is actually changed into the flesh of Jesus before it is consumed and that the communion wine is similarly changed into the actual blood of Christ before it is swallowed. This is a doctrine that is anathema to both witchcraft and Druidic lore and accounts for the often misunderstood reason why many cultures considered Christianity to be the faith of cannibals (entailing the eating of human flesh and the drinking of human blood) which, on face value, it of course is.

The ritual of sin eating, though it may be considered bizarre and unsavory by most, is not difficult to understand when placed in its correct cultural and religious context. We have seen that it is not too far removed from some mainstream religious practices that are enacted every day throughout the world, but as we shall see, sin eating is not the only unique and unusual practice that we uncovered in the Welsh Marches.

EYE BITERS

Some of the most powerful Witches of the Welsh Marches were said to be able to cast malevolent curses simply by looking at their victims. Their gaze is said to have been as effective in death cursing as if they were to bite the victim's jugular vein and watch them bleed to death. For this reason, they were known as *brathwyr llygaid* or "eye biters." Some folklorists have made comparisons between eye biting and the more widely known concept of the evil eye, though no reference to the later may be seen in the Marches.

Eye biters were, and still are, feared most among Witches and the community alike, as the accounts of their activities involve malevolent curses resulting in sick livestock, illness and death. To many folk the practice of eye biting was called overlooking, casting a glance powerful enough to invoke the most evil curses imaginable. Eye biters' alleged ability to simply stare at their victim and inflict harm has made them particularly susceptible to accusation, trial, and execution. Stories of them overlooking the judge at their trials in order to obtain acquittal are also commonplace.

Unexpectedly, an event that occurred in Ireland in 1584, when Ireland was under British rule, went some way to confuse both the history and reputation of eye-biting Witches. An unknown disease struck the country's cattle population causing them to become blind. Typically, the population accused the local Witches of cursing the cattle and striking them blind. Many of the Witches of Ireland were accused of what the courts called eye biting and those who were found guilty were executed. Whether the Irish courts created this name simply by the association of the Witches and the blindness or if they appropriated the name eye biting from what they had heard of the practice in Britain is unknown, but other than the use of the name, no similarity can be made between the Irish eye biters and those of mainland Britain.

The event of the Irish eye biting was widely known and spread to Britain where it further intensified the general witch fear that embraced the country, so much so that Reginald Scot wrote about it in his infamous book the *The Discoverie of Witchcraft,* saying: "telleth us that our English people in Ireland were much given to his idolatry in Queen Elizabeth's time insomuch that, there being a disease amongst their cattle that grew blind, they did commonly execute people for it, calling them eye-biting witches."

The reputation of eye-biting Witches is still a powerful folk memory among the people of the Welsh Marches, where they are still reputed to be the most powerful of their kind.

SPIRIT HUNTERS AND THE DOG OF DARKNESS

An even more insidious group of Witches than the eye biters are those called *helwyr ysbryd* or "spirit hunters," whose intention is to access the spirit of their victim and, in doing so, control them and bend them to their will. These powerful practitioners were known in the times of the witch terrors just as they are feared today.

Their workings are complex and arcane, known only to very few Witches, and no account of them can be found in any existent grimoires or in any contemporary publications. The only record we could find is in the oral tradition of the local folk memory and, of course, among the local community of Witches.

Another strange manifestation of the Welsh Marches is *yr gwyllgi* or the "twilight dog." This terrifying hound is known to appear as a huge black mastiff, with a baleful cry and fiery red eyes. It appears in some accounts as the Black Hound of Destiny or the Dog of Darkness, prowling the solitary roads in the darkness, and its presence is said to foretell a frightful death in the near future.

The apparition is said to inhabit the northern region of the Welsh Marches, most frequently the lonely roads of the Nant-y-Garth Pass near the town of Llandegla. Recent sightings have been reported near the heart of the Marches at Merchwiel near Wrexham, where the fearsome beast has been seen prowling the remote rural roads in the dark of night.

In a similar way, the same lonely byways are said to be visited by *yr angau,* a gruesome skeleton dressed in a long, black, hooded robe and a wide-brimmed hat and carrying a scythe. The specter drives a black coach, pulled by two black horses breathing fire from their nostrils. He roams the roadways bringing death to all those unlucky enough to catch sight of him or unfortunate enough to live in any of the homes he visits, where he carries away the souls of those that die and robs the graves of the recently buried to harvest any biding souls that he can discover.

There are many more local legends of apparitions and evildoers abroad throughout the Welsh Marches; some inhabit caves and curse wells, others frequent crossroads and ancient gallows fields. The majority are associated with death rituals and protect graveyards and burial grounds as guardians of the dead. When visiting the Welsh Marches, you will find that every small village and hamlet has its own preternatural beings, whether guarding the souls of the dead or seeking to harvest them for their own use.

9
Prominent Occultists of the Welsh Marches

Throughout the ages, the Welsh Marches has produced an impressive number of prominent occultists with a wide spectrum of worldviews. These include famous alchemists, astrologers, and occult philosophers who have influenced the kings and emperors of much of Europe and beyond. Whether this results from the turbulent history that consumed the Welsh Marches or the mysterious practices of the region's Druids and Witches is difficult to say, but it is worth looking at some of the occultists that emerged from the occult melting pot of the Marches.

JOHN DEE

John Dee (1527–c.1608/1609) was an Anglo-Welsh astronomer, astrologer, mathematician, alchemist, and occultist. Probably the most infamous of the occultists of the Welsh Marches, with a long-lived reputation that extends far beyond the shores of Great Britain, Dee was passionate about his connections with both the Marches and Wales throughout his extraordinary life.

Though born in London, he was distinctly proud of his Welsh descent. His surname Dee reflects the Welsh *du* (Eng.: black); his grandfather was Bedo Ddu, of Nant-y-groes, Radnorshire, Wales.

Throughout his lifetime Dee maintained his strong connection with the Welsh Marches and its occult traditions. His father, Roland Dee, was a prominent Mercer, meaning a person of the Kingdom of Mercer, which contained the Welsh Marches, and a member of the Royal Court of Henry VIII.

Dee maintained that he was a direct descendant of Rhodri the Great, a Prince of Wales, and was able to present his own proof of his lineage. He attended Chelmsford Chantry School between 1535 and 1542 and then St. John's College, Cambridge, until graduating with a B.A. in 1546 at the age of nineteen. It was during this period that he developed his preoccupation with alchemy and Hermetic philosophy and began accumulating what was to become one of the largest and most comprehensive private libraries in England. Dee's hunger for more and more knowledge on the occult and alchemy saw him leave the service of Queen Elizabeth and set off on a journey of discovery throughout Europe which lasted until the early 1550s.

Dee returned to England around 1552 with a unique collection of scientific instruments that he had accumulated during his travels and studies abroad. On his return to London, he befriended Gerolamo Cardano, and they jointly developed what they suggested was a perpetual motion machine. They later attracted a degree of cynicism when they claimed to have discovered or manufactured a large gemstone that was invested with magical properties.

A year later, in 1553, he became rector at Upton-upon-Severn, and although this gained him a degree of respectability, he continued his works in alchemy, magic, and sorcery. In 1555, Dee joined the Worshipful Company of Mercers, one of the most prominent guilds of London, following in his father's footsteps. In the same year, Dee was arrested with a charge of "calculating" because he had cast the horoscopes of both Princess Elizabeth and Queen Mary. The charges were later raised to treason. Dee exonerated himself but was turned over to the Catholic Church for further religious examination.

Three years later, in 1558, Elizabeth became queen and Dee was appointed as court astrologer and scientific adviser to the queen. He held the position for more than twenty years and played a major role in

England's voyages of discovery to the New World when he was said to have coined the notion and phrase "the British Empire" for the newly acquired lands the queen ruled over.

In 1574, Dee, at the age of forty-seven, wrote to the then lord treasurer, William Cecil, First Baron of Burghley, seeking his patronage to continue his occult works. He claimed to have secret occult knowledge of an ancient treasure in the Welsh Marches and of hidden occult manuscripts secreted in Wigmore Castle in the same region.

With his attention focused solely on the occult, he attempted to make contact with ancestral spirits through various methods of scrying in an attempt to gain contact with the spiritual angels he believed would guide him in his tasks. Having tried several scryers with little success, he eventually met Edward Kelley, who convinced Dee of his ability to contact the spirits Dee sought. At the time Kelley was going by the name Edward Talbot to conceal his earlier conviction for coining or criminal forgery. Dee eventually employed Kelley, and the pair began work on their pursuit of the spiritual angels. Their work progressed slowly, and by 1580 Dee claimed that the angels had dictated a number of books to Kelley in a special angelic language he chose to call Enochian.

In 1583, Dee accepted an invitation to move to Poland with Kelley and both their families, but the move proved unsuccessful. The pair then began a lengthy tour around Europe, visiting the Emperor Rudolf II in Prague Castle and King Stefan Batory at Niepolomice Castle near the then capital of Poland, Krakow. They failed in both cases to convince the monarchs of the significance of their angelic prophecies. Throughout their time in Eastern Europe, Dee was received with suspicion due to his previous association with the English queen, and it is reported that he was accused of being a British spy on more than one occasion.

Dee returned to England in 1589 while Kelley went on to become alchemist to the Emperor Rudolf II, and as Kelley's reputation grew, so Dee's declined. When he returned to the royal court, he sought the support of Queen Elizabeth who eventually appointed him as warden of Christ's College in Manchester, a post he held for ten years. Returning to London in 1605, he was able to retain his post until his death in

1608 at the age of eighty-one. Dee died in poverty, cared for by his daughter. As a final twist to his life of magic and mystery, both the parish records of his death and his gravestone are missing, so the exact date of his death and the location of his resting place remain unknown.

Dee had been married three times and had a total of eight children, though it is possible that one may have been fathered by Kelley. His first wife, Katherine Constable, whom he married in 1565, died nine years later without having any children. He married for a second time in 1575 to an unknown woman who died one year later. In 1578, at the age of fifty-one, he married for a final time. His third wife was Jane Fromond, who at the age of twenty-three was less than half his age.

Dee's life was full of mystery and occult practices, and throughout it all he maintained a strong connection with the Welsh Marches, its influence and history playing a pivotal role in his spiritual life.

For those readers with an interest in the life and times of John Dee, numerous books and online resources reveal every detail of his extraordinary life.

THOMAS VAUGHAN

Thomas Vaughan (1621–1666) was born in the small hamlet of Newton (Welsh: *Trenewydd*), located near the market town of Brecon and the Welsh village of Llansantffraed, at the center of the Welsh Marches. A renowned philosopher and distinguished alchemist, Vaughan is best remembered for his lifelong work in natural magic and that he was the twin brother of the well-known Welsh poet Henry Vaughan.

Having studied at Jesus College, Oxford, Vaughan, following in the footsteps of his family, became a staunch Royalist and fought at the Battle of Rowton Heath on September 24, 1645, under the personal command of King Charles I, where the Royalists suffered one of their most damaging defeats, incurring heavy losses. While in Oxford, he was appointed to the position of rector of Llansantffraid close to the place of his birth, a post that he held until 1650, when he was dismissed as a result of his regular drunkenness and his Royalist sympathies.

In the same year, Vaughan became involved with Robert Child in forming a "chemycal clubbe," along with the other famous alchemists Thomas Henshaw and William Webbe, with the occasional involvement of Robert Boyle, with a view to performing alchemical experimentation in their laboratory and translating ancient alchemical and chemical texts from their extensive library.

Vaughan married Rebecca Archer, the daughter of the cleric Timothy Archer, in 1651 and moved to London, where Rebecca died just seven years later in 1658. King Charles II returned from exile in Europe in 1660 and restored the Stuart monarchy to the kingdoms of England, Scotland, and Ireland, during which time Vaughan secured the patronage of Sir Robert Morey, a fellow occultist and one of the original founders of the modern wave of Freemasonry in Great Britain. When the Plague arrived in London in 1665, Vaughan and Morey left the city for Oxfordshire where Vaughan died at the house of the clergyman Samuel Kem at Albury in the same county in 1666.

Vaughan's greatest work, *Coelum Terrae: The Magician's Heavenly Chaos,* was published in 1650, the same year that he was expelled from his position as rector of Llansantffeaid. The work, a detailed and self-indulgent exploration of modern alchemy, questions many of the ancient principles of the arte and established Vaughan's reputation among his contemporaries. The work was written in the English language although Welsh would have been the lingua franca of the region where he was born and grew up. His untimely death at the age of forty-six in 1665 was the result of inhaling mercury during one of his alchemical experiments.

Thomas Vaughan's ancestors were at one time the richest commoners in Wales and were gifted Tretower Court, parish of Llanfihangel Cwm-du in the county of Brecknock, South Wales, in the mid-fifteenth century by the Earl of Pembroke. The ancient castle, manor house, and extensive lands that made up the manor remained in the family's possession for a long line of successive generations, during which time it was restored and improved to become one of the most formidable fortified manors of the Welsh Marches. As we saw in chapter 6, Tretower Court played a significant role in the history of witchcraft in the Marches and to this day bears evidence of witch marks and other protective devices designed to shield it from any malevolent influences. Tretower Court was sold by the Vaughan family in 1783 and the family's long association with the Court was broken forever.

ARTHUR MACHEN

Arthur Machen (1863–1947), born Arthur Llewellyn Jones, was a Welsh mystic and author. Machen was born at The Square (the intersection of High and Cross Streets), Caerleon, Monmouthshire, in the heart of the Welsh Marches, into a family that had produced a long line of clergymen.

Though a prominent occultist, Machen is best remembered as a writer of horror fiction. The novelist Stephen King proclaimed Machen's *The Great God Pan*, written in 1890, as "maybe the best horror story in the English language." The reader will find a plethora of references to Machen's many publications readily available elsewhere, but here we will focus on his occult works and presence in the Welsh Marches. It is, however, easy to see the influence that his upbringing in the ancient Welsh kingdom of Gwent and its Celtic Romano history had upon his writing.

From the age of two, Machen lived in the small parish of Llanddewi Fach, near Caerleon, where his father was the parish vicar. His early life was spent in the rectory where he explored his father's extensive library and discovered his interest in the occult, apparently reading his first book on alchemy at the age of eight.

When he turned eleven, his parents sent him to board at Hereford Cathedral School, a prestigious establishment offering classical education to the sons of noble men and clergy of the Welsh Marches. At some point later he sat entrance exams in an attempt to pursue a medical career but failed to achieve the required standard for a scholarship. He continued, however, to develop his writing skills and had his first poem published in 1881.

In 1887, Machen, at the age of twenty-four, married his first wife, Amelia "Amy" Hogg, a music teacher and member of the bohemian set based in London, where he first met A. E. Waite, the infamous writer and occultist. As well as being a prominent member of the Golden Dawn, a Freemason, Rosicrucian, and apparent Knight Templar, Waite was also codesigner of the Rider-Waite tarot deck, first published in 1909 and probably the most famous of the many tarot decks. The two became inseparable lifelong friends.

Just twelve years later, in 1899, Amy died following a protracted illness. During the period of Amy's illness and eventual death, Machen reportedly experienced a sequence of mystical experiences that inspired him to question his faith. During this period, under Waite's influence, he joined the Hermetic Order of the Golden Dawn where he was to exercise his knowledge of Hermeticism, along with his early interest in alchemy and the kabbalah. Throughout his adult life, Machen had held a spiritual belief in a mystical world outside and beyond the mundane, and it is also possible, for those with an interest in Machen's written works, to see the influence of the occult and Celtic Paganism is his writings during this same period.

Although he maintained these occult themes throughout his writing career, he returned to the religion of his upbringing, establishing himself as a High Church Anglican while still retaining the experiences of his mystical encounters and the fascination with ancient Celtic Christianity that had burgeoned during his youth in the Welsh Marches.

In 1903, at the birth of a new century, Machen married his second wife, Dorothie Purefoy Hudleston, and began to regenerate his writing career, focusing on his interest in ancient Celtic Christianity and the legends of King Arthur and the Holy Grail, both of which he reasoned were founded on the early rites and practices of the Celtic Church. His novel *The Secret Glory*, written at this time, was the first work to propose the notion of the Holy Grail's survival and its impact on the modern world, suggesting that it may be a metaphor for something other than a sacred chalice—a theme exploited by Dan Brown in his book *The Da Vinci Code* along with many others.

Having gone some way toward establishing himself as a writer and augmenting his income by working as a journalist at the London *Evening News,* in 1919 Machen moved to St. John's Wood, which became his home for the next ten years. Here he held literary parties attended by many of his friends and acquaintances, including the likes of Welsh artist Augustus John and English writer Jerome K. Jerome.

Machen was dismissed from the *Evening News* in 1921, and from this point until his death he never recovered any real financial stability. In 1929 he moved with his family to Amersham, Buckinghamshire, where he continued to suffer financial difficulties until, fourteen years later, in 1943, a literary appeal was launched to raise funds. It was the year of Machen's eightieth birthday, and a long list of famous names of the era responded to the fund raising, including such luminaries as George Bernard Shaw, T. S. Eliot, Walter de la Mare, and Max Beerbohm. The proceeds of the appeal supported Machen for the final four years of his life until his death in 1947 at the age of eighty-four.

Throughout his life Machen retained his affection for the Welsh Marches and the influence of his childhood years continued to inspire his occult work right up until his death. His knowledge of the occult, ancient Celtic Christianity, alchemy, and the Hermetic artes proved to be the singular driving force of his occult work as well as his literary creativity, and he attracted the admiration of such prestigious colleagues as Sir Arthur Conan Doyle, Oscar Wilde, W. B. Yeats, and later H. P. Lovecraft. Another admirer of Machen's occult works was the infamous Aleister Crowley, who is said to have believed Machen's work involved a "magickal" truth and listed his books as required reading for all his students.

GEORGE CECIL JONES

George Cecil Jones (1870–?) was of Welsh extraction with a family background in the Welsh Marches, though no accurate information on the village of his birth is available. Jones was an alchemist, occultist, and chemist who at one time also worked as a metallurgist, possibly as a consequence of his interest in alchemy.

He was a close friend of Aleister Crowley (1875–1947) and is credited with introducing Crowley to the Hermetic Order of the Golden Dawn, which Jones was a member of at the time of their meeting. Jones preferred to go by the name of Volo Noscere, which is in itself a Latin magical motto employed in a number of magical orders and secret societies.

Sometime in 1906, Crowley and Jones broke away from the Golden Dawn following a long period of disagreement and dissent, and jointly founded the new order of the A.'.A.'., based upon Crowley's teachings, his publication *The Book of the Law,* and a range of rituals and practices developed by Crowley, who became the undisputed head of the new order.

Over the subsequent years, Jones would exert a significant influence on Crowley, contributing substantial elements to Crowley's most important books and articles.

Jones remained a secretive character, with little or nothing known about his personal life. There is no official evidence available of the date or place of his death, and although he is reputed to have spent the majority of his life in the shadow of Crowley's fame, he is broadly credited with having played a pivotal role in the life and works of the Great Beast, as Crowley was popularly known.

EVAN FREDERIC MORGAN

On March 3, 1934, Evan Frederic Morgan (1893–1949) succeeded to the title of Sixth Baronet Morgan, Fourth Baron Tredegar, and Second Viscount Tredegar, inheriting his title after the death of his father, Courtenay Morgan, First Viscount Tredegar of Tredegar Park, Monmouthshire, Wales. In addition to his aristocratic titles, Morgan was a self-proclaimed poet, author, and occultist.

His mother, Lady Katherine Carnegie, was a London socialite and spent most of her time at one of their many London homes. The family estate was Tredegar House, a stately house on the outskirts of Newport where the family lived for much of Morgan's life. Among their peers, they were considered an eccentric family.

Morgan was educated at Eton College and went on to Christ Church College, Oxford. It was at Oxford that Morgan became involved with the occult and where he also entertained his homosexual preferences.

Eventually, he left Oxford under a cloud, which many of his contemporaries attributed to his "debauched" behavior and occult practices.

He converted from his family's tradition of Anglican Protestantism, becoming a Roman Catholic and moving to Rome to become a Privy Chamberlain of the Sword and Cape to Popes Benedict XV and Pius XI. He left Rome and the Vatican within a short period of time, apparently dismissed due to his further indiscretions and accusations of depraved homosexual practices.

He returned to Tredegar House where, despite his very limited artistic abilities, he became adviser on art to the royal family. Queen Mary referred to him as her "favourite bohemian." He was also a favorite of Prime Minister Sir Lloyd George and was a great influence on Brendan Bracken, Churchill's right-hand man, to whom he was related.

During the following years, he established an eclectic menagerie of wild animals at Tredegar Park, the extensive grounds of his stately home. These included a boxing kangaroo and whole flocks of birds, including his favorite parrot, whom he often introduced to his friends and visitors. Many of the animals lived inside the house rather than in the estate's enclosures. His many friends and admirers included the popular writers Aldous Huxley and G. K. Chesterton, artists such as fellow Welshman Augustus John, and the great "black magician" Aleister Crowley.

Eventually becoming known as the Black Monk, Morgan became an expert in the occult and built himself a "magik room" in the basement of Tredegar House. He chose to spell magik in this way to differentiate it from the stage magic that he so despised. During one of his many visits to Tredegar, Aleister Crowley described Morgan's magik room as the best equipped he had ever seen. Crowley took part in many extreme rituals at Tredegar Park and dubbed Morgan Adept of Adepts. It was reported that many of Morgan's rituals frightened even the Great Beast himself, and on one occasion Crowley was said to have quit Tredegar House in urgent fear for his life and sanity.

In 1929, Morgan stood, unsuccessfully, as the Conservative candidate for the seat of Limehouse in London, where he owned a large number of slum tenement houses. He never again had any parliamentary ambitions.

Despite his well-known homosexuality and many well-publicized homosexual relationships, Morgan married twice. His first wife, Lois Ina Sturt, was a society actress and daughter of the Second Baron Alington of Crichel and Lady Feodorowna Yorke, whom he married on April 1, 1928. Lois died just nine years after their marriage, in 1937.

Morgan's second wife was Princess Olga Sergeivna Dolgorouky, daughter of Prince Serge Alexandrovitch Dolgorouky. They married on March 13, 1939, and the union was annulled in 1943 by mutual consent.

During his years as viscount, in addition to establishing a formidable reputation as an occultist and master magician, he was also decorated with a number of awards, among them Knight Honour and Devotion, Sovereign and Military Order of Malta (Knight Hospitaller); Knight of Justice, Constantinian Order of St. George; and Knight of Justice, Order of St. John of Jerusalem (Knight Templar). In addition to these honors, his friend Aldous Huxley used Morgan as the inspiration for the character Ivor Lombard in his 1921 novel *Chrome Yellow.*

Morgan died suddenly on April 27, 1949, at age fifty-five, without issue, and his viscountcy became extinct. In time Tredegar House came into possession of the estate and gardens, which are well maintained and open to the general public. The family also owned Ruperra Castle, near Caerphilly, another residence in the Welsh Marches, which they considered their original stately seat.

Morgan was born and spent the majority of his life living in the Welsh Marches and acknowledged many times that the location and its heritage played a prime role in his development as an occultist and magician. He based many of his rituals on the ancient lore of the Marches and indeed can be said to have been one of its most fascinating characters.

There are many more occultists who were either born in the Welsh Marches or developed their worldview and practices while living in the Marches. While the above features occultists who achieved various levels of success and notoriety during their lifetimes and beyond, they represent a very small percentage of the many individual practitioners who worked every day in their small villages, hamlets, and farms throughout the Welsh Marches.

There is little doubt that the unique and extraordinary culture of the Welsh Marches has had a lasting influence upon the history of the occult within the Marches itself and further afield around the globe.

10
The Legacy of the Witches and Druids of the Welsh Marches

The Witches and Druids that we find today in the Welsh Marches and throughout the isles of Britain and Ireland are the products of a long and complex history, involving persecution by the Romans, the arrival of Christianity, conflict between the Catholic and Anglican Churches, acts of Parliament, the witch trials, and derision by the scientific community. Despite all this and more, the two traditions have evolved in parallel, sometimes moving closer together and other times moving further apart, to arrive at a point where each respects the other and readily acknowledges the other's beliefs and practices.

We have learned that it is valuing the differences as well as the similarities of both traditions that allows each to thrive and continue to evolve equally, and it is the recognition that being equal does not essentially mean being the same that will define the legacy of both witchcraft and Druidic lore, now and into the future. While recognizing this equality and the differences and many similarities between the two traditions, the major challenge for the future of both is the very same divergence that remains the most valuable legacy of their past.

Until relatively recently, the lore of witchcraft and that of the Druids was maintained solely by an oral tradition, passed on from generation to generation through demonstration and experiential learning. As a result, it would be reasonable to speculate that there have been as many interpretations of the lore as there have been individual Witches and Druids, each having their own understanding and each applying their learning in their own individual style. However, despite these numerous variations, the core beliefs of the traditions together with the specific formulations and rituals have, for the greater part, remained intact and unadulterated. That is until the last few centuries, when through lack of access to the original teachings of the two traditions and a perceived need to make both traditions more palatable, portable, and ultimately more marketable, they have been "repackaged" and, in some cases, completely reinvented to suit the emerging global community and the information and communication technology that feeds its insatiable appetite.

In the nineteenth century, the Druidic tradition, which had survived millennia of threats and persecution, was revived during a period of romantic fantasy to become a collection of competing orders or gentlemen's societies, closely associated with the Freemasons and other "friendly societies" that proliferated at the time. These orders bore no resemblance to the ancient Druidic lore and instead drew on its apparent romantic and learned tradition, claiming a fictitious lineage to enhance their credibility and by association gain a gravitas they did little to deserve. This romantic revival reverberates right up to the present day and will undoubtedly continue to influence the legacy of the Druids. It was responsible for representing Druids in long white robes, taken from the image of the ancient Greeks and Romans, who were equally popular in the romantic revivalist period, adding the token golden sickle and mistletoe crown for good measure.

It is these inventive groups that have evolved into the Druidic orders we see today, which in most cases have been constructed from a wide range of elements from mostly incompatible belief systems into what American sociologist Robert Wuthnow has called a "patchwork religion." Drawing inspiration from such varied sources as Eastern mysticism, Native American beliefs, and Christianity, this newly contrived neo-pagan system has adopted the title of Druidism, a misnomer that in itself illustrates a total lack of understanding of the Druid's role within Druidic lore. Despite the previously mentioned claims for an unbroken lineage to the ancient Druids, these various Neo-Druidry orders have selectively appropriated parts of the tradition, possibly from ignorance resulting from lack of access to any form of the original oral tradition or as a deliberate act to manufacture a more palatable, sanitized belief system that more readily lends itself to global distribution and dissemination through social media.

To become a member of the order, one must pay a fee; to progress through the training program and become a "qualified Druid," one must pay a fee at each stage of progression; to gain access to any information regarding their secret lore, which may not be disclosed by any member, one must—yes, you guessed it—pay a fee. This appears to be a common pattern for many of the orders. But putting this restrictive practice to one side, it is the blatant contradictions that arise from merging various belief systems into the new Druidism that is the greatest cause for concern for the future of Druidic lore. It is worth looking in some detail at just a few of these.

I mentioned earlier that using the title Druidism demonstrates a basic lack of understanding of Druidic lore and its structure, so here I will explain why this is the case. A Druid is a learned pagan, well versed in the oral tradition of paganism and the role of the Druid as a teacher and spiritual leader within in it. They are not Celtic and have never claimed to be. They originated thousands of years before the Celtic influence arrived on the shores of Britain and Ireland, as attested to by the numerous Neolithic stone circles they erected that still stand proud on the landscapes of both nations.

Druids gain their titles when they are recognized as such by the pagan community they serve (a process that remains to this day and one that I was subjected to as a youth), not by paying a fee and receiving a decorative certificate, as seems to be the case in today's orders of Druidry. As the spiritual leader of a pagan community, a Druid by definition has a congregation or group of acolytes whom they serve. Unlike many of today's orders, everyone concerned is not a Druid; you do not need to be a Druid to be a member of a pagan community. In fact, there is typically only one Druid, sometimes accompanied by an apprentice, in each community.

It is not difficult to see how many people have compared the role of a Druid with that of a priest in other belief systems, which is wholly understandable. If we then consider the terms *Druidry* and *Druidism* given to these neo-Druidic orders, we can see that this would be as appropriate as calling Christianity "Priestry" or "Priestism" or the Jewish religion "Rabbi-ism." The Druid is not the focus of or the personification of the belief systems of paganism and natural magic; the Druid is the teacher of those beliefs and practices. This is why many Druids find these terms inappropriate and offensive as their use demonstrates a total lack of understanding of the title of Druid and the role associated with it.

Finally, a few words on the patchwork of beliefs that make up much of neo-Druidic doctrine. Combining various compatible elements from a variety of belief systems and amalgamating them into a new system is not a new phenomenon, neither is it restricted to Neo-Druidism. The process, known generally as religious syncretism, is visible in varying degrees in many of the world's religions. But the governing word here is *compatible*. It is impossible to develop a credible belief system if all its elements are not compatible and do not add up to a homogenous doctrine.

For example, it is not possible to combine Christian doctrine with Druidic Paganism as they emanate from contradictory beliefs. Christianity is founded on a belief in the God of Abraham, while Druidic Paganism is based on the belief that there are no gods, just nature itself, with no deity or god in human form. This one incompatibility in itself produces a plethora of contradictions that prevent the syncretism of the two systems. For example, because there is no god predetermining the future of mankind and our universe in Druidic Paganism, each individual is the sole determinant of his or her own fate, and the universe, not being controlled by any god, is in total chaos, subject to eternal change. With no god to worship, Druids revere the forces of nature itself with no intercessor.

Furthermore, pagans and Druids do not accept that we are born into original sin and must spend our life atoning for the actions of historical figures in the distant past. It is possible to go on and on, identifying the differences between the two belief systems and how these differences are incompatible, contradictory, and cannot be reconciled in any circumstance. There can never be a cohesive argument for amalgamating the two. Neither is there a moral argument for the appropriation of the name of an ancient learned class in order to attempt to make these efforts more credible.

Having said all that, it is wholly possible to acknowledge and respect the differences between the two belief systems and accept each individual's freedom to choose whatever belief system he or she wishes. However, this is entirely different from trying to combine systems that fundamentally disagree on the very core of their doctrines.

This then is the dilemma that confronts the legacy of the Druidic lore that we have seen in the Welsh Marches together with the future of the paganism that embraces this Druidic lore. Will the Neo-Druidism orders do what the Romans, the Catholic Church, and the monarchs of Britain could not and cause the disappearance of the ancient Paganism of Britain and Ireland and the demise of the Druids who have maintained its oral tradition for so long and replace it with a confusion of disparate beliefs and concocted theatrical performances in the sacred stone circles of the original Druids? Only if we allow it to happen.

Witchcraft too has had a traumatic history, its survival threatened over the centuries. We have already seen that witchcraft shares its origins with the Druids, beginning with the natural magic of the ancient wisewomen and cunning folk. The Witches' lore is based upon the same intimate knowledge and experience of the natural world as that of the Druids, and Witches' healing powers, as well as their practical magic, is dependent upon the gifts that nature provides.

During its turbulent past, witchcraft has suffered the persecution of the Christian church, the witch hunts of the British monarchy, and accusations of daemonic possession, along with being accused of being responsible for every ill fortune that befell their community. The age of the witch terror and the witch hunt changed the Witch's reputation from one of benevolent healer, midwife, and wisewoman to that of a malevolent hag, cursing her neighbors and their livestock and possessions with the aid of her evil familiar. Even so, the many surviving Witches managed to retain the precious ancient knowledge that informed every aspect of their lives and practices.

The survival of ancient witchcraft is due in no small part to Witches rarely involving themselves in the politics of governance, which proved so fatal for the Druids. They were willing to absorb a certain level of Christian doctrine into their practices, as we can see from the evidence of the surviving written curses of the time. Many curses began to invoke the additional power of the Christian God, calling upon the Virgin Mary and other Christian saints to reinforce their curses. We also see examples of Christian imagery appearing in written curses and spells, suggesting the appropriation of Christian images to enhance their pagan magic. At the same time, we can also see the influence of Welsh witchcraft creeping into the dialogue of Christian ministers, who reportedly issued what sounded like pagan curses from their pulpits.

When we explored the evidence of the protective devices and the many witch marks to be found within the homes and buildings of the Welsh Marches, it became evident that there was a substantial population of practicing Witches apparently threatening the owners and tenants of the manors and farms that populate the landscape.

The witch terror slowly subsided, and witchcraft appears to have settled into the rural countryside. With the resurgence of the Hedge Witch, a wisewoman skilled in herbal artes, the reputation of the Witch regained some of its previous beneficial associations, though the image of the evil hag, portrayed so vividly by William Shakespeare's three Witches in *Macbeth* (also called *The Scottish Play*) still remained in the minds of most people well into the twentieth century.

As the twentieth century began, interest in the occult experienced a revival; however, this time two particular features gained prominence: the concept of Witches joining together in a coven and a new emphasis on ceremonial magic, which was a natural consequence of Witches celebrating ritual in covens. By the mid-twentieth century, a number of famous covens rose in prominence, the foremost of these being the New Forest Coven, which grew in the area bordering the New Forest in Southern England. In 1954 a new style of witchcraft emerged from the New Forest Coven propagated by a former civil servant called Gerald Brosseau Gardner, who had adopted the craft name Scire. This new pagan religion became known as Wicca or pagan witchcraft (not that there had ever been any other type). Gardner insisted he had been initiated into the New Forest Coven where he had mystically gained access to a wide range of ancient pagan practices that he had adapted by incorporating Christian and alchemical themes. In fact, the concept of Wicca had appeared much earlier in the twentieth century, but Gardner chose to take the credit for himself, further promoting himself by giving his brand of Wicca the name of Gardnerian Wicca and in doing so instigated the first major divergence from ancient witchcraft in recent history.

Gardnerian Wicca is primarily a form of ceremonial witchcraft with little reference to the natural artes that made up the ancient tradition. It has been widely criticized as a means of promoting Gardner's personal fetishes by involving bondage, whipping, and the repeated kissing of the genitals and other erogenous areas, together with naked dances and intimate bodily contacts. Many identify the practices as being perverse, not because of the gratuitous use of sexual themes and physical contact but simply because they do not use sex magic in its true natural form but choose to forgo its meaningful tenets, instead using a limited range of sexually stimulating activities pandering to very specific proclivities. It is difficult to find any substance in Gardner's brand of Neo-Paganism, which focuses solely on ceremonial magic and ritual, placing emphasis on covens sharing in ritual rather than in the individual traditional practices of the Witch, as had previously been the case. Each Wiccan coven is governed by a high priestess and a high priest of her choice, celebrating the Mother Goddess and Horned God respectively. There are three grades of initiation as there is in Freemasonry, a society that Gardner was intimately associated with.

The emergence of Gardner's Wicca prompted an explosion of similar organizations, among the most successful of them being Alexandrian Wicca founded by Ales Sanders, who used the craft name Verbius, and his wife, Maxine Sanders, in the early sixties. Other famous luminaries include English Wiccan Raymond Buckland, high priest of Seax-Wica, and Robert Cochrane, the founder of Cochrane's Craft, or Cochranianism.

The other infamous occultist who appeared during this period and owes much to the popularity and doctrine of Wicca is Aleister Crowley, whom we met earlier in our exploration. Crowley, predominantly a ceremonial magician, was the most notorious occultist of his age and, among other things, was the founder of the neo-pagan religion of Thelema.

Today, there continues to be an ever-increasing number of Wiccan groups, subgroups, splinter groups, and asides. Those who choose not to focus their energies on ceremony and ritual have taken up the banner of environmentalism and well-being, building on their heritage of nature and natural magic, but one has to search long and hard to find significant remnants of the arcane witchcraft that dominated the Welsh Marches before the end of the nineteenth century.

As with Druidic lore, the main legacy of ancient witchcraft appears to be its place as the foundation of Neo-Paganism in its various forms. Curses have been replaced by meditation and well-being exercises, potions have been superseded by herbal face packs and chamomile infusions, protective amulets, and homeopathic plant lore.

Whether the current practices of ancient witchcraft and Druidic lore maintain enough of their original tradition and learning to be considered credible and relevant in today's society remains to be seen. If, however, they are not maintained in some semblance of their original form, we run the risk of losing a culture and body of knowledge that may never be regained, an understanding of nature that was so obvious at the time and that now represents the cutting edge of modern thinking. We must never lose the ancient understanding of natural magic that served our ancestors so well, or we stand to lose not only our connection with the natural world but also the natural world and our planet, forever.

PART 2

Grimoire of the Welsh Marches

Yr Llyfr Swynion Gororau Cymru

"The Book of Spells of the Welsh Borderland"

Being the profound confutation of the commonly conceived opinion of the ancient artes of Witches, witchcraft, and Druidic lore within the Welsh Marches, together with the reinstatement of the works of natural magic that may be attributed to the same. Including diverse examples and illustrations to further the understanding and aid the application of such natural magic as will benefit humankind in all manner of ways. Notwithstanding the various methods and means of curse throwing, curse lifting, and the use of protective devices against the malevolent actions of those who wish to perpetrate hurt and harm upon innocents. Such is the stated intent of this universal grimoire.

While this grimoire is the result of a detailed comparison of witchcraft practices and Druidic lore, it must not be considered an erroneous conflation of the two traditions. It maintains that there are fundamental differences between the two, just as there are many disparate beliefs and practices within each of the individual traditions themselves. It may more accurately be described as the subtle blending of selective beliefs and practices that have an underlying unity that resonates within both traditions, allowing the merging of both without compromising the fundamental principles of either.

11
Finding Harmony between Two Ancient Traditions

We begin with a discourse on the principal differences between the ancient practice of witchcraft and the lore of the ancient Druids. Only in this way can we acknowledge that although each tradition has its own credo, beliefs, and practices, each is equal to the other. In this instance, equality does not mean that both are the same, but more importantly that both are equally effective in their practices and outcomes.

The first and most fundamental difference between the two traditions is that witchcraft, and particularly today's Wicca, holds that a pantheon of deities both govern the universe, controlling its destiny and that of the individuals who inhabit it, and may also act as intermediaries between the Witch and nature, influencing nature's forces and empowering nature's gifts. Witchcraft, both ancient and modern, accepts the deification of mythological characters such as the Horned God and the Lady of the Forest. Conversely, Druidic lore maintains that there are no gods and that to achieve our desires we must engage directly with nature itself. As a consequence, each man and woman is responsible not only for his or her own destiny but also for the destiny of all others together with the destiny of the whole of nature that we live within. In this final matter, both traditions are in accord: humankind lives within nature and not as a separate entity outside or alongside nature. This final observation is a binding belief, and in this conviction, we are able to endorse a level of syncretism and the selective blending of both cultures.

We must also scrutinize the workings and practices of each tradition. In as much as both are equal, they employ different workings and practices in different spheres of influence. It may be said that Witches work with the bounties and forces of nature through the use of what may be called natural magic and in doing so employ supernatural energies that are beyond the comprehension and perception of most ordinary people. These preternatural energies are accessed through the application of arcane knowledge and mystical skills, known only to the Witches and are passed on from generation to generation by personal initiation and intuition. This then is a hereditary arte, usually only transferred within extended family or those candidates identified as possessing the necessary essential empathy and potential.

Similarly, Druids work with the forces and materials of nature in their own way, engaging with the elements and rudimentary forces to achieve their aims. However, Druidic lore extends beyond that of natural magic, in as much as it defines a philosophical nature and universal imperatives that function within it. At times, this has seen prominent Druids involved in political and philosophical debate at a level that is not seen in witchcraft and has seen the development of a lore that permeates all aspects of human existence.

As a result, this grimoire will expound a natural magic common to both traditions that is apparent in the Welsh Marches, along with a philosophical understanding that has evolved from the Druidic lore of the region, the overarching principal being that both traditions act for the benefit of humanity and the natural world that surrounds us. This, along with the other principles and practices described in this grimoire, emanates from a nucleus of core beliefs derived from a synergy of the compatible beliefs of both traditions as they manifest themselves in the Welsh Marches. It is imperative that the reader considers these core beliefs in detail to fully understand the practices that follow.

To put the practices that follow into their correct context, the most imperative of these core beliefs is that there is no god, let alone any pantheon of mythical beings, as many Witches and occultists may suggest. There being no god to determine and direct our destiny, this responsibility lies directly with each individual. This profound responsibility relates not only to the individual's own existence, but also to the rest of humanity and the whole of the natural world. This principle reinforces the understanding that each individual must act for the benefit of humanity and the natural world we live in. We see then that, in all instances, nature must be nurtured and sustained.

To exercise this responsibility, we must further consider that all things in the natural universe are in constant flux, in a state of universal chaos, as there is no god controlling it—no first mover, no intelligent designer. This being the case, any apparent order is illusionary and temporary, ultimately returning to chaos. Even what we consider to be universal laws are only temporary conveniences, becoming inapplicable from certain unconventional viewpoints and irrelevant when seen from dimensions beyond our sensory perception. In is impossible, then, to manufacture permanance as everything will eventually return to its original chaotic state.

Here, as an example, it is worth reflecting on the destiny of a well-made earthenware jug. It is manufactured from crude materials, available from random sources in its natural form. This rude clay is meticulously crafted to refine its purity and its malleability before being fashioned into its required form. Once decorated, it is fired to change its properties and make it more suitable and durable, and then it is glazed and fired again to make it aesthetically pleasing as well as functional. The finished jug is a perfect example of form and function and is intended to have a long and useful lifetime. Inevitably, at some point in its existence it will become useless, either through a breakdown of its form (if it is broken or cracked) or because it ceases to be aesthetically pleasing (falling out of fashion or degraded to the point of becoming unattractive). Whatever the reason, the jug, having fulfilled its useful lifetime, is broken up and returned to the ground, back to the chaotic materials from which it originated. No matter how permanent the original craftsperson thought her creation would be, or how much she prayed to a god, the individual components of clay, glaze, decorative paints, and so on all return to their own natural state. This simple analogy may be applied to everything that makes up the universe, including human life, with varying time scales.

With regard to human life, we are able to conclude that each of us is born with only two fundamental instincts, survival and procreation; all other values are the product of our upbringing. There are no universal laws or moralities, only ones devised by humanity. Even those laws that define our universe are temporary and only apply in limited circumstances, for a limited time, and in our limited sensory capacity. However, within these confines, all men and women are equal in all things, though they each have their own characteristics and physical attributes that determine their relationship to one another and, to some extent, their role in society. Again, we recall the previous principle: equal does not mean the same.

The natural ambient state of nature is good; badness can only be created intentionally. Natural disasters are not a manifestation of badness or retribution for evil actions; they are the result of the chaotic nature of the universe, expressing itself as the weather, the tides, and other natural events. The only way of understanding and anticipating them is by communication with nature, either through the Old Ways or by advancing science, which is itself a modern interpretation of natural magic. This understanding is essential in the nurturing and protection of our natural planet and a fundamental responsibility of humankind.

If we are to fully understand the forces of nature and their effect on our environment, we must first understand the nature of humankind, which itself is a product of the components that make up a sentient being.

Each person is composed of three constituents. These are:

- *Physical manifestation.* Each person is the result of the coalescence of the female egg and the male sperm, which begins the creation of the physical manifestation that continues to grow until mature. When mature, the person is then capable of playing his or her part in creating the next generation, passing on his or her inherited characteristics. In this way physical characteristics are maintained and passed from one generation to the next.

- *Personal spirit or personal energy.* This is the spirit or energy that makes each one of us unique and is a component of each individual personality—the part of you that makes you *you*. This constitutent is created at conception but is initially in a naive state with no preconceived morals, beliefs, or understanding. As we gain knowledge and experience, this part grows and develops. When we die, our personal spirit dissipates, unless for some extreme reason it remains in a spectral form.
- *Universal spirit.* This constitutent is sometimes called the world spirit or *anima mundi,* which enters each of us when we take our first independent breath. It is this spirit that connects each of us to all other living and inanimate things. We only borrow it from the whole reservoir that makes up the world spirit, which permeates every element of our world, and we return it to the whole upon our death. During the time that this small part of the universal spirit occupies our being, we are capable of changing it, as we do our personal spirit, so that when it is returned to the all-encompassing universal spirit, it changes it in some infinitesimal way. It is each individual's responsibility to ensure that he or she has a positive influence on the borrowed portion of the communal spirit before returning it to the whole.

In the case of inanimate objects they of course have a material manifestation and are also imbued with the communal spirit; however, they do not have the personal spirit that all living things receive at conception.

As we have seen from the above, there is no god controlling or looking after us or our universe, no first mover who began the process of creation; no intelligent designer to design any aspect of the universe we live in. The universe and everything in it is in a state of constant flux and random chaos. Time, therefore, is a measurement of the progress of this chaos. One quality of this constant change is that it need not always change for the better, but of course when it does, it may well result in improvement. On occasion, these random changes or mutations result in an outcome that increases human survival or improves human ability to procreate. Darwinian theory defines this as evolution, a process that results from natural selection. Here though, we must remember that there is no one, neither god nor human, who is making this selection, just nature itself, a nature in which, because of these random mutations, some living things are capable of outperforming others and end up dominating the reproduction process. This process of evolution as a form of progressive development is not restricted to material manifestations alone; in fact, it is equally valid in our spiritual elements, as we shall see.

Each of our three constituents—physical manifestation, personal spirit, and communal spirit—is subject to the same random evolutionary factors mentioned above; however, like all other chaotic events, they do not evolve at the same rate or in the same way. Each has its own independent evolutionary path. Though the three constituents may be moving at the same time, they may be going in different or random directions and at different rates: at times they move closer to one another while at other times they are farther apart. When any two constituents are in close proximity and a thin space exists between them, communion between them is at a high level and they are in complete harmony. But when they are far apart, the empathy between them is critically reduced. When all three constituents are in close proximity, the individual experiences perfect harmony and has the greatest potential to unify his or her being, spirit, and energies and channel them.

If, by way of example, we consider the physical manifestation as a constant, as our physical appearance usually changes slowly rather than at a fast pace, figure 11.1 shows how both the personal spirit and the communal spirit move in a random, unrelated manner, coincidentally moving closer together then farther apart. We can see how there are times that, when two or more elements move close together, they create a thin region or veil between one another, and when all three come into close proximity, a state of harmony is created for a short period before they separate once again. Remember, nothing is permanent; any apparent order soon dissipates again into random chaos.

Plate 1. Fragments of silver birch bark and thorn discovered above the entrance doorway in a property in Shropshire.

Plate 2. The front (obverse) of the Shropshire amulet.

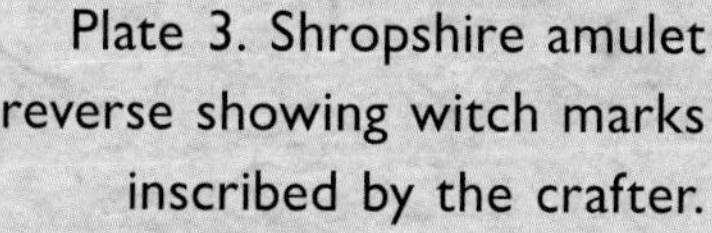

Plate 3. Shropshire amulet reverse showing witch marks inscribed by the crafter.

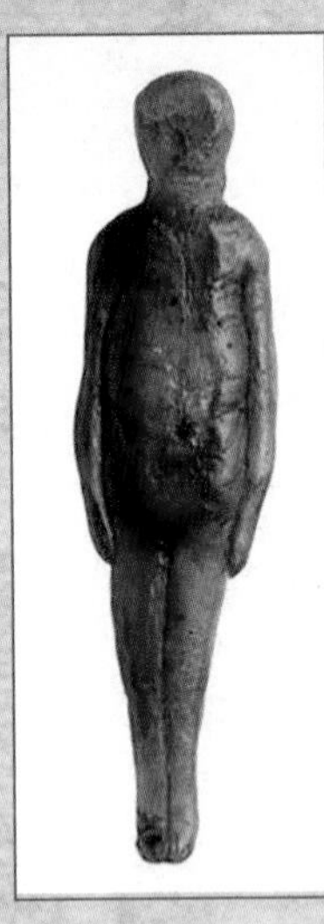

Plate 4. Miniature doll in human form made entirely of wax; formerly used to work death by witchcraft. From the archive collection of the Museum of Wales.

Plate 5. An Iron Age annular blue glass bead with white wave decoration, known as an adder stone (Welsh: *glain nadredd*) and used for healing cataracts. From the archive collection of the Museum of Wales.

Plate 6. Hereford Museum.

Plate 7. Curse doll discovered in Hereford.

Plate 8. Witch's coffin curse with small wooden poppet in coffin. Hereford Museum.

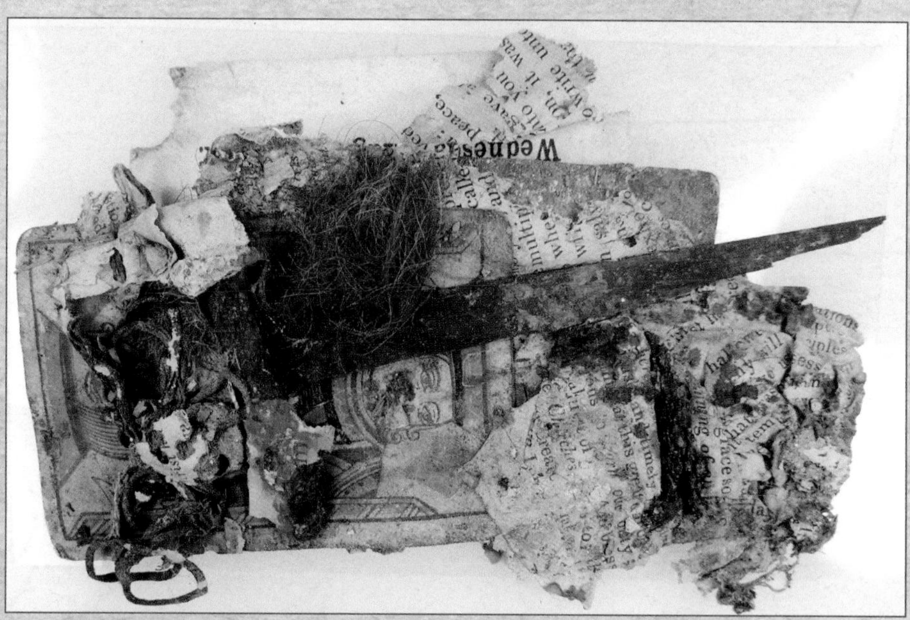

Plate 9. A collection of protective devices (assemblage) deposited beneath the floorboards in a chemist shop in Hereford.

Plate 10. Ludlow Museum at the Buttercross, Ludlow.

Plate 11. Ludlow Castle.

Plate 12. Tretower Court manor house.

Plate 13. Tretower Castle ruins.

Plate 14. Llancaiach Fawr Manor, near Caerphilly, Wales.

Plate 15. The parlor, Llancaiach Fawr Manor

Plate 16. Marian mark carved into a wooden panel in the parlor.

Plate 17. Taper burn marks in ancient door, Llancaiach Fawr Manor.

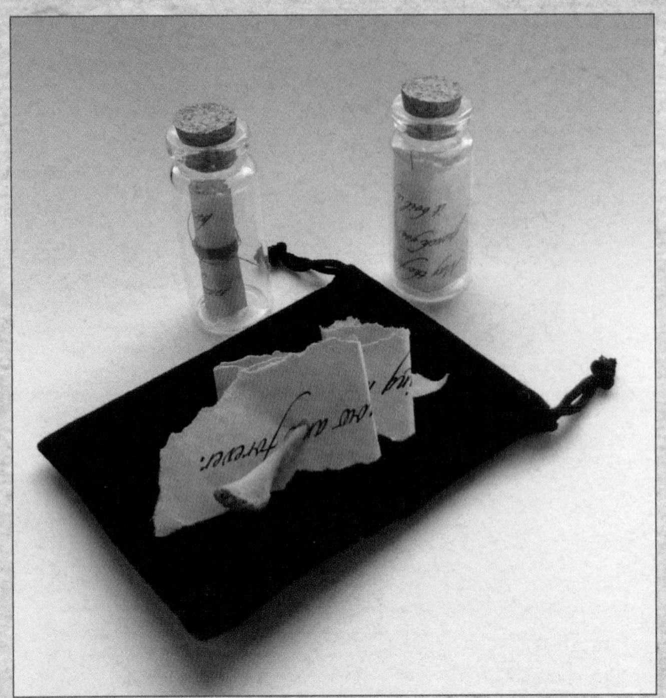

Plate 18. Written charm pierced with bone and in witch bottles.

Plate 19. Ivy macerating in the curse oil before being decanted into the blue cursing oil bottle.

Plate 20. A crude wax poppet with potential items to be used as inclusions.

Plate 21. Primrose love philter: three macerated cardinals and the fourth philter vial ready to receive the combined potion.

Plate 22. Violet, mint leaves, rosemary, and gorse flowers prior to being macerated in mead for a potentializing potion.

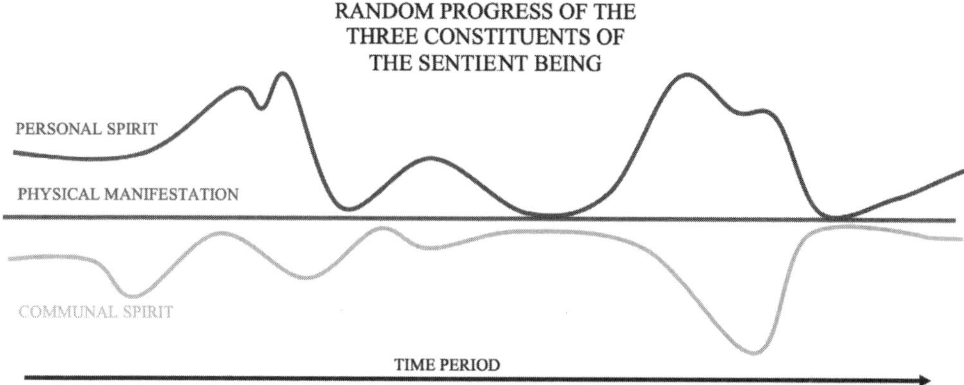

Fig. 11.1. An illustration of the random progress of the sentient being.

The random flux of all three constituents frequently causes us to feel we have lost contact with our spiritual components and can make an individual despair at any spiritual connection whatsoever. Conversely, when the three constituents are in harmony, the individual feels spiritually connected and can at times evolve into a highly informed mystical entity. We experience disharmony or harmony as individuals, but our state may also extend to a community when each individual's experience combines to create either a spiritual disconnect for a community, a society, a nation, or even an entire historical age or a period of great spiritual advancement, when the entire society finds spiritual enlightenment and develops pan-global belief systems.

It is only by harmonizing all three components that we may become spiritually aware and gain any understanding of our full potential as individuals and as entire societies. It is therefore the purpose of this grimoire to promote and explain various methods and techniques to bring all three into closer proximity and harmonize them, which is the ultimate aim of all ritual and the source of all magical power. This then is the definition of magic itself, acknowledged by ancient witchcraft and Druidic lore alike. It is the intention here to bring together the compatible elements of both traditions in the search for this harmony, while still recognizing that the differences separating the two traditions, though irreconcilable, are equal in their probity and provenance.

12

Preparation of the Workplace and Crafting Components

Each Adept will seek and find her own personal workplaces, an interior one and an exterior one. These are places where she feels close to her own spiritual being and the spirit of nature. She will also need a suitable workshop where she may undertake all her mundane work that does not require ritual empowerment at that stage of crafting. We shall see later in this chapter how to establish and equip a useful Adept's workshop, but first we must focus on creating secure workspaces for ritual practices.

In the case of the exterior workspace, first a suitable location is found and then a secure working environment is created by casting a protective circle to work within. The interior workspace could encompass a large room, which itself then becomes the protective circle, or it could just be a table surface (called a working stone) large enough to cast the circle and enable the ritual to be performed, as the Adept stands outside the circle. First, we shall explore the steps necessary to create a protected workplace within a natural setting.

FINDING AND CREATING AN OUTDOOR WORKSPACE

Finding the perfect place outdoors to craft workings is a difficult and very personal endeavor. Some simple, practical considerations are that it must have a large enough flat area to cast a protective circle and set up a working stone within it. This would typically suggest an area of around twenty feet by twenty feet, as the protective circle is normally sixteen feet in diameter, with a radius of eight feet. Often, we find megalithic stone circles established on the crest of a gentle mound, giving them a slightly raised aspect in relation to their surroundings, while others are in secluded groves of trees deep within forests. The important thing is that the Adept feels it is the right place, the place where he feels closest to nature and empowered and in harmony with the elements he intends to join with. Be aware that in this tradition the Adept will be spending most of his time alone within his protected space. There may be some occasions when he becomes part of a convocation, but mostly his practices will be solitary.

Once a suitable space has been identified and the ground cleared of any stones or other debris, the Adept is ready to cast the protective circle and describe the hexagon.

Casting the Circle and Describing the Hexagon

To establish a protective circle, several steps must be followed. First, the Adept centers the circle and then aligns it according to the direction he wants to work in and marks the first station of the hexagon. Finally, the circumference of the circle is marked and the remaining five stations of the hexagon are established.

Centering

The Adept must establish where the center point of the protective circle will be. Remember that a typical circle has approximately an eight-foot radius, so ideally the center point will be at least ten feet from any obstacles. Mark the center point with a small wooden stake.

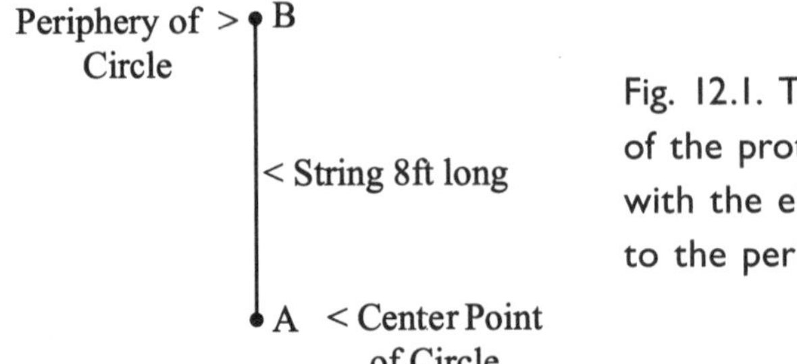

Fig. 12.1. The center of the protective circle with the eight-foot radius to the periphery.

Aligning

Next, the Adept decides which direction she wishes to focus her intended working. Typically, this would be aligned with the rising or setting sun, the rising or setting moon, or a similar significant orientation. These events happen at a different point on the horizon depending on location, date, and time. If, for example, the Adept chooses to align the working to the setting sun, she must establish the point on the horizon that marks the moment of setting. Standing at the center point of the protective circle, the Adept drives in a second small wooden stake at a point eight feet from the center point so that the two stakes align with the point on the horizon that marks the setting point of the sun. If this is done correctly, all three points—the center point, the second stake, and the setting point of the sun—are in perfect alignment.

At this point, the Adept has established:

- The center point of the protective circle, marked with the first small stake.
- The radius of the protective circle. The second stake is eight feet (the radius) from the center point.
- The focal alignment of the circle by aligning the central stake with the second stake and the alignment point on the horizon.
- The second small stake now also becomes the first station of the hexagon, that will be marked on the circumference of the circle.

Both stakes are aligned to the direction chosen by the Adept for his working. The Adept chooses this alignment based on the most effective orientation for the working. This will be discussed in the next section.

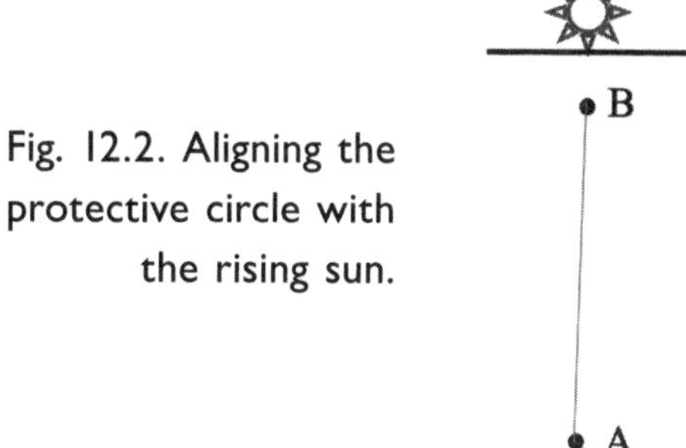

Fig. 12.2. Aligning the protective circle with the rising sun.

Describing the Protective Circle

The circumference of the circle will be described by tying a length of string to the small wooden stake marking the center point of the circle. The string is then extended to reach the second small stake eight feet from the center point. To mark the circumference of the circle, a suitable marker is attached to the end of the string corresponding to the position of the second small stake. If the surface of the circle is grass, a suitable marking tool is tied to the string. (Do not be tempted to use the second stake as a marking tool as this must stay in its position defining the alignment.) If the surface being used is concrete, asphalt, or wooden decking, then a piece of chalk or a marker pen could be used. Using the center point of the circle as the fixed point, slowly describe the circle, marking the floor or ground as the circumference is described. Continue to mark the circumference until the starting point is joined and the circle is closed.

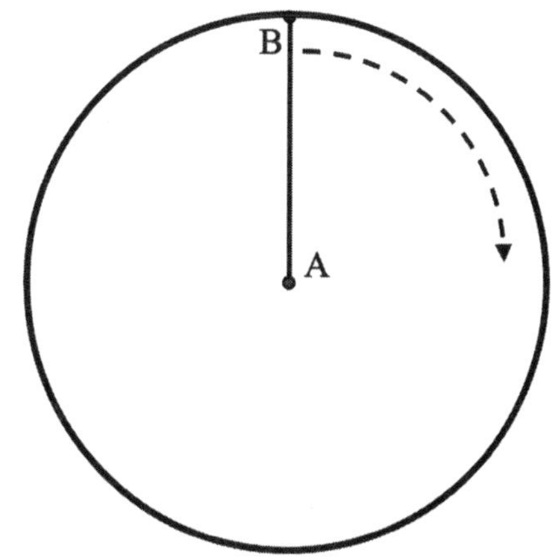

Fig. 12.3. Describing the periphery of the protective circle.

Marking the Five Remaining Stations of the Hexagon

In order to mark the remaining five stations of the hexagon around the circumference of the circle, the marker string is detached from the center point stake and, maintaining the same length (eight feet), it is tied to the alignment stake on the circumference. The first station is marked first, followed by the fifth, and then the third, second, and fourth are marked, in that order.

Using the alignment stake as the fixed point, mark the position of the first station to the right-hand side on the circumference (see fig. 12.4). Leaving the marker string tied to the alignment stake, mark the fifth station of the hexagon on the left-hand side of the circumference in the same way as before (see fig. 12.5).

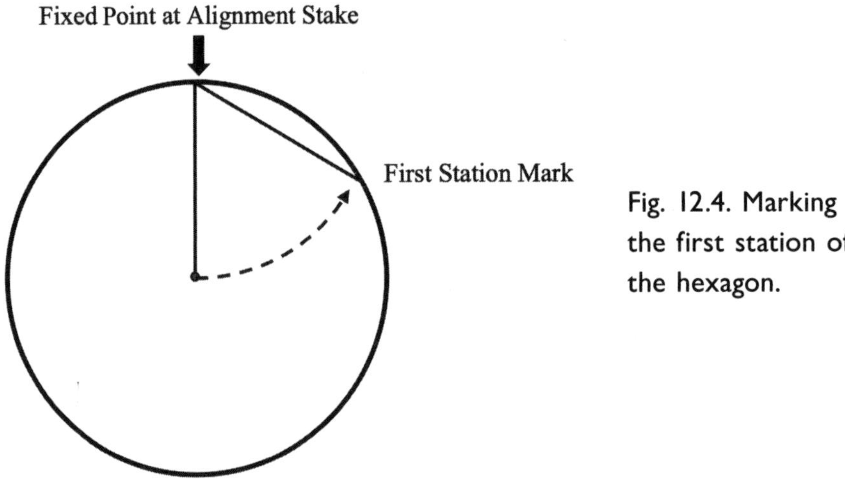

Fig. 12.4. Marking the first station of the hexagon.

The location of the third station (also known as the converse station) is determined by marking the rear of the circle in direct line with the center point stake, the alignment point stake (both still in their original positions), and the marker point in the horizon (see fig. 12.6). It is therefore directly opposite the alignment point stake on the other side of the circumference of the circle. Place a small wooden stake at the station point.

Remove the marker string from the alignment point at the top of

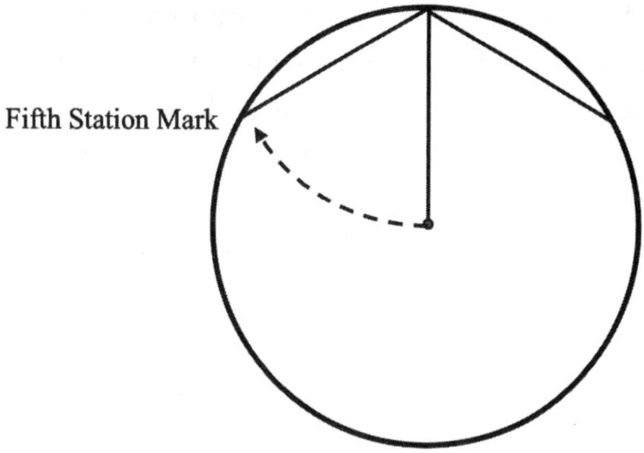

Fig. 12.5. Marking the fifth station of the hexagon.

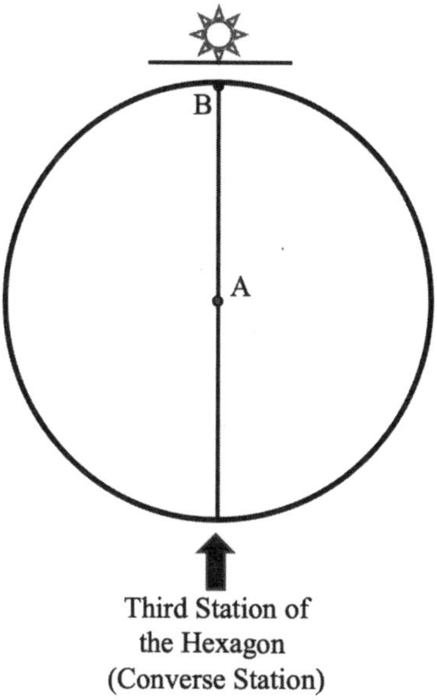

Fig. 12.6. Marking the third station of the hexagon.

the circle and tie it to the newly marked third station (converse station). Maintaining the radius length of the marker string (eight feet), mark the second and fourth station points as before (see fig. 12.7 on page 176).

The six stations of the hexagon are now marked on the circumference of the protective circle. By joining each consecutive station, the hexagon is described within the circle. The hexagon is marked on the ground either with a suitable marker such as chalk or by driving a small wooden stake into the ground at each station and joining them with string to describe the hexagon.

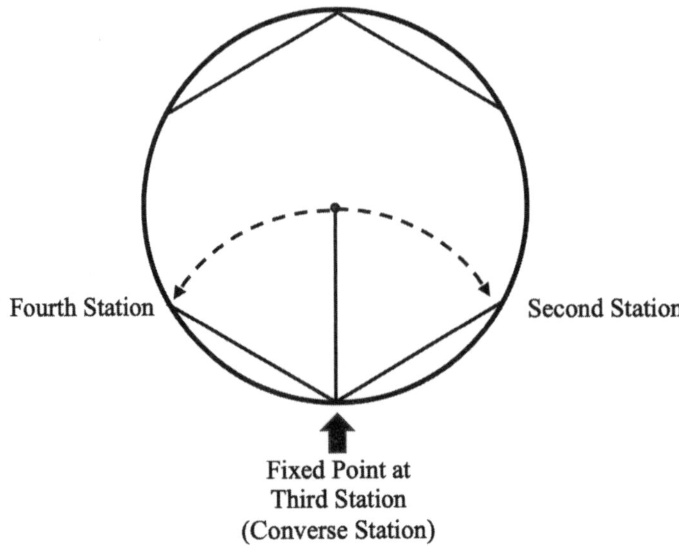

Fig. 12.7. Marking the second and fourth station of the hexagon.

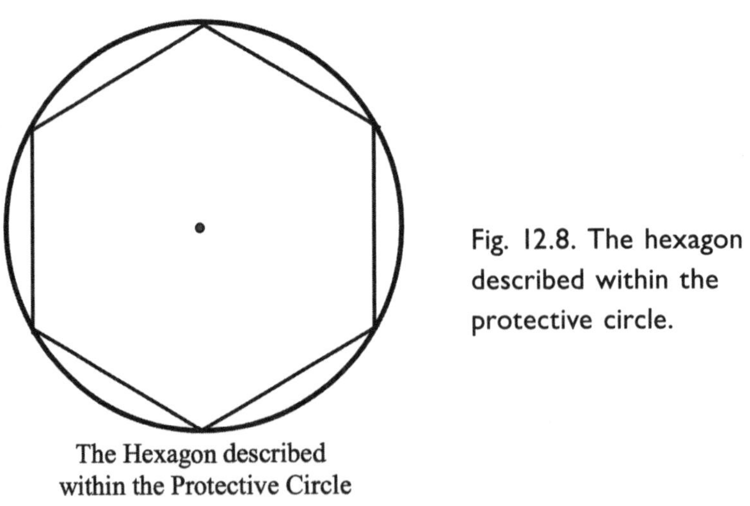

Fig. 12.8. The hexagon described within the protective circle.

When the protective circle is closed to begin a working, receptacles are positioned at each station of the hexagon to contain the six elements.

The Hexagon

The hexagon is an important sigil within the tradition. It represents a number of very significant correspondences, in particular the association with the queendom of the bee, being a representation of the cells of the honeycomb and its association with the culture of the bee. This is further confirmed when we look at the six converging points of the sigil.

At each corner of the hexagon is a convergence point; these are the six points or stations of the hexagon and each represents a sources of elemental energy. When the protective circle is closed, a vessel containing the appropriate elemental energies is placed at each station; some or all of these may be used in the working.

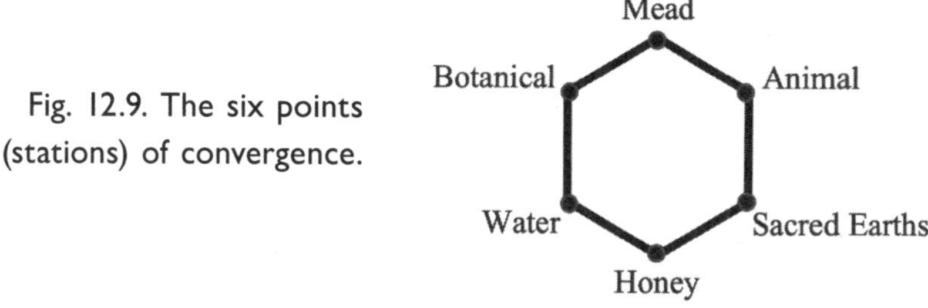

Fig. 12.9. The six points (stations) of convergence.

We have seen that the alignment station (at the top of fig. 12.10) and the third station, or converse station, directly opposite it (at the bottom of fig. 12.10), along with the center point of the circle are used to align the entire circle with the chosen celestial body (sun or moon). In addition to these two stations, there are four other major convergences.

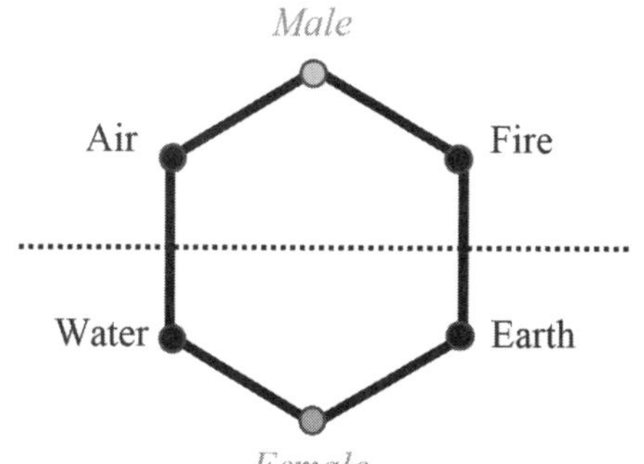

Fig. 12.10. The four convergence points describing the four elemental forces of the hexagon.

Each embodies one of the major world essences: the upper two, air and fire, being the male domain and the lower two, water and earth, being the female domain.

As well as these important convergence points or stations there are other significant elements of the hexagon. The upper chevron of the hexagon represents the male phallus, the power and force of fertilization, and the upper half of the hexagon is the male domain. The lower chevron represents the cup or chalice of the female vagina and the womb of creation. The lower half of the hexagon is the female domain. The two supporting pillars are knowledge and wisdom, while the whole illustrates how the balance between male and female is maintained through the application of wisdom and knowledge (see fig. 12.11).

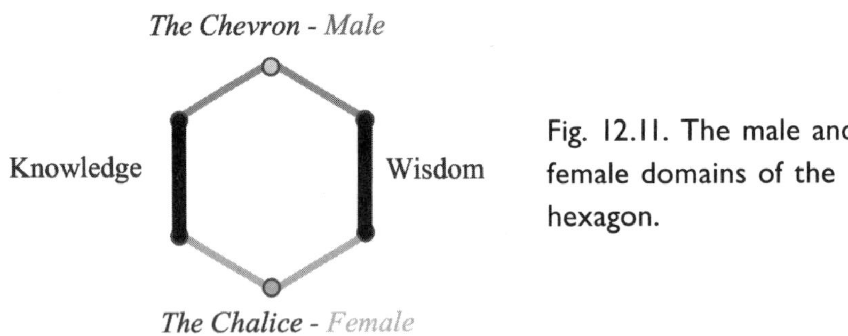

Fig. 12.11. The male and female domains of the hexagon.

The Working Stone within the Circle

At this point, the protective circle with its hexagon is ready to be cast, closed, and sealed before the Adept can begin his work at the working stone inside it. Traditionally, the working stone was exactly that, a flat stone within the stone circle where the Adept conducted her ritual workings. Many of the surviving stone circles from the period when the bulk of the megaliths that decorate the landscape were erected still have their working stone intact. It is easily recognized as the only recumbent stone within the circle, positioned opposite the circle's entry portal. Most stone circles were entered at the rear, some with two portal stones standing outside the circle through which people had to pass between before they entered the circle. Often there would be a fire at the base of each of these portal stones, and individuals would stretch out their arms as they walked between the fires, passing them through the purifying flames as they entered the circle. Nowadays, there are not many Adepts that have access to one of these ancient stone circles and their recumbent working stones. Typically, the recumbent stone of the megalithic age is substituted by a simple table made from natural wood, placed in the same spot and oriented to the same alignment as the original stone would have been.

CASTING A CIRCLE ON THE WORKING STONE

Sometimes it is not possible for the Adept to create and use a protective circle on a large scale outdoors. An alternative is to cast a protective circle and hexagon upon the working stone itself. As long as the ritual working is conducted within the protective circle, it is still shielded from any unwanted influences even if the Adept is standing outside the circle while working.

These table-top protective circles are constructed in the same way as we have already seen, but on a scale that fits the working stone while

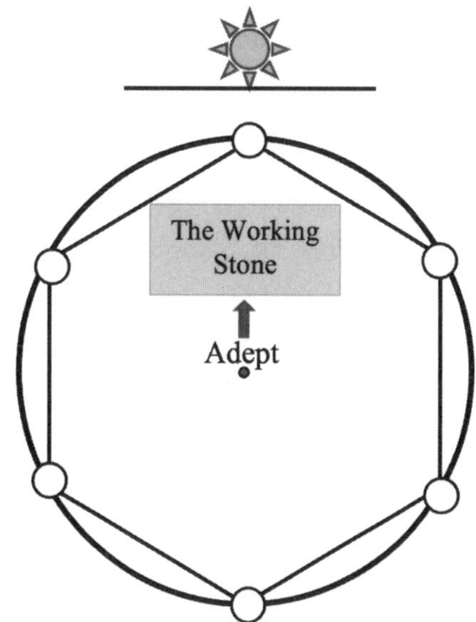

Fig. 12.12. The position of the working stone within the protective circle.

still providing sufficient space for the Adept to work effectively. It can be more difficult to orientate the circle and its stations if the Adept has no clear view of the horizon from within a building, but it is possible, by using a compass to define a bearing, to align the circle and stations accurately. In such cases it is also useful to refer to the alignments of the building's walls as a reference point.

On occasion, it may be necessary to create a working stone with a protective circle and hexagon described on its surface as a means of creating a protected workspace within the Adept's workshop. This may be required for the creation of delicate philters, potions, oils and such that need the protection of the circle as they are being made.

RITUAL AND FUNCTIONAL TOOLS AND EQUIPMENT

In time, every Adept will gather together his own cache of tools and equipment. These tools may be categorized as either ritual or functional: some will sit on the ritual working stone, and some will find their home in the Adept's workshop.

It is important that all tools are kept meticulously clean, as is also the case with all items of equipment, be they ritual or functional. All ritual tools and equipment will need further cleansing before they are used, as nothing impure must enter the protective circle of the ritual. Others will need to be charged or potentialized in order to allow their attributes to be fully accessed and utilized.

Ritual Tools and Equipment

In general, these will include:

- *Wand:* The most used and most powerful of the Adept's devices.
- *Crucible:* The ritual vessel used upon the working stone to combine and concoct the ritual materials of the working.
- *Goblet:* To hold and distribute the votive draughts of the working.
- *Spoon and blade:* To craft the potions, draughts, and other magical concoctions of the working.

- *Ritual bell:* Used to mark the progress of the ritual and to ward off unwanted influences. It is also used to reinforce the purification of the working space or protective circle.
- *Collection of bottles:* Each containing the required oils, distillations, macerations, and so on necessary to conduct the ritual working.
- *Collection of bowls and caskets:* Each containing the required powders, botanicals, minerals, and so on necessary to conduct the ritual working.
- *Two natural wax candles:* Each held in a suitable candlestick to provide the source of the ritual flame or fire used in the working.
- *Ritual burner:* Providing the ritual flame and heat source required to conduct the ritual working.

Functional Tools and Equipment

In addition to her ritual tools, each Adept will have a cache of functional tools and other essential equipment for use in her workshop. As the workshop is the place where all the potions, philters, oils, spell bottles, and so on are crafted, the Adept will need a range of equipment for distillation, fermentation, maceration, and similar processes, as well as the tools required to craft wands, amulets, charms, and talismans. Every Adept will also have an ever-growing collection of storage jars, bottles, canisters, boxes, and caskets, containing all her necessary botanicals, minerals, animal products, potions, ointments, and libations, along with all the other useful hand tools they need for their workings.

Typically, every Adept will craft the majority of his own ritual tools, so each would usually have a collection of carpentry tools kept within his workshop. It is not possible to provide a comprehensive list of functional tools and equipment that may be needed, as each Adept will have his own requirements dependent upon what workings he plans to undertake and just how much crafting he chooses to do for himself.

CRAFTING COMPONENTS

In addition to tools and equipment, crucial to the Adept's work are the materials or crafting components used. These include botanical, animal, and mineral items—some to be used in ritual, others to serve a more practical and functional purpose in the workshop.

Botanicals

One of the most important abilities of the Adept is to locate and identify the various botanicals she needs for her workings. Some plants are very common; others are particularly rare. All will be subject to their growing season and the terroir in which they grow. The subject matter of this book is located firmly in the Welsh Marches, and as such it is appropriate to restrict the range of botanicals to those indigenous to that region. While it is not possible to include all the botanicals used by the Adepts of the region (it is estimated that these would run to more than 1,150 individual botanicals), the principles and methods discussed may be used to the same effect with most of the plants in the same categories. Individual methods for the crafting of specific potions are detailed below; here we will focus attention on the universal tenets that govern the selection and harvesting of botanicals for the Adept's workshop. But first it is necessary to look at what parts of each plant is used so that we may select the appropriate plant with these considerations in mind.

As we have seen, in this tradition each sentient living thing is composed of three constituents: the physical manifestation, the personal spirit, and the communal spirit. In the same way, botanicals are composed of the same three constituents but in a subtly modified form. The physical manifestation is the most obvious of these, distinguishing each plant species from another, and the most practical tool in selecting the desired plant. The personal spirit within the botanical kingdom is as individual as it is within the sentient being, distinguishing each individual plant within a species from another and giving each plant its own unique personality. The communal spirit within each plant is the universal energy that it shares with everything else that exists, allowing it to empathize and interact with all other things, both animate and inanimate.

It is these three constituents that the Adept seeks to understand and employ in his workings. This is done by isolating each as one of the plant's cardinals, increasing the individual potency of each, and then reuniting them as a powerful and effective potion, ointment, libation, or other form of ritual transference.

In ancient Welsh, the cardinals were originally called *y calon,* which translates variously as "heart, center, core, spirit" and demonstrates not only the various understandings of what the cardinals represent but also the difficulty in precisely translating the meaning of the original Welsh words and expressions used within the tradition and why many practitioners throughout the ages have chosen to use the Welsh version rather than seeking a meaningful translation. Each cardinal is host to an elemental energy that may be utilized for the working. Each one of these elemental energies inhabits an identifiable part of the plant. The flower of the plant is where we find the elemental energy of the sun (sometimes interpreted as being heat). The leaf of the plant is where we find the elemental energy of the air, and the root of the plant is where we find the elemental energy of the earth. These elements are not to be confused with Aristotle's four universal elements, as this tradition and philosophy are completely different.

In each of these plant parts we find all three constituents comprising the plant in equal proportion. For example, in the flowerhead we find the elemental energy of the sun, while it is at the same time composed of its physical manifestation, its own unique personal spirit, and its own small share of the universal communal spirit that it possesses for its lifetime. The same is the case for the leaves and root.

In isolating each of these plant parts (flowerhead, leaves, and root), the Adept is able to intensify the elemental energy of the plant part while also increasing and focusing the personal and communal spirits that inhabit it. This is done most effectively when the cardinals are separated, so that later, when they are reunited, they are more potent than the plant would be if it had been empowered as a single component. The specific methods and techniques used in separating and increasing the potency of the cardinals and then uniting them is described in detail later in the chapter. Here, however, we need to consider how this process influences the choice of which botanical is to be selected for harvesting and when it is to be harvested.

All the features discussed above are influenced by a number of aspects of the plant's condition. The most important of these are the maturity of the plant, its life cycle, its location, and how and when it is harvested.

The Maturity of the Plant

Young plants are immature in both their physical and spiritual development, though they are overflowing with vitality and vibrance. This makes them ideal for delicate workings producing subtle products. Young plants are particularly suitable for young people. Mature plants are at the peak of their power; their cardinals are the most potent, making them most suitable for workings that require powerful and potent energies. Old plants are less energetic but may be used in preference to mature plants as their spiritual energies are more mature and their elements more powerful and concentrated. The Adept must harvest the desired plant at a time most appropriate to her needs.

The Annual Life Cycle of the Plant

Every plant has an annual life cycle. Typically, it begins its growth in the spring, flowers in the early summer, and bears seed or fruit in the autumn before it dies back and becomes dormant through the winter. This life cycle determines when fully developed leaves become available, when flowers are in bloom, and when fruits, berries, and seeds become available. And, of course, many plants are not available at all during the winter season. It is important then that the Adept plans to harvest the plant at a time when these various seasonal bounties are available.

The Environment and Orientation of the Plant

In the world of grape growing and wine manufacture, the word *terroir* is used to indicate all the various aspects of the place where the plant grows: the weather, soil content and condition, water supply, physical location and surroundings, and the influence of other plants growing around it. As well as the physical condition of the plant and, in the case of grapes, its taste complexity—aspects that preoccupy wine makers—

terroir also affects the spiritual and elemental aspects of the plant. If, for example, its root is intertwined with the root of another contradictory plant, it may well be adversely influenced in a way that will affect its potency and indeed the balance of its energies and spiritual attributes. Also crucial is the plant's orientation, both in the context of its compass orientation and subsequently to its celestial orientation with regard to the sun and moon.

The Time of Day of the Harvest

Determining whether to harvest at sunrise or sunset is the most important concern regarding harvest planning. Plants harvested at sunrise are full of energy and vitality, while those harvested at sunset have their constituents concentrated by the sunlight's energy of the whole day.

Having considered all the variables detailed above and planned the plant's harvesting in detail, the next step is to determine the harvesting technique to be used. This of course varies depending on what part of the plant the Adept plans to use. We will see later that harvesting an appropriate single branch for a living wand is a very different process to harvesting an entire flower-bearing plant along with its root. Each description for the crafting of potions and so on in the following chapters begins with an explanation of the harvesting technique employed.

The precise and confident identification of these important plants and the methods of selecting and harvesting them are regarded with such importance because of the overwhelming significance of using living plants with a known provenance. From understanding the fundamental principles described above, it becomes obvious that there is never a justification for using store-bought botanicals. Some self-harvested, dried botanicals have a place in the tradition, but never those where all the variables described above are unknown, as would be the case if using packets of dried herbs, cut flowers, and so on from stores where there is no way of knowing any of the imperative features that determine the botanical's efficaciousness.

Animals and Animal Parts

One of the most sensitive areas of the tradition is the use of animal parts and products. The first rule of practice is that no animal is ever killed or harmed to obtain the products used in ritual. Body parts are only harvested from animals that have recently been killed for food. These may include bones, hearts, livers, kidneys, eyes, etc., some of which we will encounter in the workings that follow below. In a number of workings human products are also utilized, such as blood, urine, sweat, menstrual fluid, tears, hair clippings, nail trimmings, and semen. These are commonly collected with the cooperation of a donor, or covertly acquired from a targeted donor without their knowledge, as is sometimes the case with those for whom a secret love potion is to be crafted. Once again, details of these products and body parts are included in the relevant workings that follow below.

Minerals

By far the most well-known minerals used in occult workings are crystalline or the well-documented medicinal earths of the medieval mediciners and apothecaries. Most of these originate from exotic locations and have no association with the Welsh Marches; however, there are a number of minerals that are native to the British Isles and are part of the regional tradition. We have seen above how the Druids of the Marches used fire-split quartz from a local deposit to surface a ceremonial pathway between their village and their ritual stone circle. We have also seen how alabaster shards were used as protective deposits to ward off Witches and evil daemons. Of the minerals or earths that are sourced within the region, the most significant are the compressed clays used in ointments and the common earths that are used to connect workings to their locations and cojoin Adepts in convocations to combine their power. This binding of power is a form of gestalt unison, where the total is greater than the sum of the individual elements. We shall see various minerals being purified, finessed, and potentialized in a number of workings in the following chapters.

WATER AND LIBATIONS

Water is used in every working; it is present on every working stone and plays a role in every potion, philter, and magical concoction. The most commonly used forms of water are those collected from streams, from rain fall, during thunderstorms (thunder water), and during lightning storms (lightning water). Another popular source of powerful water in the Welsh Marches is water drawn from curse wells. The region has a number of holy wells, wells that are believed to have been blessed by a local Christian saint or where a significant blessed event has occurred. Conversely, curse wells are believed to have either been cursed by a local Witch or sorcerer or where an unholy event has occurred. Ironically, several curse wells of the region acquired their reputation by an individual falling into a holy well and drowning while collecting holy water. No matter what the source of the water, it would invariably be moon cleansed before it is used in ritual or in any form of working. This is done by placing the water in a clear vessel and exposing it to moonlight for an entire night. This purification is most effective when done below a full or fat moon but never under a new or skinny moon. Tap water or bottled water are never used for reasons of provenance.

Other libations used at the working stone or workshop are simple mead, fermented from honey, or more frequently metheglyn, a unique Welsh mead infused with specially selected botanicals that imbue the libation with the physical, spiritual, and elemental properties associated with each plant. Another frequently used libation is the ancient form of ale, created by fermenting various indigenous cereals with a collection of psychotropic bittering agents. Along with these ales, a number of ciders are also employed for ritual libations and as carriers for more concentrated potions. This is one of the reasons why the central region of the Welsh Marches around Herefordshire has become one of the most famous cider-producing regions in the British Isles. Distilled spirits are used only occasionally and are crafted by distilling the various metheglyn varieties mentioned above and further enhanced by macerating selected botanicals in the spirit after it has been distilled.

13
Utilizing the Elements and the Will

Fundamental to any magical working is the bringing together of the three constituents of being we have seen above: physical manifestation, personal spirit, and communal spirit. All need to be as closely aligned as possible; without this alignment it is impossible to channel the Adept's will or to empathize with the elements in a way that they may be utilized to achieve the intended outcome of the working. The extent to which either of these objectives may be achieved is dependent upon the ability of the individual Adept, and to this end, it is worth looking at the way each Adept may develop his knowledge and skills.

Traditionally, each Adept experiences a prolonged period of learning, lasting for up to ten years, though there is no set training period as each learner progresses at a pace that is determined jointly by the learner and the teacher. Learning is achieved through an oral tradition that aims to transfer knowledge and skills through experiential learning and the use of situational parables related to the surrounding in which the learning takes place. There is no final qualification at the end of the learning (that is if the learning actually ever ends); there is no accreditation institute or certification. Instead, the learner becomes a Druid when the community in which she lives and practices recognizes her as such, acknowledging the value of her ability, and begins calling upon her knowledge and skills as a part of the society. In this tradition, there is no initiation, either by another Druid or by self-initiation, as there is no hierarchical structure to facilitate it nor is it deemed necessary. The only authority that one Druid may obtain over another is that granted through a respect for his greater knowledge, experience, and skill, and this authority is generally related to a single area of practice and not as an overall elevation. Elders may continue to teach throughout their lives as, in the same way, every Druid continues to learn until the day he dies. All Druids may be seen as solitary practitioners, there typically being only one Druid in each community. When deemed necessary, groups of Druids gather in convocation to conduct important workings, for philosophical debate, or to deliberate upon difficult issues in the community. At convocation, each Druid is accepted as equal while still acknowledging the greater experience and skill of individuals in certain areas of practice. A precursor to all these activities is the bringing together of the three constituents of being as discussed above; to do this, the first task is the casting of the protective circle.

PREPARING INVOCATIONS

We have already seen in chapter 12 exactly how the protective circle and its hexagon are described either onto the ground or onto the surface of the working stone. In this example we are using the external protective circle, described on the ground with the hexagon already marked. The circle has been aligned with the rising sun on midwinter's day and the working stone is in its correct location. The first task is to purify the inner circle and cast its circumference with purifying salt. To do this, we must prepare a simple invocation to pronounce as the circle is cast, so first a few words on invocations in general.

Preparing invocations should not be a difficult process; the most important thing is to keep it as simple as possible. As with curses, there is absolutely no need to make them rhyme; the only reason for doing this (according to bardic lore) is to make them easier to remember. We seem to remember things that rhyme better than those in ordinary prose. But as there are few occasions where an invocation is used more than once, remembering them is not really an issue. Another thing to remember is that they need not be in the Middle English of King James I. There is a lasting tendency to compose invocations and curses in the language used in the authorized King James I Bible, when in reality there is no point in using *thou, ye,* or *shalt,* so often seen and heard in spells, when simpler language makes the invocation easier to understand, and this is crucial. The Adept must understand and believe in what she is saying so that she may empower the projected energy invested in the invocation. A further risk in using unfamiliar, arcane language is that the Adept may unintentionally misuse a word or phrase, thereby composing an incoherent invocation. The single most important rule is to make the invocation simple and unambiguous, remembering that the invocation is not intended to be addressed to any god: it is a means of focusing the energies of the Adept toward the intention of the invocation.

With regard to the invocation to be used when casting the protective circle, the intention is to energize the latent energies within the moon-cleansed water used to purify the inner circle and within the natural sea salt used to protect and seal its circumference. A typical invocation to energize moon-cleansed water used to purify the circle could be:

> *I focus all my energies and spirit upon this purifying water with the intention of joining my energy with the powerful purifying vitality residing within it, liberating its latent elan so that it may purify all that it touches and that surrounds it.*

This is not a standard invocation; indeed, there are none. It is simply an example of an invocation appropriate for the occasion. Every Adept will compose his own invocation, usually a new one for each occasion, responding to the circumstances, the reason for the invocation, and his own inspiration. The imperative thing to remember is that it is not what is said that is important, as it is said only to inspire and motivate the Adept. It is not an appeal to any god(s) for assistance; it is not for the benefit of a congregation or anyone other than the Adept himself, so it should never be overelaborated or complicated. Simple is always the most effective.

PREPARING THE PROTECTIVE CIRCLE

The ritual of casting the protective circle begins by energizing sea salt with an invocation before sprinkling it in a fine line around the circle's circumference, beginning at the fourth point of the hexagon and continuing in an unbroken line clockwise around the circumference to the third point. The space between the third and fourth point is left open to allow the Adept to enter and leave the circle without breaking the protective salt barrier.

The Adept now ensures that everything required for the intended working is within the cast salt periphery. This will include all the working stone ritual items and the six bowls containing the natural elements, which will sit at each point of the hexagon. When all is in place, the Adept uses the remaining energized sea salt to close the circle by sprinkling it on the circle's circumference between the third and fourth points of the hexagon. The salt circle is now completely unbroken, and the protective circle is closed.

The moon-cleansed water is now energized with an appropriate invocation, and the interior of the circle is cleansed by the Adept dipping her fingers into the water and using them to gently sprinkle the water in every direction within the circle's interior.

The final act in preparing the protective circle is to position the appropriate bowl containing one of each of the six elemental energies at the corresponding convergence point on the hexagon (see fig. 13.1 on page 192).

BRINGING TOGETHER THE THREE CONSTITUENTS

The physical and protective aspects of the circle are now in place and the Adept is positioned within the circle in front of the working stone. All the necessary ritual tools are in place on the working table, and all that is left to do is for the Adept to focus his attention on bringing the three constituents of being previously discussed into close proximity and, by doing so, combine their energies so that they may be used with

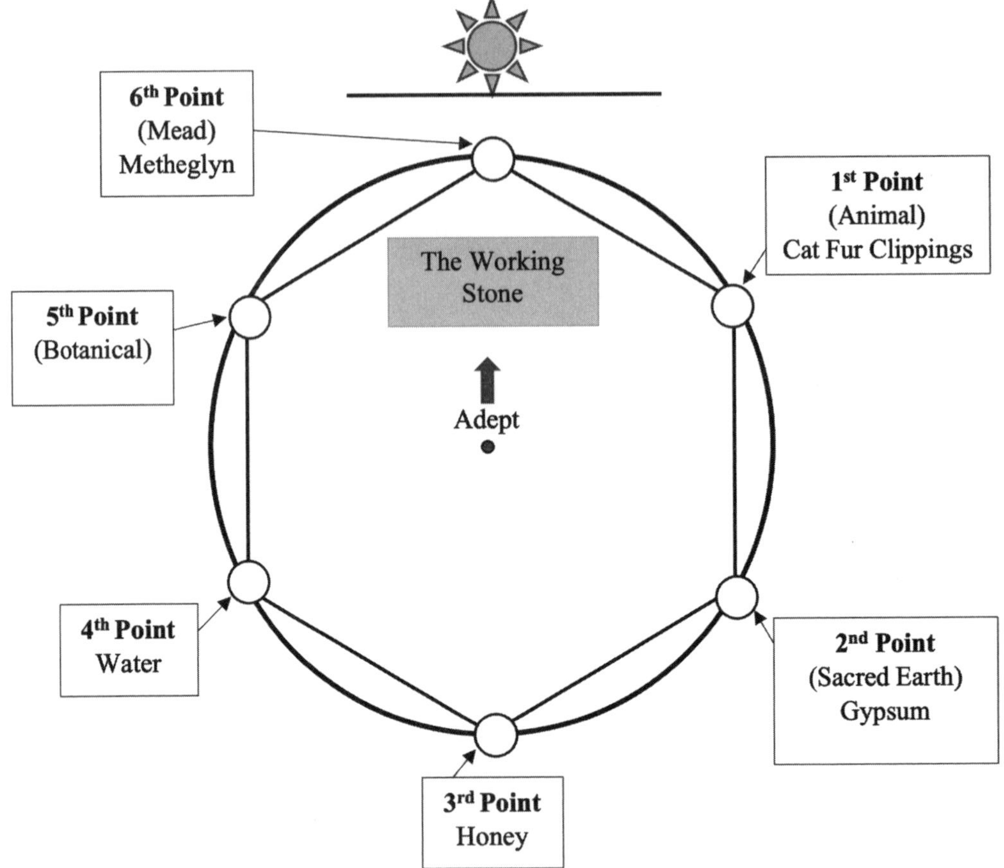

Fig. 13.1. The elements in position at the points of convergence.

the greatest effect within the intended working. This is achieved by the dual process of inner focus and meditation.

Inner focus is the process of detaching oneself from the impositions of one's surroundings and directing all one's concentration on the inner being and, in this case, its three constituents of being to bring them into closer proximity. We have seen that the closer our personal spirit, communal spirit, and physical manifestation are, the more powerful and effective our workings become. This process of disassociation is the first stage in a more complex meditation, wherein the Adept's intense focus enables her to realign her constituents, increase their psychic vitality, and amplify their inherent esoteric energies. We shall explore this in more detail when we look at individual workings below.

With his three constituents of being in close proximity and their esoteric energies at their maximum potential, the Adept is now ready to begin whatever workings he has planned, secure within the protection of the sealed circle and working within its purified interior.

The process of creating the protective circle and its secure workspace is exactly the same whether the Adept is working outside or within a small table-top circle, which is set out, cast, sealed, and purified in exactly the same manner as the outdoor circle, even though the Adept must work from outside the circle's perimeter. Similarly, if the Adept deems it necessary to create a protected working space in their workshop, exactly the same procedure is undertaken to secure a working area on a workbench.

14
Apotropaic Devices for Protection against Curses and Malevolent Energies

Protective (apotropaic) devices are essential to protect individuals, property, even whole communities against the evil intentions of maleficent actions of Witches, conjurors, or *inchaunters* (enchanters). These various devices may be worn about the body, carried, or are deposited in homes and on property to protect them.

Those apotropaic devices carried by a person may be amulets crafted in the form of mystical characters, inscribed with protective sigils or protective illustrations, or, more frequently, written with charms.

Protective talismans may also be used and differ from amulets in that they are not worn but carried about the person. They may be crafted figures, protective gemstones and minerals, bouquets of herbs or other botanicals, animal parts such as mummified feet, small animal skulls, potions, and, again, written charms.

Written charms are among the most popular of the various apotropaic devices as they are relatively easy to produce and empower, can be carried about easily, or can become a part of a protective assemblage deposited wherever it may be most effective. Written charms and curses are also often found inside witch bottles, enclosed within poppets or curse dolls, or written on silver birch bark, as is the main tradition within Wales and the Marches.

It is important for every Adept to establish a repertoire of apotropaic expedients before she embarks upon casting spells or intentions, if only for the sake of protecting herself from any rebounding influences that may occur when a neophyte first begins her workings. In the case of an experienced Adept, she will know well the need for substantial protection against unwanted influences in every area of her work.

AMULETS, TALISMANS, AND CHARMS

Although each has a different form, protective amulets, talismans, and charms are grouped together as they frequently utilize the same imagery and sigils. In simple terms, the difference between each device may be defined as follows (though it must be noted that there is considerable overlap between all three with no definitive distinction): A charm is either a written or spoken invocation. An amulet is a protective device worn about the body, typically as a necklace or bracelet. A talisman is a similar protective device that is carried in a pocket or pouch rather than worn, though they may be the same physical item or portray the same symbols as an amulet.

Charms

When written, the charm is usually secured inside a witch bottle or secreted inside a poppet or curse doll—sometimes tucked within the clothing of the poppet, other times enclosed inside the body of the poppet as it is crafted. On other occasions, the written charm forms a part of a larger deposition of protective artifacts along with old shoes, mummified animals, and other apotropaic items. Following the arrival of Christianity in the Welsh Marches, some written charms began to include Christian invocations, biblical references, and Christian prayers, though there are almost always strong pagan undertones. Spoken curses are either uttered in private by the curser or sometimes thrown or cast directly at the recipient. Again, following the growth of Christianity, they began to include aspects of Christian doctrine and were frequently uttered by Christian priests directly from their pulpits.

Amulets and Talismans

Amulets and talismans may be crafted from a wide variety of materials in any format the Adept may prefer. On occasion, they may be skillfully crafted into sophisticated artifacts, a process requiring specific crafting skills, or alternatively they may be crafted in a simple, naive form by those who do not possess such specialized abilities. One of the oldest forms of amulets inherited from the ancient classical world is the method of inscribing a written charm on a thin lead tablet. Known as a *lamella,* these tablets may be found throughout the Welsh Marches in deposits dating from well before the Roman occupation right up to the present day. Often buried or hidden in specific locations, these small lead tablets were also worn as protective devices or sewn into garments or boots to protect the person on a journey. They were often inscribed with auspicious images or carefully worded charms, composed and crafted especially for their owners. As Christianity spread and pilgrims began visiting the many shrines and holy wells, local cunning folk crafted amulets of the appropriate saint and sold them as pilgrims' medallions or souvenirs for the devoted. Slowly the ancient tradition evolved into the good luck tokens, charm bracelets, and St. Christopher medallions we see worn today.

The images that appear on most amulets and talismans are either written charms, composed by the individual crafter, or alternatively esoteric sigils representing magical intention most often inscribed by Adepts who craft the amulets in response to the specific requirements of an individual in dire need. Once again, as we have seen before, these devices may be crudely crafted in very simple form or expertly created by skilled artisans or gifted individuals. Both methods are equally effective in their use as it is the focused intent of the device that gives it its potency.

The two simple examples that follow offer the Adept a means of crafting effective amulets to be worn about the body and a rood talisman (roughly crafted) that may be carried by an individual seeking a protective device or a means of attracting good fortune in its many forms. We have examined written charms previously and these are mentioned here as another way of creating a protective device that may be carried about the person as a means of protection or attraction.

Crafting and Empowering an Amulet

A simple amulet may be crafted from a thin sliver of well-dried wood from a tree selected by the Adept for its individual attributes and virtues. The branch from which the amulet is to be created must be selected and harvested using the same criterion and methods we have seen previously, and when thoroughly dried, a section of the branch is cut and carved into a flat section with a hole at the top for the chain or thong as seen in fig. 14.1 on page 198.

Once suitably rendered, the basic amulet has its sigil or wording inscribed onto one or both sides. This must be done within a closed, sealed, and cleansed protective circle, using a simple ritual of empowerment and binding to its recipient. The wording of the incantation must be composed by the Adept in response to the needs of the recipient and may be similar to this example:

> *This amulet with its inscriptions is intended to provide protection to [Name] from any and all unwanted and hurtful ill intentions, curses, and malefic influences. May [Name] benefit from the safeguard of this amulet awake and asleep and may it protect [Name] wherever [he or she] may travel or lodge each minute of the day and night for as long as [Name] shall live.*

While this invocation may be too long to inscribe on the amulet, a shortened form or a few words with the same intention may be used on any amulet, talisman, or written charm.

An equally effective talisman, intended to be carried in a bag or pocket or sometimes sewn into garments, may be similarly crafted from a thin section of lead or pewter and empowered in the same way (see fig. 14.1).

In the same way, a written charm may be created to be carried about the person or hidden within a house to produce the same protective

Fig. 14.1. Inscribed lead talisman.

energies. Such a charm will be made up of a similar written statement, empowered and bound to its recipient in the same way as we have seen above. Frequently, these written charms are sealed within a charm bottle or witch bottle to protect them as they are being carried about.

Again, it is important to note that each of the methods detailed above are equally effective. The choice of which one to use in each individual situation is left to the judgment of the Adept.

WITCH BOTTLES, DAEMON TRAPS, AND WITCH MARKS

By far, the majority of protective devices are intended to be deposited within homes, farm buildings, and other vulnerable places to protect the inhabitants and their possessions from the malintent actions of Witches, sorcerers, and inchaunters.

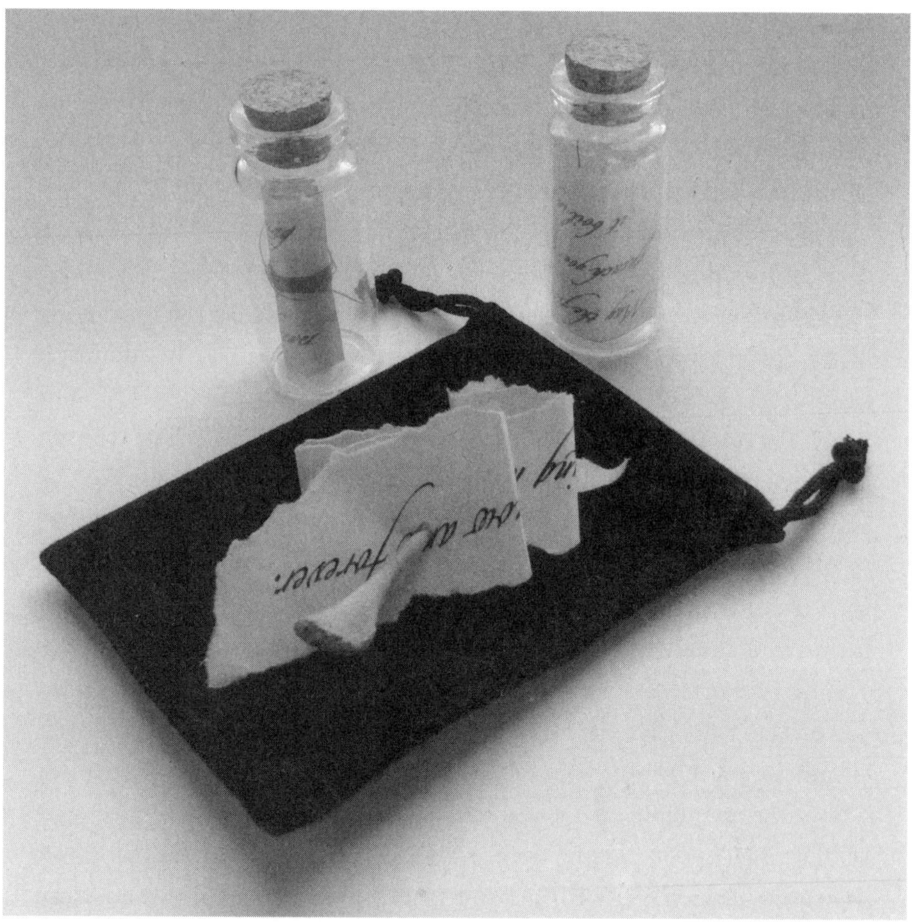

Fig. 14.2. Written charm pierced with bone and in witch bottles. (See also color plate 18.)

As we have noted in chapter 6, these devices take many forms, often including the personal, everyday possessions of the individuals concerned, simple utensils, items of clothing, shoes, toys, tools, and similar, all adapted from their mundane uses and repurposed to create apotropaic devices. To elevate a common-place item to its new purpose, the original use of the object has to be killed so that it can be adapted to its protective status. This typically involves breaking or deforming the object so that it can no longer serve its original purpose, such as deliberately blunting knives and tools, breaking tines from forks, cutting away parts of shoes, breaking parts of children's toys, and such like.

Although each object may no longer fulfill its intended purpose, such as a blunted knife, it is effectively repurposed as a magical protective object that can either deter a malevolent spirit from entering a home or destroying a precious crop stored in a barn, or it may attract a Witch's attention, distracting her from her original purpose.

Whatever the apotropaic item may be, its place of deposition is crucial. In times past, the homes of the people of the Welsh Marches were constructed around a central fireplace that was also the focal point of all the inhabitants' activities and the core of the family's domestic life—be it cooking, eating, drinking, socializing, or resting. Such fireplaces required a large, open chimney, which, in turn, provided a perfect opportunity for any malignant force to enter the home. This being the case, people often left a simple offering in front of the fireplace to placate any unwanted spirits or preoccupy any intrusive Witches as they tried to enter the property. This age-old country tradition surely influenced the idea of leaving pleasing offerings at the hearth, such as a mince pie or cookies for Santa and a few carrots for Rudolph. In the same way, protective devices are often placed at fire hearths or inside chimneys and chimney flues to deter or preoccupy spiritual intruders. The same principle of protecting vulnerable entry points gives rise to the practice of placing protective devices in or around windows, doorways, stairways, within wall spaces, between ceiling and floor spaces, underneath stairways, and inside wall cavities, all deemed as places where unwanted spirits may enter or move around a household. In the wider confines of the farm or estate, protective devices are also deposited at entry gates to fields and barn doorways, beside access roads and paths, within dairies, and in or around anywhere else the owners consider at risk from the intrusion of Witches and maleficent spirits.

The process of providing protection to the homes and the inhabitants and their possessions requires four specific steps that may be broadly described as follows:

1. *Selection* of an appropriate protective device and its intended location
2. *Crafting* the selected device

3. *Deposition* of the device or the inscription of the appropriate marks
4. *Empowerment and dedication* of the device

The most popular devices used in such cases are witch bottles, shoes, mummified cats, repurposed tools and utensils, written charms, poppets, and various forms of witch marks. Other, less frequently used devices include animal bones, knotted rope, items of clothing (whole or in part), and other personal possessions of those who feel threatened. Of these items, we shall look in detail at the crafting of witch bottles, witch marks, and a small variety of other individual protective objects. Previously, we have explored written charms and poppets, so with the addition of the items just mentioned, we have a comprehensive study of the most widely used apotropaic devices. The use of mummified cats and other animal remains is not included even though there is widespread evidence of the use of these items in many historic houses and other locations in the Welsh Marches. Cats were used because of their historic relationship with Witches as their companions and familiars, along with the knowledge that they are active at night, have excellent night vision, and have been considered to possess supernatural connections and influences in almost every belief system around the world. Importantly, there is no historical evidence or accounts of cats being specifically killed to use their mummified carcasses as protective deposits, and it has been determined that their bodies were typically mummified before they were carefully posed in prone positions as they were deposited.

Witch Bottles

As with other apotropaic devices, witch bottles are crafted in a particular way to fulfill one or more of the four general intentions of protective deposits. They are intended either to deter the entry of malevolent spirits and Witches or their familiars by scaring them away with sharp or spikey objects such as pins, thorns, sharpened twigs, and the like or to confuse the invading spirit by attracting them to an intriguing device or illustration, such as a maze or spiral, which confuse them and trap them inside. Alternatively, the Witch or spirit may be attracted to a personal possession, such as a shoe, garment, or even urine, confusing it with the actual person they seek and, in so doing, become entrapped by the binding spell attached to the object. Or finally, the Witch or spirit may be prevented from entering a house by the deposition of written charms, amulets, talismans, and so on. We shall explore the creation of a witch bottle crafted for each of these intentions.

In crafting a witch bottle, the Adept must first consider the four major tenets described above, repeated here for the sake of clarity.

1. The *selection* of an appropriate protective device and its intended location, bearing in mind its intended purpose
2. The *crafting* of the selected device
3. The *deposition* of the device or the inscription of the appropriate marks
4. The *empowerment and dedication* of the device

No matter what the protective device may be, there is a common deposition ritual for them all, which is described later in the chapter.

Witch Bottle to Protect a Household

One of the most popular uses for a witch bottle deposition is to protect a home with sharp or spikey objects empowered to hurt or impale unwanted malevolent intruders, thereby frightening them away or preventing their entry. These devices are particularly frightening to Witches and sorcerers partly because sharp instruments were used to torture and execute Witches in the early modern period and partly because Witches believed that if they were pierced by such a device their powers would be weakened or completely destroyed.

In this example, we shall assume the Adept is creating the witch bottle as a general means of protecting a household from malevolent spirits by scaring them away with a sharp object and intends to deposit the bottle in a recess within a hearth chimney. As a device intended to prevent entry, the Adept has the choice of what sharp object(s) he thinks will best deter the feared intruder. The sharp objects available to the Adept may be naturally occurring in the world of nature, such as thorns, briar, gorse, holly leaves, and the like (see fig. 14.3). They may be fashioned from natural materials, such as sharpened sticks, thorn witch axes, or similar. We can see in figure 14.4 on page 204 a witch axe that has been crafted from a short length of briar with all but one thorn removed. The witch axe is intended to hook on to the Witch, fixing her to the spot and even piercing the Witch and diluting her power. Alternatively, these objects may be repurposed household objects, like pins, pen nibs, and so on, bearing in mind that these common objects must first be altered before being deliberately repurposed. For example, a pin or pen nib may be bent.

Assuming the Adept has chosen to use a short length of spikey briar to place in the witch bottle, the device is created by simply placing the

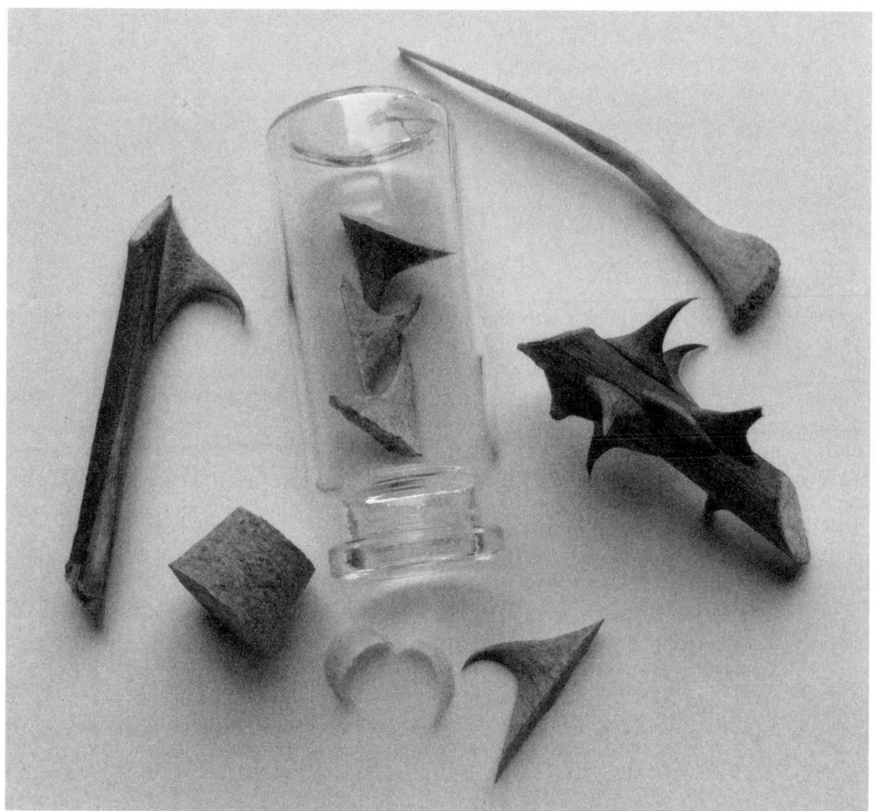

Fig. 14.3. Typical sharp and pointed items used in witch bottles.

Fig. 14.4. Witch axes, ready to be sealed into a witch bottle.

briar inside the bottle and sealing it. Very often a personal possession belonging to one of the home's residents is also sealed in the witch bottle to bond the device to the vulnerable family. Typically, this could be fingernail clippings, hair, or urine. Let us assume in this instance that the Adept has chosen to include fingernail clippings from the head of the household. Often a written spell is also included to strengthen the protective energies of the device.

When the Adept is confident that sufficient protective objects have been enclosed in the witch bottle, it is corked and sealed with sealing wax. Once sealed, the witch bottle is deposited in its designated place, in this case on a small ledge inside a chimney. The intention is to

Fig. 14.5. An assemblage of various objects in readiness for a protective deposit.

prevent any unwanted spirits, Witches, or familiars from entering the home via the chimney.

Witch Bottle to Trap Daemons

The intention of daemon traps is to literally trap the daemon within its structure and prevent it from any entry or movement around the house. These traps may take the form of intriguing complex illustrations drawn on small pieces of paper or complicated assemblages of unrelated items (see fig. 14.5). These drawings or objects are then sealed in a witch bottle. The trap is intended to attract the attention of the daemon, spirit, or familiar, draw it into the device by raising its curiosity, and then prevent it from leaving by making the exit confusing or impossible to find.

Images and illustrations are also inscribed directly on the house, such as walls, doors, window frames, beams, and such to trap daemons. When inscribed directly onto the structure of buildings, whether inside or on the exterior, these daemon traps are more commonly known as witch marks, although witch marks also take other forms with other intentions.

Witch Marks

One of the more well-known types of witch markings is the burn mark. Using a lit candle, the flame is applied to a wooden surface and allowed to burn into the surface of the wood. The resulting carbon produced by the burning is scraped away and the flame reapplied. The process is repeated until a deep, tear-shaped burn mark is created in the wood. The burn mark can then be sealed with wax polish and repeatedly polished to develop a patina. There are many examples of aged burn marks on beams, doors, furniture, and panels throughout the Welsh Marches, some being many hundreds of years old.

The purpose of burn marks is again to instill fear in any approaching Witch or malevolent spirit and drive them away. Witches in particular are known to be extremely fearful of fire and anything associated with it, a fear derived from the history of witch burnings and torture, along with many tales of their homes and possessions being burned because of their witchcraft activities. Again, burn marks are most often located at vulnerable entry points within a building or on door frames and panels, preventing Witches from accessing particular rooms or areas of a dwelling.

In addition to burn marks, witch marks may also take many other forms, for example ancient pagan devices, such as hexagons or daisy wheels, and other more recent Christian emblems, such as Marian marks and St. Andrew's crosses, though both hexagons and daisy wheels have been assimilated into Christian imagery, particularly in carvings on pews and church furniture.

Whatever the witch marks may be, they are crafted or inscribed in the same way as the other protective devices.

DEPOSITIONAL RITUAL

Every apotropaic device, be it a witch mark, daemon trap, child's shoe, or mummified cat, is deposited or inscribed at its location using an arcane ritual that both energizes (potentializes) it for its purpose and binds it to its place of deposition. The ritual comprises an invocation spoken as the device is put in place or the sigil is drawn, carved, or burned onto its host location. Once again, the invocation is composed by the Adept for each individual circumstance, using her own unique vocabulary and in accordance with the tenets defined previously. The invocation may be similar to:

> *I deposit this device with the intention of warding off any unwanted spirits or entities of malevolent spirits that may attempt to infiltrate this building or others in the possession of [Name] or [Name's] family and heirs. No unwanted spirits shall pass and may they be destroyed in their attempts. I imbue this deposit with all the essential energies needed to enable its work for as long as [Name] may live, and may it be inherited in all its potency by all those who live and work in this place for all time.*

Having spoken the invocation, the protective item is put in place or the carving or illustration is completed.

PROTECTIVE SPELLS

A building, person, or possession may be protected by using a protective spell or invocation. These may be written on a spell paper, parchment, or talisman; cast as a spoken spell or intention; or written on a spell paper and secured in a witch bottle. A number of means of casting and binding written spells may be used, and the choice of which is to be employed is left to the judgment of the Adept.

The spoken spell or intention is cast by the Adept within or about the building being protected, either by repeatedly speaking the spell as they progress around the building, or by tying the spell to a vessel of moon-cleansed water or ritual mead and sprinkling the liquid around the building and in every corner where unwanted energies may hide. Written spells may be deposited in a witch bottle, buried at the entrance to the building, such as a doorway or window, or burned in a fireplace thereby releasing the energy of the spell in the smoke, which then infuses its protection upon the chimney as it exits.

These two methods may be combined: the written spell paper may be dissolved in the moon-cleansed water by pounding the paper with some of the water in a mortar with a pestle, infusing the water with the dissolved spell, and then mixing the resulting paste with the remaining water before sprinkling the solution about the property as described above.

Whichever device and method the Adept employs, the result will depend upon the effort and intention of the person binding the spell to its location and his sincerity in energizing the deposit or spell and imbuing it with the energies and potential required for it to achieve its purpose so that it maintains its influence for the period prescribed.

15
The Casting and Lifting of Spells and Curses

To many people, the idea of casting a curse conjures up images of evil crones or sorcerers' apprentices, but in reality, it is a specific and precise undertaking that is an essential and cherished arte. In essence, it is a way of focusing the energy of a spell or intention toward or upon a specific recipient or item.

Casting may be done in a bewildering variety of ways using an equally bewildering selection of devices, but the methodology is fundamentally the same. There is an underlying commonality within the two traditions that prevailed in the Welsh Marches, and the fact that the same commonalities remain today in the wider traditions of both witchcraft and Druidic lore gives testament to its efficaciousness. Both traditions have much more in common than they have separating them, which is not really surprising, considering the shared origins and history of the two parallel traditions.

The arte of casting a curse may vary from the use of the familiar wand to a touch from a finger. It may involve the complex setting up of a pathway curse or the drinking of a love potion. In the context of this text, the word *curse* may represent both a good or not-so-good intention, which is why in the Druidic tradition it is more common to use the word *intention,* rather than *curse* or *spell,* as it has fewer predetermined connotations. Similarly, it may of course also represent a harmful or bad intention in the extreme. Both traditions avoid the word *evil* in this context as it is usually associated with the common Christian understanding of the word. Having said that, many of the texts and images from the period we have been looking at contain the descriptor of "evil," as they originated during a time when both traditions were viewed through the lens of the newly arrived Christianity, and predominantly Protestant Christianity at that.

In general, it is possible to define the casting of curses into two categories: those that simply project an intention on a target and those that use a device of some sort. The former curses typically use a wand, a touch, or similar method and are cast in a fleeting moment with the purpose of being absorbed by the recipient or targeted object. Spells incorporated into a device use a variety of objects and vehicles. The spell may be written on a piece of paper and given to an individual or placed in an auspicious place, or it may be a mark or inscription used in a similar way upon a house or an object, or it could even be a potion intended to be drunk by or used to anoint the recipient to bind them inextricably with the spell.

Each method requires the essential steps of preparation, cleansing, crafting, casting, and binding. At the same time, we must consider the potential need for releasing the recipient from the spell or removing the intention from an object, as it is only by making contingencies for this at the start that we may successfully remove or reverse the spell at a later date, if we need to. In the following sections we shall examine the most common spells and the means and methods of casting them in more detail, including the materials and tools necessary for this work.

First, however, we must consider an essential element of curse lore that is frequently overlooked or misunderstood: the Rule of Three or Threefold Law. Many readers may have heard of this law: *If a Witch or Adept casts an unjustified evil intention, it will be returned to them three times over.* While this is a useful reminder when considering the validity of casting a particularly damaging curse, it is also useful to realize that this maxim is based in a deeper ancient lore of curse crafting, a lore that governs every curse no matter how it is cast and is wholly dependent upon the reason why the curse is being cast. The reason for casting any curse is not simply the desire to impose harm or damage to a person or their property; neither is it done with the intention of punishing the targeted person for a previous transgression. The one and only reason for casting a curse or intention is to reestablish the balance of nature in response to a deliberate or unintentional imbalance. It may be considered as like for like but not in the form of vengeance or retribution. Neither may it be compared to the Christian concept of an eye for an eye, as it is not a punishment but a rebalancing—the correction of an imbalance within nature, more akin to the Newtonian principle of every action creates an equal and opposite reaction, but in this case, every imbalance requires an equal and opposite rebalance.

The *first principle* of curse lore: Every curse must be proportionate to its cause, the reason for the curse.

The *second principle:* Every curse must seek to redress the imbalance that gave rise to its creation.

The *third principle:* Every curse must be deliberately and specifically targeted at the source of the unbalance and no other person or object.

On this basis, the inevitable and sometimes unexpected consequence of inaccurate or indiscriminate curse casting is that no curse will stick or entwine itself around an *innocent* person; it will simply fall away and be totally ineffective. It will not turn itself back on to the caster as the old maxim of the Threefold Law suggests, but the results of the failure will almost certainly damage the reputation of its creator while the misuse of the various energies involved will have a dire effect on the caster's personal and communal spiritual elements.

Creating every curse or intention begins with addressing the following considerations:

- Has someone or something been badly affected by someone's actions?
- What is the reason for considering casting the cruse?
- Are you absolutely sure who or what caused the ill effect?

- Was it caused deliberately, or was it unintentional?
- Are you sure that the ill effect is a direct result of the original action and actor?
- Has the total effect of the action been assessed and quantified?
- Can the ill effect be redressed and a rebalance achieved?
- Can this be done with the use of a curse or intention?
- What would an appropriate and proportional curse or intention achieve?

Having considered all of the above, and only if the responses point toward the use of a curse or intention, the next stage is to craft suitable and proportional wordage for the curse or intention, bearing in mind that it may be used as a written curse or spoken as an incantation. This is a different process to crafting a charm, which will be dealt with separately in the section below. The tradition of the Welsh Marches has, in the past, been influenced by and included Christian references, which was common in many regional traditions and remains today in some specific regions. In this tradition, all Christian references have been removed and the content relates only to the original arcane, pre-Christian pagan tradition.

In crafting the structure of the curse, we must identify:

The target *recipient* of the curse, be it a person, an object, a place or an undertaking.

The *reason* for the curse: Reflecting the ill effect that has been caused.

The intended *outcome* of the curse: The means by which the original status quo may be recovered or reinstated. This will typically revolve around removing or diluting the influence of the person who invoked the original ill effect.

The *duration* of the curse: How long the curse is intended to remain in place.

The *link* to the natural world that will empower the curse.

The first thing the reader will note is that there is no punishment incorporated into the curse. Unlike some of the written curses from the early modern period—where the recipient may be punished with all sorts of ailments, misfortunes, or even death drawn down on them, their family, or their livestock—the tradition explained here is about returning the balance of nature, not punishing transgressors. It may well be that this resonates from the witch hunts and trials that had such a powerful influence on the region, punishing Witches (and others) as a result of the ignorance and prejudices of the judiciary of the day.

The most practical way to explain this process is by way of an example. If we believe that a certain area of a woodland has an overwhelming atmosphere of ill intent and malefaction that has been deliberately created by an individual performing negative ritual magic in the space, resulting in deleterious energies adversely affecting the surroundings both physically and spiritually, and that this can only be remedied by means of curse lore, then this may well be an appropriate situation for the use of a number of remedial curses. If, having investigated the matter in depth and applied the tenets mentioned above, we conclude that a remedial curse is the desired response and we are sure we know the person who originated the ill effect, we could construct a strategy to return the area to its original benign state. In this case it may be appropriate to cast a touch curse on the individual concerned to nullify their influence on the area, leave a written curse parchment hidden in the area, and deposit a pathway curse alongside the path leading to the area. This can be achieved by creating one curse and repeating it in each separate situation. If the curse is constructed carefully, it will be effective in each case; in fact, it will be much stronger than three individual curses, as the synergy among the three will create a single curse that is more powerful than the sum of three separate curses.

The first element of the curse is the *recipient*. In this case, it is a person who has been indisputably identified. We identify the recipient as [Name] in the suggested curse given below.

Next, we need to define the *reason* for the curse. In this case it is because the woodland has been contaminated by the maleficent energies of the recipient.

Now we have to define exactly what *outcome* we intend to achieve. Here we intend three outcomes: to disempower the recipient, to remove the maleficent energy, and to protect the space from any future malintent.

We now define the *duration* or lifetime of the curse. We confirm that we intend the curse to be effective as long as the woodland stands.

Finally, we need to *link* the curse to whatever natural energies, spirits, and powers we feel appropriate. We know from our previous exploration that we will need to combine the powers of the four natural elements and the communal spirits of the living forest to empower the curse.

Having constructed the architecture of the curse, the next stage is crafting the wording so that it incorporates all the components defined above. This is a very personal process that reflects the personality of the Adept and varies significantly from one Adept to another. As I have mentioned previously, the wording should not be overly complicated or flamboyant, as all this achieves is the prospect of misunderstanding, which will weaken the curse's power. Avoid using arcane language or Middle English words and phrases much loved by many other occult workers. Importantly, the wording should not contain any Christian references or wordage; be aware that many of these phrases and words have entered common usage in our everyday speech, so be especially careful and recheck the wording before finalizing the content. There is no specific order in which the various components should appear in the curse. Again, this is a matter of personal preference, as long as all the components are included.

The most important consideration is that the curse must be completely understood by the Adept, unambiguous, and confined to the components agreed above. Only by composing the curse in this fashion can the Adept fully empower its intention and channel her own personal spirit and energy to project and bind the curse. None of this is to say that, if it suits the personality of the individual Adept, she should not create well-crafted wording or make the curse as complicated as she wishes, just as long as it does not risk any of the pitfalls mentioned above.

Therefore, a typical composition for the situation we have suggested here may be:

> *I call upon the supreme potency of the four universal elements, directed through my personal spirit, to undo the maleficent workings of [Name] who has defiled this space, remove all [Name's] influence from this place, and diminish all [Name's] power, rendering [him or her] incapable of any further malevolent workings for [his or her] entire lifetime. Return this place to its state of natural beauty and innocence, for as long as Earth shall last. Harmonize the spirit of this place with the natural elements of our universe and protect it from any future malintent.*

Though this curse is typical of its kind, it is by no means universal. It represents my personal rendition of an appropriate curse for the circumstances described previously. It incorporates all the components as they are described above in a way that resonates with me and, as such, may not be appropriate for others. Each Adept should compose his own version of a curse that he feels reflects his personality and personal spirit. It would therefore be a useful exercise for the reader to compose his or her own version of this curse, setting it aside for a few days, revisiting it and assessing exactly how appropriate it may be, and editing it as many times as it takes to make it a powerful and fitting curse.

Only through practice and experience can the Adept obtain the skills and insight to compose and cast effective curses and suitable responses to each unique circumstance. It is not possible here to explore every potential situation that may arise or to itemize each appropriate response. I have given a simple example of what may arise and how the Adept may respond to it. It is the responsibility of each individual to formulate his or her own response as each sees fit.

We shall go on to examine a range of the most common methods and vehicles for casting, delivering, and binding spells and curses of all types. Each Adept will develop her own vocabulary of euphonic phrases from which she will compose her own unique curses and spells, whether they take the form of written charms or imprecations. To this end, we must now consider the materials, vehicles, and means by which each is delivered.

PROJECTION

The principle of casting curses is common to spells, curses, and intentions. As noted earlier, in the Druidic tradition, all spells are called intentions. An intention's purpose is to channel the intention of the Adept to a point of his body where it may be projected, cast, or thrown beyond the body (the physical manifestation) toward the recipient, be it a person, object, or place, where it is bound to the recipient with the aim of creating change by supernatural means.

The intention begins its journey as a strategically organized thought, composed by the Adept and incorporating all the considerations we have examined so far. As the Adept channels her composition through her body, the original intention is energized and amplified by her communal spirit, which adds universal energy and empowerment, and personal spirit, which fortifies the intention with the energy of the individual Adept and imbues it with her unique personality. Eventually, the Adept can feel the intention's energy arriving at the point of her body from where it is to be projected, and here it meets its first physical barrier, a barrier that must be traversed for the intention to leave the confinement of the Adept's physical being. While in some other instances the projection point may be elsewhere on the body, in most cases the projection point is the center of the Adept's right-hand palm. As the Adept feels the intention's energy building at the center of her palm, her focus is concentrated upon intensifying its energy to the level where it feels impossible to retain it within her body any longer.

The Adept's attention now briefly changes to target the intended destination for his curse. If the recipient is a person, the targeted area would be the central chest. If the recipient is an object or a place, the Adept uses his discretion to determine the target point for the curse or intention.

The most common method of casting or throwing the curse is that the Adept closes her right hand into a fist while a final concerted effort is made to concentrate the intention at its maximum power within the fist. The intention is then projected by throwing the curse like one would throw a ball, opening the hand at the finishing point of the throw and pointing the center of the palm at the intended target, visualizing the curse's energy leaving the palm in a ball, traveling through the air, and arriving at its destination. When the Adept visualizes the energy landing on its targeted recipient, she closes her fist, clenching it tightly, and twists her hand as if screwing the curse's energy into the recipient. This binds the curse to its intended recipient.

So, the method may be summarized as:

- Composing the curse internally
- Channeling the curse through the body to the center of the palm of the right hand
- Amplifying the curse's energy within the closed palm as the target point is confirmed
- Projecting the curse through the air to the recipient, extending the arm with an open hand and the center of the palm pointing directly to the recipient
- Binding the curse to the recipient by clenching the open hand, turning it as it clenches

Once the curse has been composed, and this is often done before the casting work has begun, the words of the curse are repeated slowly and quietly as a mantra throughout the steps described above. They must never be heard by the recipient.

This is the simplest method of hand cursing or hand throwing a curse and depends upon a thorough understanding of the principles and methods involved together with extensive practice to develop proficiency and accuracy. Hand throwing a curse is the simplest and purest form of curse casting. Paradoxically, it is both the simplest yet the most sophisticated means of casting curses, used only by the most experienced and skillful of Adepts. It requires the greatest skill and highly focused energy and results in the most powerfully bound curses.

In many situations the Adept may choose to employ a variety of devices to project his curses, some simple and others more complex, carefully crafted for specific circumstances. Next, we will explore some of these devices and the methods employed for their use.

CURSING WANDS

The wand is probably the most iconic device, associated by many with spell casting and the conjuration of spells. It has its own place in history as well as being a part of modern culture. Even so, it is without doubt the most misunderstood device connected to the culture of the occult.

It is important to recognize that there are many differences between the wands of the ancient witchcraft tradition and those of the Druidic lore, and by identifying these differences we also gain sight of the similarities that both traditions share, just as they have a shared origin and history.

The wands of witchcraft are of two major types: those that are roughly crafted and are most often used by country Witches, who craft the wands for themselves, and those that are finely crafted by skilled crafters who embellish them with elaborate designs and highly polished finishes equal to those of any established furniture maker or master carpenter. In both cases, it is understood that the main characteristics and attributes of the wand are imbued within the wood from which it is created, and a particular wand may be selected for a particular task in accordance with the unique characteristics associated with a particular wood type.

Many Witches of the ancient tradition believe that a wand only becomes effective once it has been seasoned by its owner, when it absorbs something of the spirituality of the owner, giving it power and influence while making it a singular device, useful only to the individual who nurtured it and to whom it has bonded. It is also commonly believed that this relationship improves and grows more powerful the longer the relationship goes on. The wands of old may well have been handed down from generation to generation through secret rites, potentially growing in energy and power as they aged. This understanding of the wand would have been the common belief of the people of the Welsh Marches and can be seen to go hand in hand with the curse casting, witch marks, and protective devices found within the region.

In direct contrast with this, the Druidic tradition of the same period and location has a fundamental belief in what translates from the Welsh as "the living wand" (Welsh: *Ffon byw*), a very different concept from the wands of ancient witchcraft. Although the iconic image of a Druid has them holding a long staff or stave, the wand holds an equally important role in Druidic lore as it does in witchcraft. Most Druidic workings involve the use of a wand, though it must be said that the staff does have a significant role to play as well. The living wand of the Druid is just that, a living branch, harvested from a donor tree, and briefly used for a particular need. It is then returned to the earth next to the donor tree, its rightful home, and ritual thanks are given to the donor for its loan with the hope that the living wand may regrow as a new and equally powerful tree of nature. The central tenet of this understanding is that the wand must be used while the branch is still living, while it still contains the vital energy of the donor tree contained within its sap and living heartwood. It is only by adhering to this understanding that the true potential power of the tree and its attributes can energize and empower the casting of intentions or any other working to which it may be applied.

If you wish to adopt the witchcraft tradition of wand lore, there are a great number of books and other online resources that explain in infinite detail the process of their manufacture and use. Alternatively, if you are not in the position to craft a wand of this style yourself, there are many available to buy in stores and online, where you may choose from a vast array of well-designed and well-made wands, often supplied with information and directions for their use.

As the understanding of Druidic living wands is far less well known, we intend to describe their crafting and use in detail below as this information is, to our knowledge, unavailable elsewhere. But before beginning, it is worth explaining that the principle of wand lore is, for the greater part, shared by both traditions we are exploring, by which we mean that the principle of the amplification of the power of the spell or intention by the wand is common to both, as is the understanding that, as the wand channels the spell or intention, it influences its effect by the addition of the energies and attributes associated with the wood from which it is crafted. So, while the basic principles are common to both traditions, the means of achieving them differs significantly.

CRAFTING AND USING A DRUIDIC WAND

To return to the crafting and use of the Druidic living wand, we may separate its crafting and use into five successive processes. Namely:

1. Selecting the donor tree
2. Harvesting the wand branch
3. Crafting the wand and potentializing it
4. Using the wand
5. Returning the wand to its natural habitat

Selecting the Donor Tree

There is a well-established understanding of the attributes and virtues of the various trees used in the occult culture of the Welsh Marches, some being used in healing practices and others in the making of mystical devices like wands and staves. There is also a widespread understanding of the responsibility we have to the natural world to undertake the selection and harvesting of even this single branch in a respectful and sustainable way.

Having established the harmony of agreement on the attributes and virtues of the trees involved, it falls beyond the purview of this work to become involved in a detailed description of each and every tree that may potentially be used in the crafting of wands. There are many resources that explore this subject in infinite detail and in order that we may progress to the other aspects of this unique form of wand lore, we refer the reader to those many excellent resources to help you decide the best possible wood from which to craft your wand.

Where the principles of the living wand differ from the wand lore of ancient witchcraft is that a much greater emphasis is placed on the *living* characteristics of the wood being used. The harvester must also consider the influences imbued upon the donor tree by the surroundings in which it has grown and lives. To borrow a reference from the world of wine making, the tree is influenced by its entire terroir, as it does not grow in isolation from its surroundings. It is useful to examine each of these influences in turn.

The first consideration is the donor tree's location. Is it growing alone or within a forest and close to other trees? If it does have close neighbors, they may influence its virtues in some way. By close we mean close enough for its roots or canopy to intertwine with the donor in a way that might affect it. In considering the proximity of the donor to its neighbors, it is useful to bear in mind that the root structure is approximately the size of the tree's superstructure above the ground. If their leaves touch, then so will their roots. The amount that the neighboring tree influences the donor depends upon its proximity, and therefore appropriate allowances must be made. In some cases, the presence of neighboring trees may be detrimental; when this occurs an alternative donor tree should be sought. Alternatively, the neighboring tree's virtues may be beneficial and therefore add to the overall influences we are looking for. Again, we refer the reader to the many resources defining the virtues and influences of the various trees involved, as they are far too numerous to list here.

Neighboring trees are not the only potential external influence upon the donor tree. The surrounding plant life in general may also influence the donor tree. Any botanical growing close enough to the donor tree's roots will affect its overall virtues and influences and any branch that may be harvested from it to craft a wand. Again, the closer to the donor tree the botanical grows, the greater its effect will be. For example, it is very common to find ivy entwined around the trunk of many trees, in which case, the ivy's influence will be significant. Similarly, mistletoe is sometimes found growing on the trunk and branches of oak trees, as we see mentioned in many of the Druidic fables and Celtic folklore. Inevitably, this has a dramatic influence upon the oak along with any branches harvested from it. Once more we refer the reader to the many external resources explaining the virtues and influences of the infinite combinations of botanicals that may be encountered on any walk in the countryside.

Another fundamental factor influencing the donor tree is the ground in which it grows. In the particular case of the trees growing in the Welsh Marches, we know there is a proliferation of crystal deposits in the locality, as witnessed by the Serpent Trail remains. If these crystal deposits are near the donor tree, then their virtues and influences must also be taken into consideration.

A further major consideration to take into account when selecting a particular branch for a wand is the orientation of the targeted branch in relation to Earth's polarity and the celestial bodies. Those branches growing on a north–south axis are most susceptible to absorbing the influences of other surrounding botanicals, while those growing on an east–west axis are more likely to resist these external influences. It is entirely appropriate to align the power of a harvested branch to influential planetary alignments, though the various permutations are always going to be determined by the individual.

Additional aspects to consider are:

- *Season of the year.* Those harvested in the spring are imbued with positive vitality; those in the summer invoke warmth and light. Branches harvested in the autumn possess a calming energy, ideal for love spells, while those harvested in the winter are best used for powerful binding spells.
- *Time of day.* If harvested in early daylight, the branch will contain the concentrated virtues of the tree; at midday it will be strong and fiery, ideal for protective workings. Those harvested at dusk will be subtle and ideal for emotional interventions while those harvested at night are most suitable for clandestine workings and secretive spells. In general, those wands harvested in daylight are

best suited to be used by male spell-workers and those harvested by moonlight are used to best affect by female spell-workers.

- *Aspects of the weather.* Branches harvested for wands during rain are imbued with the virtues of tranquility, subtlety, compassion, and gentleness. Branches harvested in thunder or lightning storms are gifted with powerful energy, strong binding power, and forceful projection and are ideal for casting spells over long distances.
- *Maturity of the donor tree.* Young sapling trees produce wands that project growth and gain, while fully mature trees yield powerful wands full of energy and vitality. Older, "major" trees donate wands best used in workings requiring knowledge and maturity of thought and intention and those that will benefit from experience and are ideal for workings relating to relationships, well-being, and future prosperity.

Being fully aware of all these aspects is imperative, as once the branch has been harvested its attributes cannot be changed. We must remember that our ancient ancestors, be they Witches or Druids, had an intimate involvement with nature and a profound understanding that is unrivaled in today's civilization. They considered themselves as an equal part of nature and worked *within* nature and the natural world and not, as we often hear in today's culture, alongside nature. They were therefore an integral part of nature, not its partner. To fully understand the principles of selection outlined above, one needs to understand nature itself. The relationship with the potential donor tree must never be entered into in haste; one must be prepared to return to the tree a number of times before any final decision is made to harvest a particular branch. This process may take a number of seasons extending over several years before a decision is finally made. This will be necessary to understand all the subtle changes the tree and its branches respond to over the days, months, and years while it is being observed. Returning during different types of weather and at different times of the day will also benefit understanding and insight. Here, the importance of making the correct selection cannot be overemphasized.

Harvesting the Wand Branch

Having selected the specific branch that best matches the Adept's requirements and in the light of all the variations examined above, the Adept must now plan and undertake the harvesting. There are only two working tools required for the harvesting working: a sharp knife, which may be the Adept's preferred ceremonial knife if it is sharp and sturdy enough, and a measure of sealing wax together with a suitable flame to melt it with. Both are common tools in every Witch's and Druid's tool cache. The knife is to be used to cut off the branch; the sealing wax is used to seal the open wound on the donor tree left by the harvesting and also the cut end of the harvested branch (the intended wand) to seal in its sap and vital energies. It is customary to speak an invocation of thanks to the tree and forest on completion of the harvesting. This is composed by the Adept in a way that embraces the circumstances prevailing at the harvest time.

Crafting the Wand

The crafting of the wand is typically undertaken in the Adept's workshop, but in the case of the living wand, there is rarely any decorative work employed, as the wand is seen purely as a functional tool to be used for a particular task and then returned to nature. This being the case, it is the functionality of the wand, rather than its form, that takes priority, so it is imperative that the Adept fully understands how the wand functions in order to craft it correctly.

Using the Wand

The purpose of the wand is to channel the energy of the spell or curse from the Adept toward the recipient. In doing so, it both amplifies the energy and imbues it with the virtues and attributes of the wood from which it is crafted. Earlier in the chapter, we have seen how the curse is composed by the Adept and then channeled to the center of the palm of her right hand where it encounters its first major barrier, the need for it to leave the Adept's physical manifestation. As the curse's energy sits in its location, it is reenergized and amplified by the Adept so that it may be powerful enough to leave the body and be projected to its recipient, where it is bound to its host. In the example above, we explored how this is done by hand throwing, casting the curse by using the hand. If the Adept wants to project the curse more powerfully and enrich it with further virtues and attributes, then she uses a curse wand crafted from a wood that empathizes with and magnifies the intention of the curse. The selection and harvesting of such a wood was described earlier; now we need to explore how this wood, in the form of a curse wand, functions to the benefit of the Adept.

In order that it may influence the projected curse with its own attributes, the crafted wand must channel the curse's energy through its length, amplifying it and adding its virtues as it does so. If we think of the wand as an electric cable and the curse's energy as the electrical current, then we can see that, like the cable, the wand needs to carry its current along its length, retaining it within its structure as it moves and protecting it from any external forces or influences that may obstruct or delay its progress. In the case of the wand, the curse's energy travels through the core of the wand, the natural core sap and heartwood of the branch that it has been crafted from. It is insulated from external influences by the body wood and bark of the branch as its energy is imbued with the wood's attributes as it travels through the heartwood core.

Having seen above how the curse's energy is held within the natural barrier of the Adept's palm, the Adept must bring the wand's core into direct contact with the center of his palm, in the same way that an electrical cable is brought into contact with its power source. To achieve this, the heel end of the wand must be cut at a diagonal, exposing the core and sap so that it may make direct contact with the Adept's palm (the curse's power source). The bark of the branch should not be cut or decorated along its length as it acts as an insulating barrier for the wand. The tip of the wand must be cut cleanly, again exposing the wand's core so as not to obstruct the curse energy's progress as it is projected toward its recipient, and finally, it becomes very apparent that the wood must be newly harvested and must still retain the wood's sap and vital energy if it is to work effectively.

As the Adept prepares to project the curse, focusing intently upon the energy at the palm while using his will to amplify its power, he also visualizes the barrier between his palm and the core of the wand held within it. This is done with the wand held vertically in the raised hand, pointing skyward, so that the energy may multiply at the point of contact between the wand core and the Adept's palm. At the appropriate moment, when the Adept judges that the curse's energy is at its maximum, he projects the curse through his palm, along the length of the wand toward his intended recipient, lowering his arm and pointing the tip of the wand at his target as he does so. The composed curse is repeatedly recited, quietly and slowly, from the moment the wand is put in contact with the palm until it is projected and bound to the recipient. The binding is achieved by moving the wand's tip in a decreasing spiral, as if wrapping the curse around the recipient, securing it with a flip of the wand's tip.

Gaining this insight into how the wand functions gives the Adept a greater understanding of how the harvested branch should be crafted into a wand. Once it has been crafted and before it is used, the wand must be potentialized, raising its intrinsic energies and mobilizing its natural vitality to its maximum potential. This is achieved by bringing the core of the wand at each of its ends (tip and heel) into contact with the palm of each of the Adept's hands, closing the connection of the body and wand, making one fully connected energy circuit. The Adept then channels her spiritual energy through and around the closed circuit, energizing it and raising its potential as she does so. An appropriate invocation is gently spoken as this process proceeds. Once the Adept judges that the wand is energized to its maximum potential, the wand is released and is ready to be used. A wand that has been crafted and potentialized in this way is suitable for almost every purpose that may arise.

Returning the Wand to Nature

Following its use, the wand is immediately returned to its original habitat where it is pushed back into the ground next to its donor tree with the intention that it may grow into a tree over time. Again, a suitable invocation of thanks is spoken as the wand is replanted.

CURSING WATERS

Water has been associated with both blessings and curses from the beginning of time and can still be seen in use in the rituals of all the major global belief systems from Japan to Europe, Africa to India, and beyond. As an indispensable requirement for human existence, it is easy to understand how it plays such a prominent part in so many mystical beliefs, where it is regularly used right up to the present day in baptisms, anointing, votive offerings, initiations, and cleansing rituals. Various waters are used at their natural sources or, in other cases, they are collected and used later in ceremonies within churches, temples, and other places of worship and devotion.

The supernatural energies of water are at their strongest at the water's source, and this has resulted in a long history of pilgrimage to water sources all over the world where people seek to benefit from the spiritual powers of water as it emerges from the earth. When water is collected and removed to another location, it is then often reenergized by some form of blessing or charging to restore its original vitality. Many places of worship are specifically placed close to significant water sources, most sharing their name with the saint, deity, or ancient god to whom the water source has been dedicated, usually in recognition of a miraculous event or perceived benefit attributed to them. Subsequently, many of these locations have become places of pilgrimage for devotees and the abode of holy men or hermits, while many of the water sources themselves have gain the title of holy well, holy stream, and so on.

The Welsh Marches, like many other regions of Britain, has more than its share of these holy wells and holy streams, and to fully understand the history and purpose of these holy wells, we shall look at one of the best known in the region, Ffynnon Elien or St. Elien's Well in the parish of Llandrillo-yn-Rhos.

This small well in the north of the Welsh Marches sprang into existence to save the life of St. Elien as she was dying from thirst on her journey through Wales during the sixth century. The well quickly became famous as a holy well, with its waters providing miraculous healing for a varied collection of illnesses. The healing process involved draining the well three times and anointing the sick person with its healing waters. The well proved a popular place of pilgrimage and provided a welcome source of income for the farmer whose land surrounded the well.

Around 1723, for some unknown reason, the well developed a reputation as a cursing well, where vengeful individuals sought to curse those who, for whatever reason, had offended them. The curse was created by inscribing it on a small slate shard and casting it into the well; as long as the shard remined within the well, the curse would be sustained. Pilgrims traveled from far and wide to throw their imprecations into the well as a means of righting injustices and rebalancing their lives. Local records show that over the following thirty to forty years, thousands of pilgrims visited the well, making it a source of annoyance for the local inhabitants and the local parish church until, in 1828, the congregation of the local Methodist chapel destroyed the well and planted potatoes in its place. Soon afterward, the stream was redirected, and a substitute well was constructed nearby, though this never regained the reputation of the original curse well.

Most cursing wells began their existence as holy wells before going through some perceived disaster or calamity and gaining a new reputation for malediction and being recreated as cursing wells, offering opportunity for large numbers of seemingly wronged individuals to rightly or wrongly seek revenge upon their offending neighbors. The practice of inscribing maledictions on slate shards and depositing them in cursing wells continues to the present day and examples may be found throughout the British Isles, but of course not all people have access to these ancient arcane resources, in which case one alternative is the use of a curse binding casket.

Crafting and Using Cursing Waters

The curse binding casket consists of a suitable receptacle that may be securely covered and sealed, capable of holding water and a curse tablet in the form of a small slate shard. The working should be undertaken inside a closed, sealed, and purified protective circle to prevent the intrusion of unwanted influences and the escape of any random influences from the curse tablet itself. The first stage of the working is the crafting of the cursing water, the more accessible alternative to the waters of the cursing well.

The working begins with the Adept collecting a good measure of water from a natural source such as a river or stream that the Adept knows to be pure and unpolluted. The water should be collected from as near as possible to the source. The water is sealed in a clear glass vessel and placed in an exposed position under the moonlight for at least one night, a process known as moon cleansing. This cleansing removes any unwanted influences and creates the pure cleansed water base needed for this working and others.

This water is poured into the chosen casket, which may be any preferred opaque vessel deep enough to hold the water and slate shard and have a close-fitting lid or top that allows it to be secured with a water-tight seal. The vessel or casket should not be overfilled with the water, allowing enough space so that the water displaced when the shard is immersed does not overflow. Once the water is in the casket, the slate curse tablet should be prepared.

A short, concise curse should be composed by the Adept in preparation for inscribing it onto the slate tablet. It is best to record this short composition on paper first, so that it may be finessed before it is inscribed. When the Adept is confident that the wording of the curse is what he wants (bearing in mind the fundamental tenets described above), the wording is carefully and clearly inscribed onto the slate curse tablet; this may be as simple or as intricate as the Adept chooses. The curse is quietly and repeatedly spoken as the inscribing proceeds. Once completed, the curse tablet is ready to be united with the water in the casket. This is the most profound part of the working.

The uniting requires the working stone within the protective circle to be prepared with:

- Water-filled casket with lid
- Inscribed slate curse tablet
- Thread to secure the lid in place
- Sealing wax to seal the binding
- Ritual candle to melt the sealing wax

Fig. 15.1. The various components assembled in preparation of working.

The slate curse tablet is held with the fingers of both hands, and the curse is spoken as the tablet is carefully passed through the tip of the candle flame to gently purify it, removing all unwanted influences before it is united with the water. When this is done to the satisfaction of the Adept, the tablet is carefully and gently slid into the water within the casket, making sure that it is totally submerged and none of the water overflows. As this is done, a suitable incantation composed by the Adept is spoken. This may be similar to:

> *As I immerse this tablet beneath these purified waters, may it bind itself to [Name] so that [Name] will not prosper until [his or her] ill actions are overturned and the balance of nature returned. May this curse bind to [Name] until this is brought about and for as long as this tablet remains beneath this pure water.*

Fig. 15.2. Stone curse tablet inside casket.

Once the tablet is in place, the lid is placed on the casket and it is secured with the thread, which is tied at the top center with a knot. The sealing wax is slowly heated until it becomes malleable; it is then used to seal the knot as a suitable incantation is spoken, such as:

As I bind this casket and seal it, may the curse I inscribed within be bound to [Name] and remained sealed there until its perfect outcome is achieved.

Fig. 15.3. Casket containing curse tablet sealed with sealing wax and imprinted with seal.

When the time comes to remove the curse, this is achieved by simply breaking the seal, opening the casket, and removing the curse tablet from the water inside. The curse tablet is destroyed by breaking up the slate with a hammer or suitable rock. A countercurse or *anti-defixio* is spoken as this is done, which may be something similar to:

As I remove this curse tablet from its casket and cursing water and destroy it completely, so may the curse it bound to [Name] be removed and destroyed in the same way.

The shattered shards of the slate tablet are finally discarded over a suitable natural space, large enough to ensure no two pieces accidentally come into contact with each other.

Curse wells in the Welsh Marches are also a popular place for people to leave curse rags, small lengths of fabric tied to trees alongside the chosen well. A curse rag is crafted by obtaining a small length of material from the person the curse is to be bound to. The rag is dipped into the waters of the curse well and tied to the branch of a tree close to the water source. As the rag progressively decays, the curse is bound tighter and tighter to the recipient until the rag falls from the tree and returns to nature, at which time the curse is fully bound. If a suitable length of fabric cannot be obtained, then a small length of natural fabric may be substituted. This rag must, at some time before its use, have come into contact with the intended recipient, either by coincidence or deliberately brought into contact with the recipient by the Adept. On occasions these substitute rags have been soaked in the urine of the intended recipient, touched with his or her blood or sweat, or subjected to other means of infusing it with the personal spirit of the recipient.

Whichever method has been employed, the curse is spoken as the rag is tied to the tree branch. The curse may be worded as the one described above, including the fundamental tenets of all curses, but in this case should include the wording:

As I bind this rag to this tree, so may my curse be bound to [Name]. As this rag decays, my curse will be bound tighter. As it finally returns to nature, may my curse increasingly smite [Name] until such time as [Name] remedies [his or her] wrongdoing.

CURSING OILS

The principle of using oils as carriers for curses is known worldwide and employed by a wide range of belief systems, including that of the Welsh Marches. Indigenous oils such as walnut and hazelnut are used either as carrier oils or as host oils. To create and use a carrier oil, the oil is first infused with botanicals, potentialized, and charged with a spoken curse and then diluted and brought into contact with the intended recipient to bind the curse. As a host oil it is sealed into a vessel along with a written curse or other *materia magica,* with the sealing of the vessel corresponding to the sealing or binding of the curse.

In this instance the most potent botanical used in an oil infusion is ivy. The binding nature of the ivy enhances the binding property of the curse, while its poisonous leaves and bark mitigate the menacing potential of the recipient ignoring the curse's intention. Here it is also worth noting that a good many poisonous botanicals like deadly nightshade and yew are used in the crafting of cursing agents.

Crafting and Using a Curse Oil

To create a curse oil using ivy the Adept will need:

- Freshly harvested ivy leaves
- Bottle or jar with a secure cap or cork
- Enough oil to fill the bottle

The crafting process is a simple one. As many ivy leaves as possible are pushed into the bottle or jar, leaving enough space for the oil. The oil is slightly warmed and then poured into the bottle, covering the leaves completely. The vessel is then securely sealed and placed in a warm, dark place for the infusion to macerate. After a minimum of one week, or up to three weeks if possible, the leaves are carefully removed from the vessel, leaving the infused oil behind. The leaves are then returned to the location from where they were harvested and placed on the ground with a thankful invocation, as we have seen above. The remaining oil is now infused with the ivy's virtues and attributes and may now be diluted to be used as a carrier oil for a curse or as a host oil used to contain a written curse. *Be aware that this oil is now poisonous!* and must be sealed and stored with this in mind. It is *not* to be taken *orally or applied directly to the skin!*

Before being used as a curse-carrying oil, or touch oil, the infused oil must be first diluted, potentialized, and charged with the individual curse it is intended to carry. To dilute the curse oil, mix one part of the curse oil with four parts of any pure, natural botanical oil. Once diluted, it is safe to use as instructed. The charged oil is then potentialized in

Fig. 15.4. Ivy macerating in the curse oil before being decanted into the blue cursing oil bottle. (See also color plate 19.)

the same way as we have seen above to energize both the natural oil and the botanical it is infused with. Once potentialized, the oil is then charged with the specific spell it has been created for.

To do this, the curse must be passed from the Adept to the carrier oil. This may be done by the Adept touching the oil with her finger or, alternatively, the Adept may employ her wand as a conduit, touching the oil with the tip of her living wand. In either case, the curse is spoken, slowly and gently. The curse itself is composed using the tenets defined above. When all these processes are complete, the carrier oil is sealed in a small vial until it is needed. The oil must be used as soon as possible following its charging and is bound to the recipient by dropping or touching a few drops of the curse oil on to the skin or hair of the recipient while repeating the curse exactly as it was spoken during the charging. The amount of oil that comes into contact with the recipient is not important as the same charge is held in every drop. Therefore, as long as contact is made between the oil and the recipient, the circuit is closed and the spell is bound.

As with other potions, an amount of the curse oil must be retained in case the curse needs to be reversed. This is done in the same way as explained above when the oil is again brought into contact with the recipient. Any remaining oil *must* be disposed of *safely* and not introduced into the household wastewater system.

As a host oil, the infused oil is used undiluted but will still need to be potentialized to energize the oil and the botanical within it. This again is done in the same way as explained above. In this case the infused oil is to be the host for a curse tablet or written curse to amplify the curse and imbue it with the energies and attributes of the infused oil. To achieve this, a measure of oil is poured into a suitable vessel, large enough to also contain the curse tablet or script. The composed curse is then inscribed onto the tablet (or written onto the curse script), charged, and then immersed in the host oil. The vessel is sealed with a sealing spell as described above. The curse remains in place for as long as the curse tablet remains sealed and immersed in the vessel of oil.

CURSING CAKES

Cursing cakes are often the most difficult method of casting and binding a curse as the recipient must eat the cake that has been charged with the curse to bind it to him or her. Cursing cakes are useful in cases where the Adept casting the curse is not in regular close contact with recipient of the curse.

Cursing cakes are most usually made as griddle cakes, that is, small individual cakes baked on a bakestone or iron griddle heated on top of an open fire. There are abundant recipes available for griddle cakes, so there is no need to explain the method of baking them here. The important difference, however, is that as the griddle cake bakes, the curse is recited slowly and quietly, baking it into the cake where it remains until the cake is eaten. If the Adept thinks it appropriate, botanicals used in curse magic such as rosemary, mint, sage, thyme, or parsley may be included in the cake mixture to infuse the attributes of the plant into the cake to enhance and energize the overall curse.

The curse is cast by allowing the recipient to eat the cake, thereby binding the curse to the recipient. Of course, if the curse is to be reversed or lifted, a further griddle cake will need to be crafted and potentialized with a curse-lifting invocation. The recipient will then need to eat the second cake to remove the curse. Similar griddle cakes are used by sin eaters as explained in chapter 8, the main difference being that sin eaters most often leave the cake on the chest of the deceased overnight to allow it to absorb the sins of the corpse. When the sin eater removes the cake and eats it, he takes upon himself the sins of the dead person and then works to absolve himself after the corpse has been buried.

When using botanicals, great care must be taken in correctly identifying and harvesting them and determining the quantities used. Curse cakes cannot be baked at the same time as other bakestone cakes, as elements of the curse may infuse anything cooked in near proximity. The curse cake must be eaten within the day it is baked, so careful planning is essential.

CURSE BOTTLES AND POUCHES

Curse bottles are probably the most common and well-known means of casting and binding curses, though similar devices are used in protective spells and intentions throughout the Welsh Marches. Sometimes known as witch bottles, they have been found in a large number of houses, farms, and other locations where they have been secretly deposited either as protective devices, guarding against unwanted witchcraft and maleficent spirits, or as a means of binding a curse to a place, its occupants, and/or their properties.

We discussed the use of witch bottles as apotropaic devices in chapters 6 and 14 and have seen a number of examples from a broad range of historical buildings within the Marches, so here we will focus on the crafting of curse bottles as a means of casting and binding a curse.

The purpose of sealing a curse into a curse bottle is that the curse remains in place as long as the curse tablet or script is sealed in the bottle. This is exactly the same as when a witch bottle is used as a protective deposit. The curse is composed in the same way as we have seen before, and in consideration of the tenets described above. The wording of the curse is then either written on a script, which may be a slip of paper or, more formally, a piece of parchment or silver birch tree bark, or, alternatively, inscribed on a small rectangle of lead sheet (a curse tablet) with a pointed scribe as the curse is spoken. In either case, the written curse is then folded or rolled and pushed into the bottle. The curse is again repeated as the bottle is closed with a cork or similar and sealed with sealing wax. Finally, the curse bottle is secreted securely so that it will not be accidentally broken or opened, in which case the curse would be lifted. Some Adepts have a large cache of curse bottles, each binding a different curse to its recipient.

Curse pouches fulfill the same purpose, only instead of sealing the curse tablet or script inside a bottle, the Adept seals it into a small pouch, tying it tightly and sealing the secure knot with sealing wax, as we have seen above. On occasion the Adept may choose to include appropriate botanicals and small personal items related to the recipient, such as nail and hair clippings and the like, to reinforce the connection between the curse and the recipient and increase the binding power.

CURSE STONES OR SLATES

Curses may also be cast and bound by using curse stones and curse slates. On some occasions these stones or slates are secreted in the homes or farm buildings of the recipient so that they remain close to the recipient and the influence and binding of the curse remains at its strongest.

In either case, the curse is composed as we have seen previously and then inscribed onto the stone or slate (the carrier) while repeatedly speaking the curse slowly and quietly. The curse stone or slate is then hidden in a place that is as close to the recipient as possible, within his or her house or in a garden next to the house. The inscribed curse then binds to the recipient on every occasion that he or she moves close to it, which maintains a renewed and constant binding as long as the curse stays in place. The curse is lifted by removing the hidden curse stone or slate and destroying it.

These devices are also used as pathway curses, by secreting them beside a path that is frequently taken by the recipient, thereby renewing the curse every time the recipient walks past it. On other occasions the curse stone or slate is used to cast and bind the curse by depositing it in a curse well, where the curse remains bound to its recipient for as long as it remains in the well.

Fig. 15.5. An inscribed curse stone along with a similar curse slate shard.

POPPETS

A poppet is a small doll representing the recipient of the curse. It may be crafted as a simple representation of the person, made from a few sticks bound together in the shape of a human form, or at the other extreme, it may be a skillfully crafted, detailed figure with the likeness of the recipient, even wearing miniature clothing sewn from fragments of the clothing of the targeted individual.

The purpose of the poppet is to create a spiritual connection between the doll and the recipient; once this is achieved, the poppet then serves as a conduit for casting and binding the curse projected by the Adept. After it is crafted, the poppet undergoes two rituals: the first to forge the link between it and the recipient and the second to project and bind the particular curse to the linked recipient. Once cast and bound, the curse remains effective as long as the poppet exists; consequently, to lift the curse the poppet must be destroyed. This being the case, the poppet is usually kept safely by the Adept for as long as the curse is to remain in place.

Remembering that the curse, as we have seen previously, is a means of reestablishing the universal balance of nature and is only effectively bound to one who is responsible for creating the original imbalance, it is common for the curse to inflict consequences upon its recipient, not as a means of retribution but as an incentive for the recipient to redress his or her malevolence. Quite often, this involves cursing the recipient to ill fortune, loss of fortune, poor health, the suffering of pain, or even, in extreme cases, death. The means of inflicting these consequences vary considerably, but all include the crafting of the poppet (sometimes known as a curse doll), the fixing of the poppet to the recipient, and finally the projecting and binding of the spell and its consequences. There are well-known legends of poppets being pierced with pins or blades to inflict pain in the same limb or organ of the recipient; others mention binding to restrict breathing or free movement, blindfolds or gouging the eyes to impair eyesight, and, in some extreme cases, cutting off the limbs of the poppet, burying it, or sealing it in a miniature coffin. The latter are designed to end the recipient's life if the malefaction is not rectified. Historical examples of each of these are spread around the various regional museums of the Welsh Marches.

As there are so many diverse forms of poppets, each crafted with a particular intent, we will confine our interest here to just two: the first a simple wooden form and the second a molded wax poppet, one of the most common forms of curse doll.

Simple Wooden Poppet

This simple form of poppet is crafted from a carefully selected branch formation found on a suitable donor tree. As with harvesting a branch for a wand, the branch formation for the poppet must be sought out on a donor tree that contains the necessary attributes to enhance the spell. To achieve this, all the considerations and tenets set out for the harvesting of a wand branch will apply in exactly the same way, but in this case, the Adept is not looking for a single branch but a group formation to represent the form of a person. This selection process must

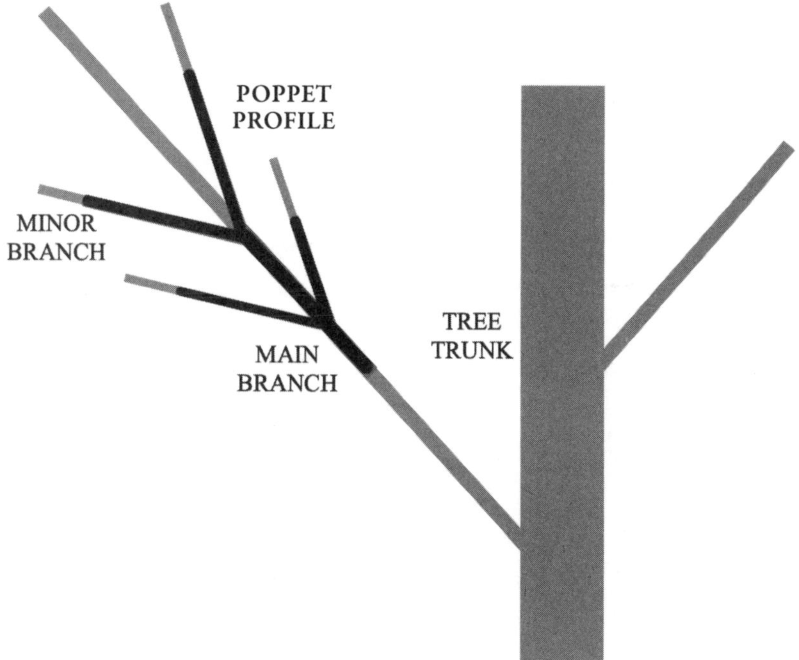

Fig. 15.6. Illustration of poppet formation identified on a tree.

not be hurried and may require repeated trips to the forest or woodland to find the most appropriate tree and formation.

Put simply, the formation should consist of a central branch with two suitably positioned off-shoots that represent the arms and a further two offshoots that represent the legs. Figure 15.6 may help in identifying a suitable formation, bearing in mind that the formation will need to be trimmed to form the resultant poppet.

Once the initial branch formation is harvested, it is trimmed so that it resembles a human form. The branch representing the body is allowed to extend above the "shoulders" of the form so that the head may be formed. Figure 15.7 shows a poppet with the head crafted from twine.

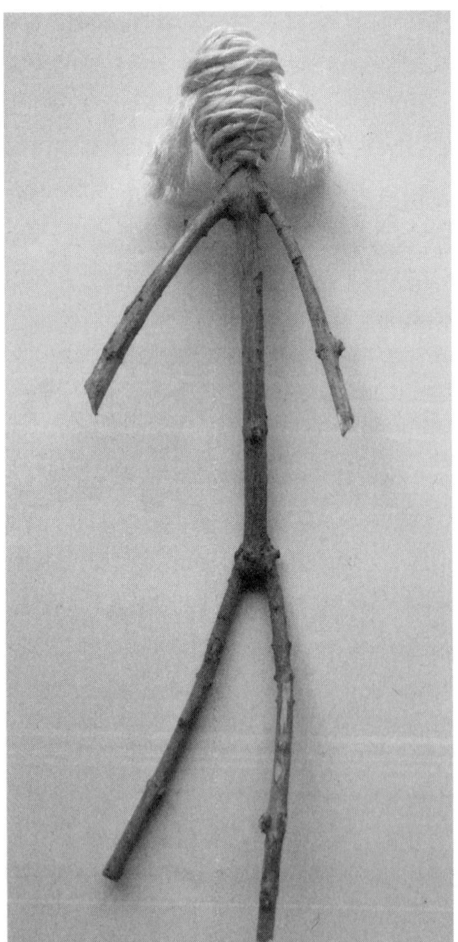

Fig. 15.7. A simple wooden poppet with a head made of wool twine.

At this point, as we shall see again later when we consider the wax poppet, we must focus on one of the main methods of tying the poppet to the recipient and that is by attaching items belonging to the recipient to the poppet, be it hair, nail clippings, teeth, or items owned by or worn by the individual targeted. This is the strongest way of creating the bond between the poppet and the recipient. Sometimes the poppet may be dressed in miniature dresses, smocks, or other attire made from fragments of the recipient's clothing, bedsheets, or any items previously worn or touched by the individual. In the case of the poppet in figure 15.7, strands of the recipient's hair have been interwoven with the twine of the head and hair. Having crafted the poppet, it is then tied to the intended recipient to create the spiritual conduit to cast and bind the curse. The tying is conducted within the protective circle, cast, closed, and sealed as we have seen previously. The tying item, be it hair (as in this case), nail clippings, or clothing, is attached to the poppet as a simple invocation is spoken. Such as:

> *By bonding this [name of item] to this effigy of [Name of recipient], so do I tie them each to the other and open the path to cast and bind my future intentions.*

Having tied the poppet to the recipient, it now becomes time to compose the curse itself. In doing this, the Adept takes into consideration all the tenets described previously. The curse may then be written on a script, simply by writing it on a small rectangle of paper or silver birch bark, as it is slowly and quietly repeated by the Adept.

The next stage is to attach the curse script to the poppet. It may be simply tied to the poppet, hidden within the poppet's clothing, or fixed by any other means to the curse doll. As it is being attached, the Adept will speak a binding spell such as:

> *As I fix this curse, that I recite again now [recite complete curse] to this effigy of [Name], so may it be bound to the person as it is bound to their image. May [Name] suffer the consequences as they have been spoken should [Name] fail to recant [his or her] ill actions and return the balance of nature in whole.*

As this ritual is spoken, any actions relating to the consequences are carried out, such as inserting pins or thorns into a particular limb, the eyes, and so on, as described in the curse. If it is a death curse, the poppet may be sealed in a miniature coffin or immersed in a vessel of water or whatever consequence the curse itself invokes. Importantly, the poppet is then hidden or stored in a place where it will not be interfered with but where it may still be retrieved should the curse need to be reversed.

Wax Poppet

A number of historical examples of wax poppets are housed in the regional museums of the Welsh Marches, some still enclosed in their miniature coffins. These poppets are more complex and more faithfully represent the recipient; however, this need not be a precise rendition but is normally intended as a broad characterization of the individual who has been targeted.

As with the wooden poppet, the first stage in creating the wax curse doll is the crafting of the doll itself. It is important that the wax poppet is crafted from natural, untreated beeswax and not paraffin wax or any other form of candle wax. The crafting is a delicate process that requires an amount of skill and patience as the doll is modeled by manipulation and not cast as other figurines may be. The wax is heated to a temperature that makes it malleable enough to mold by hand into the required shape but not to its melting point. This is done by heating the beeswax in a bain marie or double boiler, allowing for the precise control of the temperature as the wax heats. If the wax melts, it must be allowed to cool again until it is possible to manipulate it as a block, molding it and adding more wax as needed as the form is shaped into a miniature human body. Once a rough form is achieved it can be refined by carving with a sharp knife or by using a heated knife or spatula to craft the desired shape and details.

Having crafted an acceptable representation, it is then necessary to add to it a similar personal possession as we saw previously. Strands of the recipient's hair may be fixed to the wax of the head or other items sealed within the doll to tie it to the recipient. To enclose personal items

Fig. 15.8. A crude wax poppet with potential items to be used as inclusions. (See also color plate 20.)

within the poppet, an incursion is made with a heated blade where the heart of the poppet would be and the wax lifted to form a cavity. The size of the cavity created depends upon exactly what is to be inserted and is left for the creator to judge. Items commonly enclosed within the poppet to form a tie include: a lock of hair, nail clippings, teeth, or small possessions belonging to the recipient, like a ring, hair pin, or similar, all serving to tie the poppet to the intended individual. Once the item is safely secured within the poppet, the cavity is sealed either by folding back the flap of wax previously cut away and sealing it with a hot blade or by filling the remaining cavity with molten wax and allowing it to cool and harden. A similar tying invocation as we have seen above is recited as this ritual is done.

Following this, the Adept composes the curse in the same way as before, giving due consideration to the tenets already described, and crafts a curse tablet with a curse written on a paper script or the bark of a silver birch tree or inscribed on a small tablet of lead, copper, or slate. The curse tablet may be attached to the poppet or enclosed within the doll in the same way as the personal items we have described earlier. As the tablet is attached or enclosed within the doll, the same binding curse is chanted as we saw with the wooden poppet, binding the curse to the recipient via the poppet and prescribing the consequences of failing to comply. The wax poppet is then securely stored for as long as the curse is in place. If the curse is to be lifted or reversed, the wax poppet must be destroyed.

In some cases, rather than craft a complete doll effigy, the part of the body upon which the consequence of not fulfilling the command of the curse is tied may be crafted in isolation. Typically, a leg may be crafted if the consequence of ignoring the curse is an ailment of the leg; similarly, effigies of arms, heads, hands, feet, eyes, and most other parts of the body may be crafted and empowered in the same way.

Wax poppets may also be pierced with pins or blades and sometimes thorns to inflict pain if the curse is ignored by the recipient. Poppets crafted from other materials such as carved wood, carved root vegetables, and corn dollies may be tied and empowered in the same way.

To assist the neophyte, here follows a brief selection of various wordings for curses and the like, presented with the intention of inspiring the original compositions required by the Adept for her workings.

MALEDICTORY FORMULARIES OF THE DRUIDS AND WITCHES OF THE WELSH MARCHES

While it is always the prime responsibility of every Adept to compose his own curses, charms, and maledictions as he finds appropriate to his needs and circumstances, history provides us with a record of the words and phrases used by those individuals of the past who occupied themselves with the task of creating such execrations. By consulting these arcane texts, the Adept may enter the world of the ancient curse casters to his own benefit and education, even taking the more potent compositions and entwining them within his own.

It is not surprising that a good number of these antique curses were voiced by the Christian clergy, who frequently used their powerful offices to speak curses and maledictions from the security of their pulpits. This was not confined to the parish clergy but became systematic within the papist Church of Rome, which enthusiastically embraced the universal practice of curse casting, even including profane maledictions in their ordination liturgy for their nuns and bishops as well as the anathema or the rite of excommunication. The practice of throwing curses from the pulpit was enthusiastically encouraged by bishops and cardinals, who themselves used their holy office to cast "God's curse" upon their acolytes, quoting from the text of their Holy Bible.

Among "God's curses" were warnings uttered by priests, recorded in parish churches as late as 1851 CE, that sinners be struck blind and deaf or pained when sitting or standing or have their crops and goods taken from them.

Although many priests may have ignited the flames of fear within the hearts of their parishioners with their pulpit curses, it was those of the wisewoman, Witch, and Druid that instilled the most potent terror in their targets. It was also said that a curse cast by these powerful individuals bound the curse to their target with great effect, and history confirms that many countryfolk sought out their local wisewoman in preference to their priest, doctor, or pharmacist. Other curse casters included beggars, blacksmiths, millers, orphans, widows, and those approaching death. Each of these groups of curse casters had their own idiolect, sometimes referring to their trade and often relating to their role in the community. In the lexicon of curses below, many of which date from the nineteenth century, some of these are more obvious than others.

Let her beware the widow's curse.

The widow's curse will meet him at the threshold and wither him.

May the squeezing hand of death be upon you, now and forever.

May you never prosper.

May the first drop of water quench your thirst then may it boil in your bowels.

May the flesh rot off your bones.

May your flesh fall away and putrefy before your eyes.

May your limbs wither.

May the stench of your rotting body be too terrible for starving dogs.

May your family be cursed through all their generations for all time; this I pray.

Whoever has stolen my goods, I ask that you punish them. Whether it is a girl, a woman, or a man who stole.

Do not allow sleep or health to him who has done me wrong, whether man or woman, unless he reveals himself to me.

I commit whoever has stolen my goods may they burn if they do not return it.

Just as this stone is lifeless and cold, so may they be lifeless and cold.

Bring agony and a lingering death to this person who has wronged me and my kin.

May his crops rot in the ground and may he decay in the same manner.

Now poor health and penury shall befall this person for all his days and beyond.

Make his food decay in his field and putrefy in his mouth, until starvation slowly takes him.

If he walks, let his limbs be wracked with pain, if he rests, let his body be consumed by flame, if he eats, let his bowels rot and fall from his body. All this I wish with all my heart.

CURSE LIFTING, BREAKING, AND REMOVAL

Curses cast by an Adept may be lifted or even reversed if the circumstances demand it. In anticipation of such circumstances, the Adept makes provision when casting the original curse so that it may be removed at a later date. In cases where potions, oils, waters, and botanicals are used in projecting and binding curses, a portion of the original material is kept so that it may be used in the curse lifting. In other cases where the curse itself is retained by the Adept, such as in curses using poppets or sometimes curse bottles and curse tablets, the curse may be removed by simply destroying the curse vessel.

When the Adept wishes to lift a curse projected and bound by a potion or the like, the remaining portion of the elixir is removed from storage and reinvigorated by a ritual designed to return it to its initial state. In a similar ritual to the original casting and binding, the potion is potentialized once again and the lifting intention projected to the original recipient using an invocation such as:

> *I return to this [Name] the [potion, oil, etc.] to remove the binding of the original curse bound to [Name]. I now understand and accept that the malefaction that existed has been remedied and the balance of nature restored to its original state. I release [Name] from the binding of this curse in the hope that [Name] will live out the remainder of [his or her] lifetime with good intent and actions.*

The potion or item is then destroyed.

It is also within the Adept's abilities to lift or remove a curse projected and bound by another, if she feels the curse has been cast without sufficient reason or with ill intent or if the Adept believes the malefice has been remedied and the natural balance returned. Having said that, the Adept must be most certain that she is correct in her judgment of the situation as there are many obvious—some not so obvious—ramifications of lifting another Adept's curse.

The first thing the Adept must ensure is that he knows for certain all the facts surrounding the situation, reasons, circumstances, and people involved, along with the intended outcome and consequences of the curse and the methodology of its casting and binding. If he is firmly convinced that the curse must be lifted, then the method of doing so must be determined and the lifting spell carefully composed, bearing in mind that if the lifting is not justifiable or is misjudged and if an imbalance of nature is therefore not corrected, the curse may well be redirected quite justifiably toward the Adept, as his work will be against that which strives to retain the universal balance. But if as a result of all due consideration and research such a lifting of the curse is judged as necessary, then it may be effected as follows.

The simplest and most effective lifting of the curse may be undertaken if the method of casting the original curse is known. Ideally, this means the wording of the original spell, the materials or objects used in its creation, whether any remnant of the original curse potion or similar has been retained and, if so, where it may be located and what the consequences of the curse would be. If all or any of these are known their information must be woven into the wording composed to lift the curse. This is done by special ritual within a protective circle, a circle that must be scrupulously secured, as the risk of contamination by interference with the original malediction is particularly high. Within the protection of the circle the Adept crafts a purification elixir by crushing fresh mint leaves, rose petals, and lavender flowers in equal measure in a pestle and mortar, adding the bruised compound to a flask of moon-cleansed water and placing it aside on the working stone. Next, if the wording of the original curse is known, it is inscribed on a curse tablet or written of a script of paper or preferably silver birch bark. The curse tablet or script is then placed into a suitable bowl ready to be anointed with the cleansing elixir. The Adept then lights the working stone candle.

The bowl with the curse tablet is held up in the left hand, while with the other hand the Adept lifts the flask and passes its neck through the candle flame, purifying it as it passes. Lifting both vessels high, the Adept speaks the lifting spell as the water is poured over the curse tablet to cover it, purify it, and nullify the bound curse. This spell is composed by the Adept and may be similar to:

> *I am satisfied that, following my scrupulous and strict investigation, the curse written here is ill advised, misplaced, and, above all, unnecessary. I now focus my intention upon removing this curse written as [recite the original curse in total if it is*

known; if not, simply state that the exact wording of the curse is not known]. If the intention of this curse was, as it should have been, to reestablish the balance of nature, then let that be done. Whatever the consequences of ignoring this curse were, let them be undone and removed. In final recompense, let this curse be entirely unbound from [Name], and if it brings about the rebalancing of the natural state, then let this curse be redirected to the person who cast it.

The curse tablet is then removed from the bowl and destroyed, meaning, of course, that the curse cannot be redirected as the words of the ritual request. However, if the original curse was cast with deliberate ill intent, the original curse potion, tablet, or other materials still exist and remain in the original Adept's possession and will bind the curse to the Adept until they are destroyed. This again underscores the need for any curse to be well founded and bound with good intention; otherwise, the Adept must be prepared to suffer the consequences of her own malediction.

16
Elixirs of Love

The most frequently requested of all potions within witchcraft and Druidic lore is undoubtedly the love philter. As with other potions, the finished philter may be given as a drink or dropped onto the skin, clothing, or a possession that the recipient will come into contact with. When taken as a draught, it would commonly be referred to as a potion; if administered through skin contact, then it is called a philter.

In either case, the liquid is crafted according to the principle of the three cardinal elements contained within the selected botanicals, extracted either by maceration, distillation, or a combination of both. This therefore means that we must have a minimum of two constituent parts for extracting each cardinal: the effective botanical part (flower, leaf, or root) from which a cardinal is to be extracted and the carrier or solvent used both to extract the cardinal and as the carrier liquid, initially infused with the cardinal. When the three extracted cardinals are reunited, it becomes the active philter. There may be occasions when more than one botanical is used to combine the attributes of each to create a more powerful philter.

Here we will see just one example, but it must be remembered that other botanicals and solvents may be used; indeed, on some occasions philters also contain minerals, animal products, and sometimes the hair, nail trimmings, and so on of the targeted recipient. This example is crafted from the primrose and mead, a potent combination that creates a powerful philter to be administered through skin contact, though it may also be taken as a draught, given as two to three drops in a beaker of wine or similar.

PRIMROSE LOVE PHILTER

The primrose (*Primula vulgaris*) is one of the first flowers to appear in the spring, when its small yellow flowers provide the first flashes of color to an otherwise dull countryside.

It is most frequently found growing on embankments, by hedges, and beside pathways, where the small flowers grow in compact bunches of multiple flowerheads. As the first flower (*prima,* "first," *rosa,* "flower") of spring, its cardinals contain the vibrant energy and vitality of the burgeoning summer growth and its light-yellow color portrays it innocence and uncomplicated nature. Because primrose blossoms so early in the year, it is not influenced by other contradictory plants that appear later in the season and so it retains its purity. For these reasons, the primrose has always been associated with love, innocence, and fertility, three ideal virtues for a love philter.

Fig. 16.1. A cluster of wild primroses growing beside a pathway.

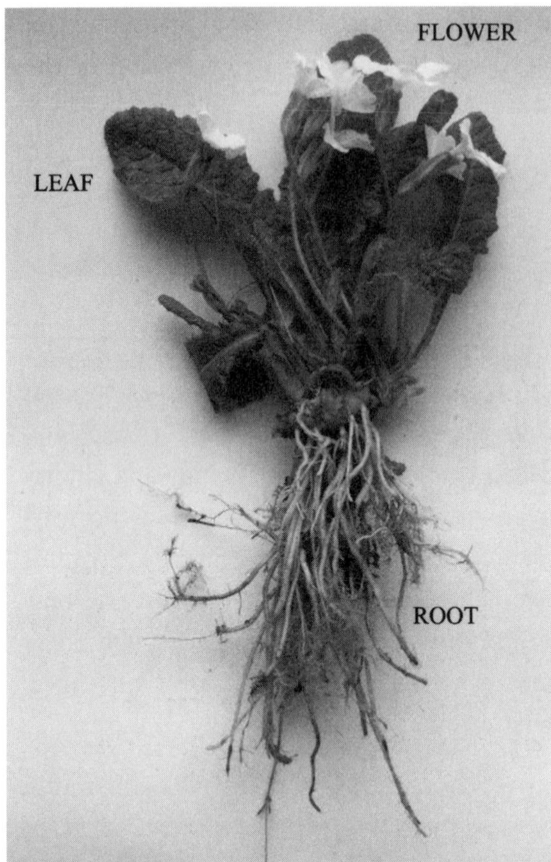

Fig. 16.2. An illustration of the parts of the primrose used in crafting the potion.

As with most other flowers, the primrose retains each of its cardinals in a separate section of its structure: the cardinal of the element earth is held in its roots, the cardinal of the element air is retained in its leaves, and the major cardinal of the element of the sun (fire) is held in the flower-head, where we also find the male and female reproductive organs of the plant. From this we can see that we must therefore harvest the entire plant when it is in full bloom to enable the extraction of all three cardinals.

To enable us to fully utilize all the virtues of the plant to best effect, it must be harvested at dawn, when there is still dew on the leaves and flowers. The donor plant is only harvested from an area where there is a substantial population of established primroses, so that due respect is shown to the balance of nature and there is no lasting impact on the conservation of the species.

When harvesting the primrose, a suitable invocation may be said by the Adept. Though this should be a personal composition of the individual Adept, a typical incantation may be:

> *I thank the whole of nature for its bounties and in particular for the primrose with its delicate virtues. I undertake to return all the elements of this primrose to its home soil when my work is complete.*

Having spoken this invocation, the Adept must harvest the primrose with great care, gently digging up the entire root system without damaging the flowerhead or leaves. The harvested plant must be used as soon as possible so that its virtues remain intact. Returning to the workshop, the Adept carefully washes the roots of the primrose to remove any remaining earth, at which point the plant is ready to be crafted into a philter.

The solvent liquid in this case is mead. It is equally important that the Adept crafts the mead he uses. Although there may be a variety of proprietary meads available, it is impossible to determine the exact provenance of any store-bought version, even if it is produced locally and the Adept knows the fermenter.

Mead is produced by fermenting honey and water using airborne yeast in a wholly natural process. The main constituent of mead is honey, and it must be harvested from a known source where the bees are not fed supplements or sugars but are free to gather pollen from the surrounding countryside. The importance of the relationship among Witches, Druids, and bees cannot be overstated. Much of the arcane magic imagery of the Druid tradition involves the use of the hexagon, the same six-sided shape that bees instinctively use to construct their wax honeycomb cells. There is a specific section of a bees' nest (only human-made bee homes are called hives) where they store the honey they have produced in hexagonal cells. This honey, sealed in individual wax cells, becomes the bees' winter food source, kept for the time when their usual flowers are no longer available. The Adept harvests this honey along with the wax honeycomb structure, both of which are used in a number of ritual activities.

When mixed with water, in the proportion of one part honey to two parts water, and allowed to stand in the open air, natural airborne yeast settles on the liquid and reacts with the sugars in the honey to produce alcohol. During the fermentation process, the mixture produces carbon dioxide and other by-products, which make the liquid look cloudy and effervesce as it is working. As the fermentation comes to an end and most of the natural sugars have been converted into alcohol, the liquid begins to clear, and this is the sign to siphon off the clear mead from the residual solids at the bottom of the fermentation vessel. The resultant mead is bottled and may be kept for as long as necessary, sometimes even years, before being used.

It is worth mentioning metheglyn, the other alcoholic drink associated with the Druidic tradition about which much has been recorded. This ritual drink is made by fermenting honey with a mixture of magical botanicals. Because of this it must never be used in crafting other potions or philters as the botanicals used will disproportionately influence the virtues of any potion it may be used for.

To craft the philter, the Adept will need:

- One freshly harvested primrose plant
- Three small bottles or jars that can be tightly sealed
- A good measure of mead (fermented in advance)

The working of crafting the love philter must be done within a protective circle and hexagon as detailed previously. This may either be an entire external protective circle or within a table-top protective circle, whichever suits the Adept's circumstances to best effect.

Assuming the protective circle has been suitably closed, sealed, and cleansed, the working begins by separating the three cardinal parts of the primrose: the root, the leaves, and the flowerheads. As mentioned previously, the primrose grows a number of flowerheads; there will typically be five or six on each stem with its root bulb. The flowerhead and leaves are best separated by squeezing the stem tightly between the forefinger and thumb, using the thumbnail to sever them. The root is then separated from the stem in the same way.

Fig. 16.3. The separated parts of the primrose prepared for the working.

The remaining stem and its root bulb is replanted in its original growing location where it may grow and bear more flowers. The flowerheads, leaves, and roots are then placed in separate bottles and generously covered with mead. Each bottle is sealed and left to macerate for a minimum of fourteen days, or longer if possible.

Fig. 16.4. Bottles containing the three individual cardinal parts macerating in mead.

If no other workings are planned, the circle is dispersed, and the working tools returned to their cache.

When the philter is required for use, assuming the cardinals have been macerating for a minimum of fourteen days, the three cardinals must be reunited to create the finished philter. This reuniting working must once again be conducted within a protective circle constructed and cleansed as detailed above.

To reunite the three cardinals, the Adept will need:

- Three bottles containing the macerated plant cardinals
- Fourth bottle to contain the finished philter

Inside the protective circle, the Adept begins the working, pouring a small amount of each of the three cardinal essences into the empty fourth vial. While doing so, the Adept must speak (or recite internally) a suitable self-composed incantation, such as:

> *In reuniting the three cardinals of the primrose, I call upon the profound elements of nature, channeled through my personal spirit to empower and energize this philter and give it the potential to secure the love and affection of any it may be directed to, whenever it may be needed.*

The philter vial is then sealed. Importantly, the philter must be used before sunrise of the day following its crafting.

The person who commissioned the philter must apply a small amount of it to the skin of the target recipient, thereby transferring the philter's virtues and binding properties to the recipient. A brief binding incantation must be spoken as the philter comes into contact with the skin, but this must be spoken softly so that the recipient does not hear it. The secrecy of the ritual is very important as it is imperative that the recipient believes he or she has formed the emotional bond and is not being forced or cajoled into an artificial relationship. The overall intention of the ritual is to promote the bonding of the individuals concerned by stimulating a permanent love and physical

Fig. 16.5. The three macerated cardinals and the fourth philter vial ready to receive the combined potion. (See also color plate 21.)

attraction between them. A typical binding incantation to be spoken quietly by the person applying the philter may be:

> *With this philter I bind you to me by magnifying your love and desire for me and me alone for the rest of our lives.*

This entire methodology may be used in the same way for either male or female recipients and is best applied by the subtlest means possible.

The philter may be crafted from a variety of botanicals, particularly if it is to be crafted at different seasons of the year. A seemingly obvious candidate for crafting the philter is the rose. Frequently associated with love and passion, the rose is a popular token of affection at Valentine's Day and on birthdays and the like. Surprisingly, however, it is not used in philters. Although wild rose or dog rose (*Rosa canina*) petals and buds are used in some formulas, any flower that grows on a bush is unsuitable for a philter. The main reason for this is that blossoms on a flowering shrub share all their leaves and roots, so unless the entire bush is used simultaneously, with all its flowers, leaves, and roots, the overall effect is diluted and the virtues are out of balance. As it is not practical to harvest a bush, only flowers or flowering herbs where the *whole* plant can be used will make a potent and focused philter. Other appropriate candidates for love philters are sweet violet (*Viola odorata*), wood anemone (*Anemone nemorosa*), and daisy (*Bellis perennis*).

Another important tenet in making a philter is that a portion of each separate cardinal essence (*not* the united philter) must be saved and stored for the future. These saved portions provide the only means of undoing the binding at any time in the future should it be desired or necessary. Releasing the philter's binding is achieved by uniting the retained three original cardinal essences in the same way as it is done for the binding working and discreetly reanointing the recipient while reciting a release invocation composed by the Adept. This may be:

> *With this philter I negate my previous binding, disengaging your love and desire for me and releasing you from my original intention, for as long as we both shall live.*

Again, this invocation must not be heard by the recipient. Any remaining philter essence should be returned to the location of the original flower it was made from.

ATTRACTIONS AND GLAMOURS

It is not always the case that someone wants to attract another person; often, it may be an object, like a new home, a change in circumstances, or even a new feeling, such as attracting happiness or increased energy. Obviously, none of these things can be attracted with a love philter or potion as many of these desires are not necessarily physical items or individuals and there is no way to "touch" the desired target, so a method of casting and binding the spell to a concept rather than an object or person must be employed.

Attraction working may be used to draw things or concepts to a person while glamours are workings used to instill a fascination between two individuals (different from instilling love with a philter), or to encourage friendship and bonding, even within a family or group. Fortunately, both intentions may be achieved through very similar workings, requiring the same magical devices and ritual.

Here, we will focus on an attraction working, within a protective circle, using a hook wand as its principal magical device. The hook wand is crafted from a specific branch conjunction where a smaller branch emerges from a larger one or where two similar-sized branches diverge. When seen in its natural state on a tree, the formation will appear as a V shape or checkmark formed by the branch junction. The schematic in figure 16.6 illustrates a potential hook wand formation on a tree.

The donor tree should be selected using the considerations detailed

Fig. 16.6. The location of a potential hook wand on a tree.

earlier and are exactly aligned with those used to select any other wand. The most appropriate tree species for attraction are the oak (due to its wisdom and longevity), the rowan (a tree of attraction, other than to Witches and sorcerers), and the sycamore (another tree of attraction and binding). Consideration may also be given to crafting an entwined hook wand, using ivy for its attribute for binding. As we have seen before, an

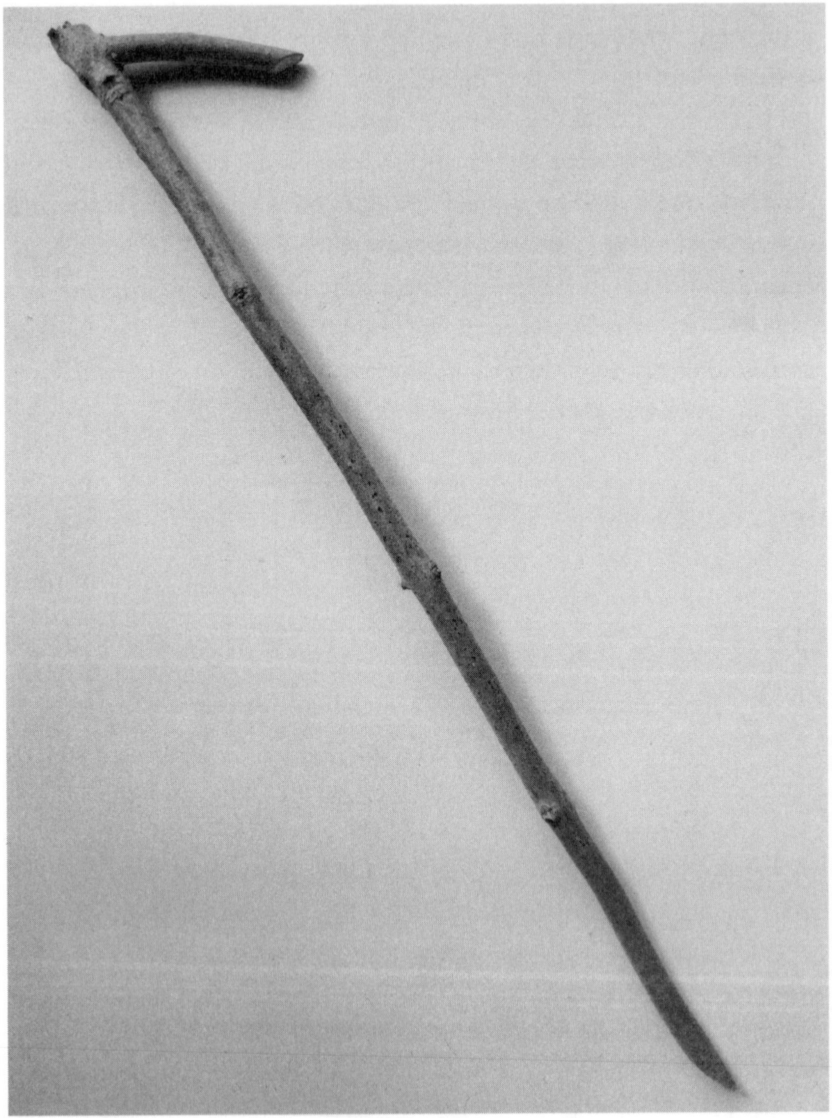

Fig. 16.7. A crafted hook wand.

invocation of thanksgiving is spoken as the branch is harvested, and any small twigs and leaves are trimmed and left at the foot of the donor tree.

Once the hook wand has been harvested, the Adept refines its shape in her workshop. The heel end of the wand, opposite the tip, is cut at a diagonal so that the maximum surface area of its core may be brought into contact with the Adept's palm when the spell is being cast and bound. Again, like all other living wands, the hook wand is crafted for a single specific purpose and must be used while all the living sap and vitality is still held within the branch.

Having crafted the form of the hook wand, it must now be potentialized, used for its desired purpose, and then returned to nature at the location where it was harvested. The hook wand is potentialized within a protective circle that has been closed, sealed, and cleansed. The working is done at the working stone, and as with other wands, it begins with the wand being energized and empowered. Energizing amplifies and liberates the wand's inherent attributes and vitality, while empowerment imbues the wand with the specific spiritual energies of the Adept, giving it the potential to project and bind the spell to its recipient or objective.

In this case, the Adept potentializes the hook wand by anointing it with a potion while speaking an invocation. The potion, which both cleanses the wand and elevates its spiritual energies, is crafted from a compound of mint, rosemary, violet, and gorse flower, each known for its cleansing and empowering virtues (see fig. 16.8 on page 264). The four botanicals are macerated in honey mead for a minimum of seven days, which further elevates their inherent energies and compounds them into a powerful potion.

Within the protective circle, the Adept begins the working by slowly and reverentially anointing the newly harvested hook wand with the potentializing potion, while slowly and quietly speaking an invocation of the Adept's own composition, which may be similar to:

> *Now that this wand has been harvested and thanks given has been spoken to its donor, I seek to free it of all unwanted influences and elevate its inherent energies and virtues so that it may aid me in my working.*

Fig. 16.8. Violet, mint leaves, rosemary, and gorse flowers prior to being macerated in mead. (See also color plate 22.)

This continues until such time that the Adept is confident that the wand is ready to be used in the attraction working. It then becomes important that the hook wand is used within as short a time as possible to utilize its maximum potential.

Again, within the protective circle and stood before the working stone, the Adept prepares for the attraction working by lighting two ritual candles, one at each side of the working stone, with the wand lying in between. Prior to the working, the Adept will have composed a suitable invocation, taking into consideration all the tenets described above. When suitably focused, the Adept raises the hook wand in both hands, dedicating it and his working to the universal forces of nature and concentrating his own personal spiritual energy upon the task at hand. The Adept then concentrates the energy of the invocation upon the center of the palm of the right hand where it is held at the boundary of the physical body, as we have seen before.

The hook wand is then held firmly in the right hand, using the diagonal cut of the wand's heel to maximize its contact with the Adept's palm. The wand is then moved in a hooking motion, attracting the targeted object, person, or circumstance toward the Adept. As this is done, the invocation composed for the working is spoken. Having recited the invocation three times, the wand is moved in three small circles, thus binding or tying the spell to the recipient. Having completed this, the hook wand is immediately broken, completing the binding and rendering the spell permanently bound, as the wand cannot be reused to lift it.

The same working can be used as a glamour working, where only the wording of the invocation need be changed.

APHRODISIAC, SEXUAL ELIXIR, AND AMATORY ESSENCE

The tradition of the Welsh Marches is very precise in its interpretation of its most effective sexual elixir, one that originated with the wisewomen and sorcerers of pre-Celtic Wales and its borderland and has been maintained by both Druids and Witches. Known in the native Welsh of the borderland as *canolbwyntiau carwriaethol,* this powerful amatory essence is crafted from violet, lavender, mint, and blackberries macerated and combined in an elixir of honey and short mead. Made in small amounts, the potion is very concentrated and typically diluted in wine, mead, or ale before it is given to drink. It is crafted by a complex method of extracting, magnifying, and reuniting the cardinals of each of the botanicals, but each plant's essence is kept separate until finally being combined to create the final elixir.

Understandably, this crafting of this elixir is one of the most complex in the tradition, involving, as it does, four different plants producing twelve discrete cardinals, each to be crafted individually. Before describing the process, we must first look at each of the botanicals being used and the reason each is included in what is literally the final quintessence: the fifth essence created from the original four.

- Wild sweet violet (*Viola odorata*) has distinctive heart-shaped leaves with blue-violet flowers that bloom from March to May. The violet is included in this potion to add a loving component to the elixir. The violet plant has the virtues of enduring love and romantic attachment. Its heart-shaped leaves underscore the plant's strong passionate attributes and fulfill an important role in a well-balanced amatory essence.
- Lavender (*Lavandula)* in its wild form grows as a small bush bearing clumps of individual flowerheads, each containing rows of small individual florets. Popular for its fragrance and protective virtues, it is also a sexually stimulating plant with the additional attributes of enhancing focus and concentration, empowering physical vitality, and heightening the mind's ability to be aroused by visual stimuli.
- Common mint (*Mentha spicata*) is also known as spearmint, lamb's mint, and mackerel mint. The mint plant brings its virtues of vitality, virility, and stamina to the elixir, helping create the balance between the physical and spiritual aspects of the philter.

Each of these botanicals brings its own virtues to the final elixir, helping create a potent but controllable energy, along with the vital and sustained stimulation necessary for an effective aphrodisiac. These three essential botanicals are eventually intermixed with the elixir's core essence crafted from blackberries macerated in wild honey and mead to create a potent and *puissant* philter.

Blackberries are an especially powerful sexual stimulant and, as with other berries and fruits, are used in isolation from the other elements of the plant. As with all other botanicals, their harvesting requires the same consideration of the plant's terroir, time of harvesting, and so on, but we do not need to separate its cardinals for it to be potentialized. All berries, fruits, nuts, and seeds are a fundamental part of the reproductive process of the individual botanical and carry the concentrated energies and virtues that enable the plant to reproduce. These reproductive energies are essential in any effective aphrodisiac. Even though the intended purpose of the aphrodisiac may not be reproduction, these energies are an imperative force in any sexual elixir.

Honey has a long and well-deserved association with love and sexual pursuit. Its virtues include its ability to promote feelings of love and affection as well as being a potent sexual stimulant. The idea of newlyweds having a honeymoon is believed to have originated in Wales, where traditionally the newly married couple would spend their first lunar month together eating copious amounts of honey to enhance their sexual potency and vitality, with the hope that their efforts would provide them with their first child. The moon part of honeymoon refers to the monthly cycle of the moon, it being the most apposite period for the couple's successful lovemaking and a period that covered a complete female reproductive cycle. Over time, the original meaning and very practical philosophy of the honeymoon has been lost, but the sexual potency of honey has not suffered the same fate.

The final component of the elixir is mead, a honey-based fermented drink that was the first alcoholic drink known to be available to the ancient Druids and cunning folk. Mead is made in two forms: long mead, a less potent version, similar to cider or perry and created as a "long" thirst-quenching drink like ale, and short mead, a more concentrated, wine-like drink, higher in alcohol than long mead. The short version is frequently used in arcane ritual and also forms the base for the medicoreligious libation metheglyn, where short mead is infused with herbs, flowers, barks, and other botanicals to add to its existing virtues. Short mead is the most common base for aphrodisiacs as, being borne from wild honey, it already contains its own attributes while also having the ability to amplify and enhance the attributes of anything that may be added to it.

The process of crafting the final elixir begins with the extraction, enhancement and reuniting of the three cardinals of the individual violet, lavender, and mint plants. As we have seen previously, this requires the harvesting of an entire plant of each species to retain their natural balance, even though the elixir will only be crafted in small volume. Each plant must be harvested complete with its flower, leaves, and root, as each contains its own cardinal. Care should be taken where individual plants grow together in communities, where their roots and stems may intertwine. In such cases, the harvested flower, leaves, and root must all come from the *same plant* and not include any parts of neighboring plants, even if they are of the same species. Each of the three cardinal parts of the harvested plant, its flowers, leaves, and root,

Fig. 16.9. Blackberries macerating in mead to create the host solution.

are separated and macerated separately in short mead, using the method described in detail above, resulting in the crafting of three cardinal essences for each plant, giving nine in total.

While this is being done, the harvested blackberries are macerated in a solution of equal parts of wild honey and short mead to extract their attributes, which become absorbed within the solution. Be aware, once again, that the blackberries are harvested alone, without the leaves or roots of the other botanicals, as the the berries' amatory virtues are most concentrated within the berries themselves. The maceration and extraction process takes a minimum of fourteen days, during which time the dense color of the berries migrates to the honey and mead solution. When complete, the honey or mead should be an intense purple-black color and the consistency of a syrup. When ready, the syrup is strained to remove any solids and stored in a vial until it is needed. Only a small amount of the syrup is needed to craft the final elixir; three to four teaspoons is sufficient as no more than a few drops of each united cardinal will be added to it during the final stage.

At this point, all the components of the sexual elixir should be ready for the final working: the three individual cardinals of the violet, the three individual cardinals of the lavender and the three individual cardinals of the mint, along with the vial containing the solution of blackberry, honey, and mead. The next stage is reuniting all these individual elements in the correct order and the ritual potentializing of the united elixir prior to its casting and binding.

The final reuniting ritual must take place as near as possible to the time the elixir is to be used and not more than four hours before being cast. The ritual is conducted at the working stone within a protective circle that has been closed, sealed, and cleansed, as previously described in chapter 12. The working stone is set, ready for the working. Figure 16.10 on page 270 illustrates the process of reuniting the cardinals and crafting the elixir.

First, the three cardinals of the violet are reunited within a single vial. Each cardinal is slowly poured into a fourth vial while the Adept speaks the incantation she has previously composed for the working. Only a small amount of each cardinal essence is required to create the

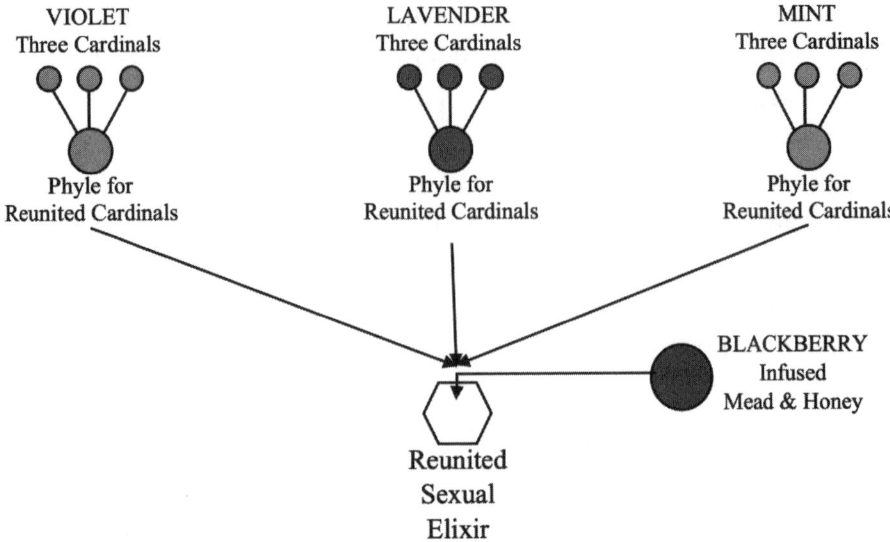

Fig. 16.10. A schematic illustrating the process of reuniting the cardinals in the host solution in order to craft the elixir.

reunited essence. The remaining liquids are filtered into separate clean bottles and carefully stored in case the working needs to be reversed at a later date. The solid matter that was filtered out, now considered a *caput mortem,* is assembled together and returned to the locality from where it was harvested with a brief incantation of thanks. This completes the reuniting of the cardinals of the violet and leaves the Adept with one vial containing the reunited cardinal essences, to be kept on the working stone for the completion of the working, and three bottles, each containing one of the separate cardinals of the violet.

This process in then repeated in exactly the same way for the three cardinals of the lavender and the three cardinals of the mint plant.

At this point, the Adept has before him three vials, each one containing the reunited cardinals of one of the plants used. He will also have decanted and stored the original nine separate cardinals in case they are needed at a later date, remembering that the working may only be lifted or reversed by using the same original cardinal that bound it in the first instance. Also on the working stone will be the vial containing the host solution of blackberry, honey, and mead, which had been crafted previously in preparation for the working. The intention of the final part of the working is to combine the three reunited cardinals with the host solution, thus creating the powerful synergy that empowers the sexual elixir.

With the vial containing the host solution open, the reunited cardinals of the violet are lifted by the Adept and three drops are slowly and precisely dropped into the host solution while the Adept speaks her invocation, which may be similar to:

> *With this begins the fashioning of the elixir and so with the combining of each of these essences may the whole be empowered and imbued with the vitality, energy, and passion gifted by these natural plant spirits. Let each add its own, and may the whole be greater than the parts it is composed from.*

Having completed this action for the violet, the same is done with the reunited essences of the lavender and, finally, the mint. When three drops of each essence have been dropped into the host solution, the vial is sealed and gently rocked to mix the elixir while the Adept speaks the final incantation, which may be similar to:

> *With all the elements combined and their energies entwined, each will magnify the other, and the whole will impart its vital energies to whomever may be bound by it.*

This completes the working. Now the Adept *must* ensure that the elixir is cast within the same day it is potentialized. The elixir may be given within a draught, where only *nine* drops within a glass or cup are the required amount. Alternatively, *three* drops may be placed upon the skin, or *nine* drops dissolved in an amatory bath. Whatever the means of absorption, a binding invocation must be spoken as it is administered, similar to:

> *I bind this philter, its powers, energies, and spirit, to [Name].*

The effect of the philter may be felt within an hour of its ingestion or application.

Fig. 16.11. The completed elixir in its blackberry host solution.

Finally, in considering the use of this working and sexual elixir, the Adept must be aware of whether the recipient(s) of the elixir are to use it voluntarily or if it is to be cast secretly, and due consideration must be given to the implications and ramifications of its method of use. As with the use of all potions and philters, it is the Adept's responsibility to ensure that his creations, be they material or spiritual, are only used safely and to the mutual benefit of those involved. As always, this is a profound and sacred responsibility and must not be undertaken lightly.

17
Other Spells and Workings: Attachment Nosegays and Druid's Breath

There are, of course, many more curses, spells, and other workings employed by the Witches and Druids that still dwell in the Welsh Marches, but having seen above the principal tenets and methods used in the majority of these workings, it will be possible for the Adept to compose, cast, and bind spells and intentions for her own use.

It is, however, useful to look at just two more techniques frequently employed that may be of great benefit, the first being the use of attachment nosegays and the other the secretive working known as Druid's breath or breath of the Druids (Welsh: *anadl y Derwydd*).

ATTACHMENT NOSEGAY

An attachment nosegay is a simple posey that has been assembled from carefully selected living botanicals, freshly harvested and tied together with twine that also holds in place an amulet or charm with appropriate sigils inscribed upon it. Though the reasons for employing these nosegays may be manifold, they are exclusively used as attraction devices, drawing good health, good fortune, wealth, and other benefits to the person who receives them and binding these good fortunes to him or her for as long as the nosegay survives. Many of these nosegays are therefore dried and cherished for many years, even gifted from generation to generation. This ancient tradition, dating back to pre-Roman times, may well be the predecessor to the bridal bouquet and the broader cultural tradition of gifting bunches of flowers as a goodwill gesture. Unusually, this traditional working is not confined to males presenting their nosegays to females but is used equally to attract good fortune to both genders and it is just as common for a Druid to gift an attachment nosegay to a fellow male and, in the same way, for a female Witch to present a similar nosegay to another female.

The crafting of an attachment nosegay is achieved through the same working as many of the other attraction workings we have seen above. First, an appropriate range of botanicals is decided upon, and then each specific individual plant is targeted using the same tenets we have seen previously. Having identified each plant, the particular plant part required is harvested, again using the same criterion we have employed previously. It is important that the botanicals are harvested as near to the time they are to be empowered as possible so that their individual vitality and potency is retained.

In the meantime, a suitable amulet is prepared with an appropriate invocation having been composed so that it may be immediately inscribed onto the amulet or charm.

The empowerment working is conducted inside a closed, sealed, and cleansed protective circle, prepared exactly as was described in chapter 12. At the working stone, the nosegay is secured with the twine and the amulet attached to complete the attachment nosegay. As the Adept secures the nosegay, he speaks the same invocation that he has inscribed on the amulet or charm along with an empowerment invocation of his choice. Once the nosegay has been securely tied, which concludes the empowerment working, the nosegay is ready to be presented and bound to its recipient. As the Adept offers the nosegay, he speaks a binding invocation that binds the energies of the gift to its recipient for as long as the nosegay survives, a binding that may be passed on to any subsequent descendant in the recipient's bloodline.

In reflecting upon the method and intention of this traditional working, it is not difficult to see how the existent practice of celebratory bouquets and flower giving, although much more informal, has descended from the same philosophy.

DRUID'S BREATH

The concept of Druid's breath, however, has no such surviving hereditary tradition. A working that is not entirely confined to the Druidic tradition, Druid's breath is both a method and means of casting a curse or beneficial intention and binding it to the recipient. It requires the crafting of a powder potion, compiled from a collection of specifically chosen botanicals, minerals, and/or animal products, which are chopped to a fine consistency or dust containing all the virtues and attributes of its combined ingredients.

In some very specific instances, the powder potion is burned to ash and ground to an even finer dust before it is cast and bound. The purpose of the burning is the same repurposing as we have seen before, killing the initial function of the material and repurposing it, dedicating it to its new purpose, eliminating any confusing elements, and focusing the burned compound solely upon its newly designated intention.

In both cases, whether the constituents are fresh or ash, the intention is cast by blowing or throwing the dust at the recipient, thereby binding the intention to the intended person, object, or place. This need not be done in a flamboyant, ritualized way—the dust may be surreptitiously sprinkled directly on the recipient's skin, whether an arm, back of the neck, or other location, without the recipient's knowledge. In the same way, the binding invocation may be softly spoken or whispered as the potion powder is cast, thereby achieving the same casting and binding without any formal or ritualized episode.

The reason the working is called the Druid's breath is that the potion powder is more formally cast by the Druid placing the powder on the palm of his hand or on a small wooden platter and then blowing it onto the recipient in a cloud of dust that lands upon the recipient as the Adept speaks the binding invocation. Some believed that the dust emanated directly from the Druid's body as a magical breath carrying its curse or spell within it.

As a first step, we shall craft a typical potion powder to be used in a banishing working; next we will make a burned powder to be used in a secretive attraction working and then, finally, we shall explore the means of casting and binding that epitomizes the Druid's breath technique.

CRAFTING AND CASTING POTION POWDERS

Typically, potion powders are not crafted from a single natural resource but contain a mixture of herbs, flowers, barks, earth, and animal products, such as bone, fur, feathers, and the like, all compounded into a single potion. Care is taken in selecting the appropriate elements so that their particular virtues and attributes are brought to the curse or spell. This means that these potion powders may be used to cast and bind particularly complex and meaningful intentions and frequently absorb powerful and potent energies that are bound to the recipient in an exceptionally influential way. In the same way, the means of casting and binding the curse or spell can be very dramatic and as such will be perceived as particularly powerful to those who cast and receive it as well as those who witness it.

In crafting both a banishing working and an attraction potion powder, consideration should be given to the fact that only small measures of each constituent will be needed, so care must be given to collecting *only* the amount intended to be used. Any surplus amounts should be returned to the earth with an invocation of thanks at a point before the potion powder is empowered.

Crafting a Banishing Working

In crafting a potion powder to be used as a banishing working, the same tenets and principles are used in identifying the constituent parts and harvesting and collecting them, the main difference being that in this case we select appropriate mineral earths and animal products as well as botanicals. For a banishing working, we would typically select rowan tree leaves, stinging nettle leaves, briar (blackberry) leaves, and holly bark. To these botanicals, we add gypsum earth as a forceful binding mineral, together with a goldfinch feather and a pinbone from a cockerel's leg to instill the potion with an element of movement and flight. The botanicals should be harvested in the same way as we have explained previously, with due consideration to their location, terroir, age, and so on. Gather the gypsum from local sources if available; if not, a similar binding mineral such as clay may be used as a substitute. The goldfinch feather may be gleaned from the ground near a nest location. In either case, the wild bird must not be disturbed or harmed. If a goldfinch cannot be identified, then a feather from most any small, attractive wild bird may be substituted. The cockerel bone may be obtained from the carcass of a bird that is to be used for food or one that has died from natural causes. *Do not harm or kill* any birds to create this potion; the killing will invalidate the potion completely because, as with the living botanicals, all animal products must be obtained from ethical sources to maintain the integrity of the working.

Once all the constituent parts have been gathered, they are finely chopped and mixed together to produce the potion powder. Contrary to its name, it is virtually impossible to chop the fresh ingredients into a powder, as many of them contain a small amount of moisture that will tend to produce a paste-like substance rather than a dry powder. The intention is to create a fine compound that can be easily dispersed by blowing on it. Once this has been achieved, little will be gained by continued chopping. Bear in mind that the potion must be cast as soon as possible once it has been crafted before it dries out and becomes a moisture-free powder. The completed potion powder is then poured into a small vessel and sealed until it is energized (potentialized) just prior to being cast.

The Adept energizes the potion powder by holding the vessel between her hands and speaking an empowerment invocation of her own composition, created specifically for its specific intention. This may be similar to:

In creating and empowering this potion, I manifest my intention to banish [Name] in body and spirit from this [Name of house, town, country] for the duration of [Name's] existence. In doing so, I release all bonds holding [Name] and sever any connections that may prevent [his or her] leaving or isolation.

Having been empowered, the potion must be cast as soon as possible. The means of casting and binding the potion are discussed below.

Crafting an Attraction Potion Powder

The burned potion powder is prepared in exactly the same way, but in this example, we are crafting an attraction potion, intended to create a binding fascination between the recipient and a named individual that goes beyond a physical lustful attraction of the aphrodisiac or sexual elixir we have seen previously. As this is a powerful, emotional bond, the Adept needs to use the most potent means available to him; burning the potion powder focuses its intention on the spiritual plane.

The attraction potion would typically be crafted from rose petals, forget-me-not flowerheads, lavender flowerheads, and purifying spearmint as the botanical agents; a small measure of earth from around a primrose root as mineral content; and ground swift eggshell from the animal kingdom. The component parts are first ground and then burned to ash before being ground once again to a fine powder and stored in a small vessel before it is empowered.

As before, the Adept empowers the potion by holding the vessel in both hands and speaking an empowerment invocation she has composed specifically for the intention. This may be similar to:

The energies of this potion have been reduced to their most intense by the burning of the components, redirecting their purpose and focusing them upon their newly designated intention. May they attract, fascinate, and bind [Name of recipient] to [Name of intended partner] in an unbreakable unity for the whole of their lives and may they live in mutual harmony for as long as they both shall live.

Again, the empowered potion must be cast as soon as possible after it has been empowered.

Casting Potion Powders

Casting both types of potion powders by the Druid's breath is done in the same way. A measure of the empowered potion powder is poured into the Adept's cupped palm and a suitable binding invocation is spoken. This may be similar to:

> *I bind this potion and its intent to [Name] by using the power of my breath and the energies contained within me. May it bind with all good intentions as it has done for those who have preceded me.*

Having spoken the invocation, the Adept blows across the potion powder so that it lands on the intended recipient. This working may be done as an open ritual with witnesses and a degree of dramatic effect or conducted secretly, with the invocation spoken quietly and the potion powder gently blown on to the recipient without his or her knowledge. Either way, it is equally effective.

Spells cast in such a way are usually done following prolonged consideration and not entered into lightly; in such cases, they are rarely reversed or lifted. If reversal is to be anticipated, a measure of the original potion powder is retained before empowerment as the spell can only be lifted through a reversal working using that powder. The details of a typical reversal working have been described in chapter 15.

These are just two of the many curses, spells, and workings that are available to the Adept, and reference may be made to the descriptions of the tenets and methods employed above so that he may craft, cast, and bind suitable invocations to match whatever circumstances he may encounter. In every case, it is imperative that the Adept selects the most appropriate workings, composes well-considered invocations, and casts and binds only those spells or curses he is confident are well suited, measured, and above all safe and well intended in every way.

18
Scattering the Workplace and Caching Apparatus

Whenever a working is completed, the Adept finds herself inside a sealed protective circle, surrounded by the apparatus and material she has been using. Because of the magical nature of the work, she cannot just simply walk away from the circle without due ritual. The three imperatives are that she reopen the protective circle in the correct manner and, if necessary, disassemble the physical items used to create it. She must also cleanse and store the tools and equipment she has been using and, finally, she must dispose of the materials that have been accumulated for the ritual working. Each of these tasks must be undertaken correctly, or the integrity of any future working may be jeopardized. All three of these tasks are cojoined into what is commonly called the scattering, being the correct dispersal of all the necessary equipment and materials used in the working.

REOPENING OF THE PROTECTIVE CIRCLE

If the Adept intends to return to the circle in the short term to complete the working or to begin another ritual, then the circle may be temporarily opened by simply brushing away the salt used to close the circle at the entry portal after he entered at the beginning of the working. The entrance portal may be resealed whenever the Adept wishes by repeating the original sealing ritual as he did when the circle was first cast. The decision as to whether the protective circle needs to be cleansed once again is left to the discretion of the individual Adept and his assessment of the situation at hand. If the protective circle is to be permanently dispersed, then it must be done in the correct manner, bearing in mind that it is best to cleanse the tools and equipment that have been used before the circle is opened, so that they may benefit from the protection of the circle during their individual cleansing.

The first step in dispersing the protective circle is to gather together the six containers holding the representations of the elements from the six points of the hexagon within the circle and pour their contents into a storage vessel pending their return to nature. The containers may then be cleaned and placed aside pending their return to the Adept's cache. At this point, the protective power of the circle is compromised, so the remaining tasks should be carried out as soon as possible. Assuming the various materials and tools have been cleansed and stored, the salt seal of the circle is brushed away, and once this is done, the circle is considered dispersed.

CLEANSING THE RITUAL EQUIPMENT AND TOOLS

Each ritual tool that has been assembled for the working must be individually cleansed so that it is immaculately clean when it is returned to the cache. Once the physical cleansing is complete, the items are spiritually cleansed by placing them all together on the working stone where the Adept, with both hands extended over the tools, speaks a cleansing invocation of her own composition, which may be similar to:

> *I thank these pieces, who have been part of me during this ritual, for their fair use and deft assistance in my workings and place them aside until their qualities are again needed in the works of nature.*

With this, the tools are wrapped in clean linen, tied securely, and set aside, ready to be returned to the Adept's cache.

Any remaining materials, whether botanical, mineral, or animal, must also be dispersed in the correct way. Having already collected together the six deposits representing the elements from the points of the hexagon within the circle and deposited them in a storage vessel, any remaining materials from the working stone are added to the same vessel. Any other containers, jars, or bottles are cleansed, as mentioned earlier, in preparation for their return to the cache. The combined contents of the storage vessel are then returned to nature in the correct manner. Here, we will take a moment to consider the rationale underpinning their method of return.

As we have seen previously, it is the resonating belief of both the ancient traditions of witchcraft and Druidic lore within the Welsh Marches that all natural materials are imbued with three essential components: their physical manifestation, their personal or individual spirit or energy, and their portion of the universal spirit or energy that we call the communal spirit or universal spirit (world spirit). At the moment of their harvesting, each material is permeated with each of these components in their living state, but as soon as they are harvested, their individual component parts begin to decay and disperse. Their physical manifestation begins its inevitable decay, their individual spirit or energy begins to slowly dissipate in a process of entropy, and their communal energy or spirit begins its slow return to the overall universal spirit where it is absorbed into the whole. This being the case, it becomes apparent that there is no purpose in retaining the materials or storing them for future use, as their potency degrades as they grow older when they lose their vitality and as their virtues and attributes decay.

However, it is important to acknowledge that other traditions, even within Wales and the borderland, do not subscribe to this understanding, and this is seen in its most simple form in comparing how wooden wands are used in the various traditions. In line with what has been described previously, the tradition explored here maintains that a wand only retains its potency during the short period following its harvesting and while it fully retains it vital energies within its sap and living spirit, all of which disperses and atrophies as the wood dries and eventually decays. Another theory contends that a wooden wand may absorb the spiritual energies that surround it as it grows older and concentrate them as it matures, thus becoming a more potent tool as it ages. Here we must state, however, that this later theory is incompatible with the overall philosophy of our living tradition, and we do not agree with it.

This being the case, the assembled residual materials from the completed workings are transported within their storage vessel to the natural location where they were originally harvested and returned to their natural habitat by the Adept, who does so with a suitable invocation of thanks, as we have seen previously.

In closing this discourse, we may see that the tradition described throughout this grimoire was developed from a long-standing history of belief and practice and that although our exploration here has been confined to the tradition of the region of the Welsh Marches, many other traditions exist and are equally as important in governing the lives of those who are dedicated to them.

England, Wales, and the borderland that have separated them for millennia all have a socioreligious background that has evolved in a tempestuous mixture of paganism, politics, conquest, and Christianity, both in its Catholic and Protestant forms, but two forms of paganism have survived as living belief systems that still flourish in today's modern world. This grimoire is the product of these two traditions, in the belief that ancient witchcraft and Druidic lore will continue to guide the beliefs of insightful individuals into the future.

Bibliography

Aubrey, John. *The Remaines of Gentilisme and Judaisme.* Reprint. London: W. Satchel, Peyton for the Folk-Lore Society, 1881. First published 1687.

Bodin, Jean. *De la Démonomanie des Sorciers.* Antwerp, Belgium: Chez Arnould Coninx, 1593.

James I, King of England. *Daemonologie, In Forme of a Dialogue, Divided into three Bookes: By the High and Mighty Prince, James &c.* Edinburgh, Scotland: Robert Walde-graue, 1597.

Kramer, Heinrich. *Malleus Maleficarum.* Speyer, Germany, 1486.

Puckle, Bertram S. "Wakes, Mutes, Wailers, Sin-Eating, Totemism, Death-"Taxes," chap. 4 in *Funeral Customs: Their Origin and Development.* London: T. Werner Laurie, 1926.

Scot, Reginald. *The Discoverie of Witchcraft.* Reprint. London: Elliot Stsock, 1886. First published 1584.

Sinclair, Catherine. *Hill and Valley: Or, Hours in England and Wales.* Edinburgh, Scotland: Robert Carter, 1838.

Vaughan, Thomas. *Coelum Terrae: The Magician's Heavenly Chaos.* Reprint. Whitefish, Mon.: Kessinger, 2010. First published 1560.

Index

Page references in *italics* indicate illustrations.
Numbers in *italics* preceded by *pl.* refer to color insert plate numbers.

Act Against Conjurations, An (1563), 52
adder stones, *pl. 5,* 84, *84*
Adepts. *See also* Druidic tradition; Witches
  learning period of, 188–89
  tools and equipment of, 180–87, 280–83
  workplaces of, 170–80, 280–83
Age of the Saints, 122
Agricola, General, 121
alabaster, *84,* 186
alchemy, 7, 17
alewives, defined, 64
Alexandrian Wicca, 158–59
amatory essence, 265–72
amulets, 194, 196–98
  crafting and empowering, 197–98
Andrews, Ian, 97
Anglesey, 120
animal bones, in witchcraft, *82*
animals and animal parts, in rituals, 82–83, *82,* 186
anima mundi, 167
aphrodisiacs, 265–72
apotropaic devices, 194–208. *See also* protective devices
  defined, 3, 19, 194
  terminology and interpretation for, 19–22
Archer, Rebecca, 144
Arundel, Thomas, 35
"as above, so below," 17
attachment nosegays, 273–75
attractions, 260–65
  attraction potion powder, 278–79
  defined, 261
Aubrey, John, 133
Avebury, 117

banishing working, crafting and using, 276–78
bees, and Witches and Druids, 255
Bible
  Gutenberg Bible, 38–39
  King James version, 47–49
blackberries, 266–67, *268*
Black Hound of Destiny, 138
Black Monk, 7, 149

blacksmiths, and magic, 67, 70
Bodin, Jean, 40–41
"Book of Spells of the Welsh Borderland, The," 162–283
boots, in witchcraft, 81, *81*
botanicals, in rituals, 182–85
bottles, 181, 237–38
Boudica, 121
bowls, 181
Bracken, Brendan, 149
Brown, Dan, 146
Buckland, Raymond, 159
burn marks, *pl. 17,* 76–77, 98–99, *100*

Caesar, Augustus, 119
Caesar, Julius, 117–18
cakes, cursing, 236–37
  reversing the curse, 237
candles, 181
canolbwyntiau carwriaethol, 265
Caratacus, 121
Cardano, Gerolamo, 141
cardinals, 183
Carnegie, Katherine, 148
caskets, 181, 228
casting a curse, 209–51
  prevalence in Welsh Marches, 60
  summary of steps, 217
  two categories of, 210
castles, in Welsh Marches, 12
Catherine of Aragon, 92
Catholic Church
  curses in, 33–34, 247
  and post-Roman Britain, 122
  and witchcraft, 32–35
cats, mummified, in Ludlow, 92–94, *93*
cattle-blinding incident (Ireland), 137–38
caul, in witchcraft, 83
Cecil, William, 142
Celt, meaning of term, 119
Celtic Christianity, 123, 125
Charles II, 54, 104, 113, 144
charm bracelets, 17, 196
charms, written, 194–98
  defined, 194–95
  in witch bottle, *pl. 18*
Child, Robert, 143–44
chimney, 71, 200
Christianity
  becomes religion of Rome, 118–19
  Celtic, 123, 125
  and charms, 33, 195–96
  Christian curses, 78, 247
  and curses, 157
  and Druid tradition, 155–56
  Eucharist and sin eating, 136
  Jesus Christ as sin eater, 134
  King James Bible and, 48–49
  in medieval Britain, 122
  witchcraft and, 32–59
Chrome Yellow (Huxley), 150
Church of England, formation of, 35
circle. *See* protective circle
Claudius, invasion of Britain, 118
cleansing ritual equipment and tools, 281–83
Cochrane, Robert, 159
Cochrane's Craft, 159
Coelum Terrae (Vaughan), 49–50, *49,* 144
common mint, 266
communal living, in period homes, 70
conjurors, defined, 63
Constable, Katherine, 143
Constantine, Emperor, 118–19
constituents of humankind (three), 166–69, *169,* 182–83, 188, 282
  bringing them together, 191–93

Consumer Protection from Unfair Trading Regulations, 59
convergence points, 177–78, *177–78,* 191–93, *192*
Cor Tewdws, 124–25
countercurse, defined, 21
Covenanters of Scotland, 54
COVID-19, and research for this book, 5–6
crafting components, 181–86
Crowley, Aleister, 147–48, 159
crucible, 180
crucifix, 17, 19
crystalline, 186
cunning folk, 6, 13, 15, 62, 67. *See also* Druidic tradition; witchcraft; Witches
  parallel development with Druidic tradition, 117
curse bottles, 237–38
curse doll, *pl. 7. See also* poppets, for witchcraft
curse lifting, 248–51
  removing a curse cast by another, 249–50
curse pouches, 238
curse rags, 233
curses, 4, *5*
  casting and lifting, 209–51
  Christianity and, 33–34, 157
  defined, 20–21
  desired outcome of, 214
  devices for protection against, 78, 194–208
  duration, 214
  effectiveness of, 78–79
  five elements of, 213–14
  lifting, breaking, and removal of, 248–51
  link for, 214
  maledictory formulas, 246–48
  as means of rebalancing nature, 211, 213, 240
  pathway curses, 239
  projection of, 216–18
  protection from, 78
  and punishment, 212–13
  reasons for casting, 210–14
  recipient, 213
  sample curses, 247–48
  on silver birch bark, 4
  three principles of, 211
  wording of, 246–48
curse slates, 238–39
curse stones, 238–39
curse tablets, lead curse tablet, 129–30
curse wells, 187, 239
cursing cakes, 236–37
  reversing the curse, 237
cursing oils, 233–36
cursing wands. *See* wands, cursing
cursing waters. *See* waters, cursing
cursing wells, 228

Daemonalogie (King James), 44–47, *47*
daemons/daemonology, daemons operate under control of God theory, 45
daemon traps, 76, 104
Dafydd ap Richard, 104
daisy, 260
daisy wheel, 75–76, *75, 102*
Darwinian theory, 168
David, St., 122–23
Da Vinci Code, The (Brown), 146
Ddu, Bedo, 140
dead cake, 132

Dee, John, 7, 140–43
De Heretico Comburendo, 35
De la Démonomanie des Sorciers, 40–41, *41*
depositional ritual for protective devices, 207
disassociation, 192–93
Discoverie of Witchcraft, The (Scot), 41–44, *42,* 137–38
Dog of Darkness, 138
Dolgorouky, Olga Sergeivna, 150
doll, for witchcraft, 80–81, *80. See also* poppets, for witchcraft
  at Hereford, *88–89*
  witch's coffin with, 89, *89*
doors, as vulnerable points, 70–71
Druidic earth sigil, *26*
Druidic history
  early history, 117
  and Romans, 117–25
Druidic places, 126–31
  Rotherwas serpent, 127–29
  Walton Basin, 126–27
Druidic sigils, *26, 27*
Druidic tradition, 164–65. *See also* Druidic tradition and witchcraft
  acts for benefit of the world, 164
  becoming a Druid, 188–89
  current non-authentic versions, 153–54
  direct association with nature, 135
  Druidic "university," 124
  Druids of the Welsh Marches, 116–31
  early history, 117
  fundamental belief that all are inseparable parts of nature, 135, 163–64, 223
  intentions in, 209–10
  legacy of, 156
  nineteenth century romantic version of, 153–54
  no gods in, 135, 155, 163–67
  occult practitioners of Welsh Marches chart, *65*
  origins of, 116
  parallel development with cunning folk, 117
  reputation for memory and learning, 118
  true Druidic tradition, 154–56
Druidic tradition and witchcraft
  finding harmony between the two traditions, 163–69
  principal differences, 163–69
Druid's breath, 275–76
Dwarf's Hill, 129

Edward I, 12
Edward IV, 12–13, 92
eglwys, defined, 123
elements, in rituals, 191–93, *192*
Elien, St., 227–28
elixir, purification, 250
elixir, sexual. *See* sexual elixir
elixirs of love, 252–72
Elizabeth I, Queen, 52–53
  and John Dee, 141–42
Enochian language, 142
equipment, ritual, 180–81. *See also* protective devices; workplace
essences, world, 27–28
eternity sigil, *29*
Evans, Professor, 133–34
evil, 37, 210
evil eye, 137. *See also* eye biters
evolution, 168
eye biters, 137–38

familiars, 51
  defined, 21–22
Farchogor Illtud, 124
fawr, defined, 123
Ffynnon Elien, 227–28
Fian, Dr., 46–47
fireplace, 200
  as vulnerable point, 71
focus, inner, 192
folk medicine, and magic, 15
foundation sacrifices, 73
Fraudulent Mediums Act 1951, 59
Fromond, Jane, 143
funeral biscuit, 132

Gallic Wars, 117–18
Gardner, Gerald Brosseau, 158
Garnerian Wicca, 158
George, Lloyd, 149
George II, King, 59
Germain, St., 124
Gildas the Wise, 125
glamour, 261, 265
goblet, 180
God, 36–37, 58
  and daemons, 45
  nonexistence of, 135, 155, 164–65
Golden Dawn, Hermetic Order of the, 147–48
gossip's bowl, 133
Great God Pan, The (Machen), 145
Great Scottish Witch Hunt of 1597, 49
Grey, Lady Jane, 52
grimoire of the Welsh Marches, 161–283
Gutenberg Bible, 38–39
Gwen ferch Ellis, 56–57

Hammer of Witches, 39–40
hanging loop, functions of, 30
harmony, perfect, 168–69
harvesting plants, 185
Hedge Witch, 157
Henry VIII, 35, 50, 52
Herbert, William, 95
Hereford Museum, *pl. 6,* 87–91, *87*
hexafoil, 75–76, *75*
hexagon
  describing the, 171–78
  importance of, 177
  marking stations of the, 174–78, *174–78*
  meaning of, 76
  and six points of convergence, 177
  symbolism of, 27
hexagon of harmony of the bee, 27, *27–29*
Hobbit, The (Tolkien), 131
Hogg, Amy, 145–46
Holy Grail, 146
Holy Inquisition, 34–35
homeopathy, 16
homes, vulnerable points of, 70–71
honey, 255–56
  association with love, 267
hook wand, 261–65
hook wand potion, *pl. 22*
Hopkins, Matthew, 53
horses
  horse skulls, 74
  magical function of, 74
horseshoe, as protective device, 68–70
Howlett, William, 134
Hudleston, Dorothy Purefoy, 146
humankind, three constituents of, 166–69, 182–83, 188, 191–93, 282
Huxley, Aldous, 150

icons, in Catholicism and witchcraft, 33
Illtud, St., 122–25
image magic, 16–17
images, in Catholicism and witchcraft, 33
imbalance, correcting, 211, 213, 240
inchaunters, defined, 194
individual and whole, *29*
instincts, two fundamental, 166
Institoris, Henricus, 39–40
intentions, 216
  in Druidic tradition, 209–10
  rightful reason for casting, 210–13
interpretation, and protective devices, 19–22
invocations, 189–90, 190
Ireland, west, living in, 5
Irish cattle-blinding incident, 137–38
iron, in magic, 69–70
ivy, *pl. 19*
  in cursing oils, 234, *235*

James I, King, 47–49, 53
  and the *Daemonologie,* 44–47
Jessup, Alicia, 104–15
Jesus Christ, as sin eater, 134
Jones, George Cecil, 147–48

Kelley, Edward, 142
"killing" protective objects, 72–73
King, Stephen, 145
King James Bible, 47–49
kitchens, as gathering place, 99–101
Kramer, Heinrich, 39–40

lamella, 196
language, in invocations, 190
Lanyon, Emma-Kate, 93
lavender, 266
Law of Contact, 16
Law of Contagion, 16
Law of Correspondence, 16–17
Law of Similarity, 16–17
Law of Sympathy, 16
libations, in workings, 187
"like produces like," 16
living wands, 219–26
  crafting and using, 220–26
  harvesting a wand branch, 224
  potentializing, 226
  returning them to nature, 226
  selecting a donor tree, 220–23
  using the wand, 224–26
Llacaiach Fawr, 104–15, *105*
  burn marks at, *pl. 17,* 106, *108, 109*
  carved cross at, *110*
  manor, *pl. 14*
  Marian mark at, *106, 111, 113*
  mesh marks at, *107*
  shoes discovered at, *112*
  spaces in, *pl. 15, 105, 107, 109–13*
  St. Andrew's Cross at, 114, *114*
llan, defined, 123–24
Llanwit Major, 124
Lord of the Rings (Tolkien), 131
love philters, 252–72
  primrose love philter, 253–60
luck, defined, 19–20
Ludlow, 91
Ludlow Castle, *pl. 11,* 91–92, *93*
Ludlow Museum, *pl. 10,* 91–94, *92*
Lydney Park Estate, 129–31

Mabinogion, 97
Macbeth (Shakespeare), 157
Machen, Arthur, 145–47

magic. *See also* Druidic tradition; witchcraft
black magic, 61
circumstances for use of, 14
defined, 14, 20
and folk medicine, 15
history of, 15–16
image magic, 16–17
indispensable role for countryfolk, 15
principles of, 14–18
relationship to scientific world, 14–15
transference magic, 18
uses of, 15
white magic, 61
maledictory formulas, 246–48
malefice, defined, 61, 63
Malleus Maleficarum, 39–40, *40*
manor houses of the Welsh Marches, 94–115
Marches law, 12
Margaret ferch Richard, 57
Marian mark, 76
defined, 104
at Llancaiach Fawr, *pl. 16*
Mary I, 34–35, 52
Mary Queen of Scots, 52–53
mead, 267–68
production of, 255
metheglyn, 187, 256, 267
minerals, in rituals, 186
mole's feet, *82*
Mona, massacre of Druids on, 119–21
moon sigil, *27*
Morey, Robert, 144
Morgan, Evan Frederick, 7, 148–50
Munslow, Richard, 134

National Museum Wales, 3
artifacts of, 79–87
natural selection, 168
nature
belief that humankind lives in nature, 163–64, 223
as good, 166
Neo-Druidism, 155
Newes from Scotland (King James), 45, 46
New Forest Coven, 157–58
Nodens, 129–30
Normans, invasion of Welsh Marches by, 10–12
North Berwick witch trials, 44–45
Noscere, Volo, 147–48

oak, 262
occult practitioners of Welsh Marches, chart, *65*. *See also* Druidic tradition; witchcraft; Witches
Offa, King, 10
Offa's Dyke, 10
oils, cursing, 233–36, *235*
crafting and using, 234–36
reversing the curse, 236
Ordovices, 121
original sin, 156
outdoor workspace
aligning, 172–73, *173*
finding and creating an, 171–79
overlooking, 137

palm, 225
as projection point, 216
paper birch, 4
pathway curses, 239
Paulinus, Gaius Suetonius, 120
personal spirit, 167, 282
pewter, use of, 23

physical manifestation, 166–67, 282
Picard II, Roger, 95
Picard family, 95
pilgrimage, 17
plants, 182–85
  annual life cycle of, 184
  environment and orientation of, 184–85
  maturity of, 184
  time of day to harvest, 185
poppets, for witchcraft, 17, 80–81, 240–46
  defined, 240
  donor tree for, 241–42, *241*
  reversing the curse, 246
  simple wooden, 241–44, *242*
  wax poppet, 244–46, *245*
positive thinking, 69
possession, daemonic, 21
potion powders, crafting and casting, 276–79
pouches, curse, 238
preparation of the workplace, 170–81
Prichard, Edward, 94, 104, 113
  ghost of, 114
primrose love philter, *pl. 21,* 253–60, *254, 257, 259*
  crafting, 256
primroses, *253*
  harvesting, 255
  parts used in love philter, *254*
printing revolution, 38–39
projection, of curses, 216–18
projection point, 216
protective circle, *179*
  casting on the working stone, 179–80
  casting the circle and describing the hexagon, 171–76
  centering, 171–72, *172*
  describing the, 173, *173*
  external protective, 189
  preparing the, 191
  reopening the, 280–81
protective deposits, 70–72
protective devices, *pl. 9,* 194–208
  botanicals as, 72
  collection of, found in Hereford, 90, *90*
  crafting of, 200–201
  defined, 194
  deposition of, 200–201, *205,* 207
  empowerment of, 200–201
  four steps in home protection, 200–201
  horseshoe, 68–70
  "killing" the objects, 72–73
  reason for, 78
  selection of, 200–201
  terminology and interpretation for, 19–22
protective spells, 207–8
Protestant Church, and witchcraft, 35–37
publications regarding witchcraft, 37–50
Puckle, Bertram S., 133–34
punishment, not a reason for curses, 212–13

quartz, fire-split, 186

rag offerings, *85*
Red Book of Hergest, 96–97
relics, veneration of, 33
religious syncretism, 155
Remaines of Gentilisme and Judaisme (Aubrey), 133

repurposing items for magic, 199–200, 275
research for this book, and COVID-19, 5–6
rheibes, defined, 62
rheibwr, defined, 62
Rhodri the Great, 141
Rhydderch ap Evan, 57–58
Rider-Waite tarot deck, 146
ritual belt, 181
ritual burners, 181
ritual tools, 180–81
  cleansing, 281–83
Romans
  end of British occupation, 122
  invasion of Britain, 117–22
  misinterpretation of Druids, 119, 135–36
roses, not suitable for love philters, 259–60
Rotherwas serpent, 127–29
rowan, 262
Rowton Heath, Battle of, 143
Rule of Three, 210–11
Ruperra Castle, 150

Sacred Oak Groves, 135
Samson of Dol, 124–25
Sanders, Ales, 158
Sanders, Maxine, 158
scattering the workplace and caching apparatus, 280–83
Scire, 158
Scot, Reginald, 41–44, 137–38
Scott, Walter, 58
Scottish Witchcraft Act of 1563, 52–53
Scottish Witchcraft Act of 1649, 54
scowles, 129
Seax-Wica, 159
Secret Glory, The (Machen), 146
Senicianus, 130
sexual elixir, *272*. *See also* love philters
  crafting, 265–72
  reuniting cardinals for, *270*
shadow, defined, 25
Shakespeare, William, 157
shoes, in witchcraft, 81, *81, 91*
Shropshire amulet, *pl. 2, pl. 3*
Shropshire farmhouse findings, 2–5, *5*
  amulet, *24,* 25–31, *26–31*
  interpreting, 23–31
sicut regale, defined, 12
sigils
  in Shropshire amulet, 25–31
  of witch marks, 75
Silurist, the, 97
Silvanius, 130
silver birch bark, *pl. 1,* 4
sin, concept of sin arriving in Britain, 133
Sinclair, Catherine, 134
sin eaters, 132–36
  function of, 132
  last surviving sin eater, 134
slates, curse, 238–39, *239*
Snakestones, 84
spells
  casting and lifting, 209–51
  lifting spells, 237, 239–40, 246, 248–51
  protective, 207–8
spirit, personal, 167
spirit, universal, 167
spirit hunters, 138
spoon and blade, 180
stave of power, 30
St. Christopher image, 17, 19, 196

St. Elien's Well, 227–28
steward's attica, defined, 104
St. Fagans National Museum of History, 80–87
stone circles, 178–79
Stonehenge, 117
stones, curse, 238–39
Sturt, Lois Ina, 150
sun sigil, *27*
superstition, defined, 19
sweet violet, 260
sycamore, 262

Tacitus, on Mona massacre, 120–21
talismans, 194, 196–98, *198*
target point, of curses, 216
terminology, of protective devices, 19–22
Thelema, 159
thorn branch, as protective device, 4
Threefold Law, 210–11
Tiberius, makes Druidic practice illegal, 119
Tolkien, J. R. R., 130–31
Tompson, Agnis, 46
tools, ritual, 180–81, 281–83
torture, used to extract accused Witch confessions, 56
transference magic, 18
transubstantiation, 136
Tredegar Park, 148–49
trees, selecting a donor tree for a living wand, 220–23
Tretower Court and Castle, 94–103, *95, 99*
  castle ruins, *pl. 13, 96*
  daisy wheel mark at, 102, *102*
  gifted to the Vaughans, 144–45
  manor house, *pl. 12*
  manor house interior, *98, 100, 103*
  taper marks at, 98–99, *100, 101*
trwysog, defined, 12
twilight dog, 138

universal spirit, 167

Vaughan, Henry, 49, 143
Vaughan, Roger, 95–96, 97
Vaughan, Thomas, 7, 49–50, 97, 143–45
Vita Sancti Samsonis, 124–25

Waite, A. E., 146
Wales, adjoined to England, 13
Wales, people of, 9–10
Walton Basin, 126–27
wands, 180, 218–26, 261–65
  use in various traditions, 282–83
wands, cursing, 218–26
  living wands, 219–26
  seasoning, 218–19
  two types, 218
wands, hook, 261–65, *261, 262*
  defined, 261
  potentializing, 263
  potion for, 263, *264*
water
  supernatural energies of, 227
  traditional associations of, 227
  in workings, 187
waters, cursing, 227–33
  assembled components for, *230*
  casket with curse tablet sealed, *232*
  countercurse, 232
  crafting and using, 228–33
  stone curse tablet inside casket, *231*
wax poppet, *pl. 4, pl. 20*
wells, cursing, 228
Welsh language, 62

Welsh Marches. *See also* Welsh Marches arcane traditions; Witches of the Welsh Marches
- acceptance of occult in, 13, 115
- castles in, 12
- Druids of the, 116–31
- history of, 9–13
- holy wells and streams in, 227–28
- legacy of Witches and Druids of, 152–59
- manor houses of the, 94–115
- map of, *11*
- Norman Marcher barons, 12
- prominent occultists of, 140–51
- system of laws in, 55
- Witch artifacts of the, 79–115

Welsh Marches arcane traditions, 14–22. *See also* Druidic tradition; witchcraft
- as continuing, 6
- decision to explore history of, 7
- grimoire of the Welsh Marches, 161–283
- legacy of Witches and Druids of, 152–59

Wenham, Jane, 58
Wheeler, Mortimer, 130–31
White Lady of Tretower, 97
whitesmith, defined, 24
Wicca, 6–7, 20, 158–59
wild sweet violet, 266
William III, 13
William the Conqueror, 10, 94–95
windows, as vulnerable points, 70
witch axe, defined, 4
witch axes, 203, *204*
witch bottles, 18, 85–86, *85, 86,* 198–206, *199,* 237–38
- items for, *203*
- purposes of, 201–2
- to trap daemons, 205–6

witchcraft, 59, 209. *See also* witchcraft and Druidic tradition
- acts for benefit of the world, 164
- argument that it does not exist, 43–44, 58–59
- belief that humankind lives in nature, 163–64, 223
- Catholic Church and, 32–35, 34–35
- Christianity and, 32–59
- critique of, 36–37
- evolution of, 13
- as fraud, 58–59
- as heresy, 39–40
- historical publications regarding, 37–50
- imagery in, 33
- legacy of, 156–59
- pantheon of deities in, 163
- Protestant Church and, 35–37
- social role of, 36
- supposed link to evil, 37
- vilification of, 36–37, 50–52
- what is a Witch?, 38
- witch artifacts of the Welsh Marches, 79–115
- witches' evidence in homes and farms, 68–79

witchcraft acts, 50–52
- An Act Against Conjurations (1563), 52
- after Henry VIII, 52–54
- Fraudulent Mediums Act 1951, 59
- laws from King George II to the present, 58–59
- Witchcraft Act of 1542, 50–51

Witchcraft Act of 1604, 53
Witchcraft Act of 1735, 59
witchcraft and Druidic tradition
evidence of combination of, 3
finding harmony between the two traditions, 163–69
merging of, 31
principal differences, 163–69
similiarities of, 25, 209–10
witchcraft laws. *See* witchcraft acts
witchcraft trials, in Wales, 55–58
Witches, 45. *See also* witchcraft; Witches of the Welsh Marches
belief in, 60–61
defined, 42–43
fear of, 61
fear of fire, 99
origin of word, 62–63
and "pact with the devil," 41, 45
powers of, 42–43, 43
recognizing (*Malleus Malificarum*), 39
three kinds of (*Malleus Malificarum*), 39
what is a Witch?, 38
Witches of the Welsh Marches, 79–115
and occult practitioners (chart), *65*
profile of, 62–67
witchfinders, 53
witch hunts, 50–52
witch marks, *31,* 74–79, 206
origin of, 74
on Shropshire amulet, 30–31
Witch's familiars, defined, 21–22
witch terror (Western Europe), 38–39
comparative events of (chart), *66*
wits, defined, 62–63
wooden poppet, *pl. 8*
working stone within the circle, 178–80
workplace. *See also* outdoor workspace
defined, 170
preparation of, 170–80
Worshipful Company of Mercers, 141
Wuthnow, Robert, 153

Yerbius, 158
Ynys Mon, massacre of Druids on, 119–21
yr angau, 138–39
Yr Llyfr Swynion Gororau Cymru, 162–283